Critical Mass

Critical Mass

Transport, Environment and Society in the Twenty-first Century

John Whitelegg

LONDON • CHICAGO, ILLINOIS

in association with WWF

First published 1997 by Pluto Press
345 Archway Road, London N6 5AA
and 1436 West Randolph, Chicago, Illinois 60607, USA

British Library Cataloguing in Publication Data
A catalogue record for this book is available from the British Library

ISBN 0 7453 1083 4 hbk

Library of Congress Cataloging in Publication Data
A catalog record for this book is available from the Library of Congress

Designed and produced for Pluto Press by
Chase Production Services, Chadlington, OX7 3LN
Typeset from disk by Stanford DTP Services, Northampton
Printed in the EC by Redwood Books, Trowbridge

About WWF

WWF is the world's largest independent environmental organisation, with a global network active in 96 countries.

WWF aims to conserve nature and ecological processes for the benefit of all life on Earth. By stopping, and eventually reversing, the degradation of our natural environment we strive for a future in which people and nature can live in balance.

This mission can only be achieved if people recognise and accept the need for sustainable, just and careful use of natural resources. WWF-UK believes that education has a key role to play in this process. We are therefore working with schools, colleges, further and higher education, community groups, and business and industry. Our comprehensive environmental education programme includes resource development, IT projects, curriculum development, professional and vocational training, business toolkits and work with local authorities.

If you would like further details about WWF-UK's education programme, please write to: WWF-UK, Education and Awareness, Panda House, Weyside Park, Godalming, Surrey GU7 1XR. Telephone: 01483 426444. Fax: 01483 426409. Web site address: http://www.wwf-uk.org

Contents

List of Tables viii
List of Figures x
Preface xi

1. Perranporth and China 1
2. A Faustian Bargain 17
3. Free to Choose and Free to Grow 34
4. A Word with the Driver 50
5. What Time is This Place? 59
6. What Place is This Time? 76
7. Sustainability 97
8. Environment 114
9. Transport and Equity 128
10. Traffic and Health 147
11. Resolutions 170
12. Solutions 200

Bibliography 227
Glossary and Abbreviations 237
Index 244

Tables

2.1 Estimates of Resource Usage of Air and Road Transport (in kilograms) 26
2.2 Summary of Energy Consumption and Emissions: Life-cycle Analysis (per car) 29
2.3 External Costs of Transport in the UK (1993) 32
6.1 Global and Route Group Passenger Forecasts 87
6.2 Relative Importance of Different Modes of Transport in their Contribution to Global Warming 89
6.3 CO_2 Emissions from Passenger Car Traffic at Heathrow Airport 93
6.4 Heathrow Airport's CO_2 Inventory (data in tonnes) 94
6.5 NO_x Emissions at Heathrow Airport at present and in 2016 94
8.1 The Selected Environmental Impacts of Principal Transport Modes 116
8.2 Main Sources of Greenhouse Gases 118
8.3 Forest Damage in Europe (%) 120
8.4 Trends and Projections of Urbanisation (1950–2010) 121
8.5 Length of Road, Rail and Waterway per $1000km^2$ of Land Area 123
8.6 Comparison of Different Modes of Passenger Travel 124
9.1 Number of Injured Child Pedestrians and Child Cyclists by Age Group and Ethnic Definition 143
10.1 Summary of Short-term Exposure–response Relationships of Sulphates, $PM_{2.5}$ and PM_{10} with Different Health Effect Indicators 157
10.2 Health Outcomes Associated with Changes in Peak Daily Ambient Ozone Concentrations in Epidemiological Studies 160
10.3 Number of Europeans Living in Places where WHO Guidelines were being Overstepped in the early 1990s 163
10.4 Percentage of Population Living with Noise Levels Greater than 65 dB(A) 164
11.1 Transport Fuel Consumption in Brazil 180
11.2 The Benefits of Alternative Fuels Compared with Gasoline 183

11.3 Location Policy Categorisation 193
11.4 Percentage of Journeys by Different Modes of Transport in Selected European Cities 194
12.1 The Economics of Production and Transport (CALIDA) 208
12.2 The Environmental Effects of Basic Scenario 2015 and the New Course Scenario Set Off Against the Target for Sustainable Development. 211
12.3 Transfer of Road Freight to Shipping and Inland Waterways 214

Figures

2.1 Time Spent Travelling Per Day (number of trips per day and distance travelled) 20
3.1 Average Social Speeds (taking into account the total amount of time spent in transport) 38
3.2 Transportation Relationships: strawberry yoghurt, 150g 40
3.3 Transportation Relationships: strawberry yoghurt, 500g 41
3.4 Transportation Relationships: chocolate pudding, 125g 42
4.1 Modal Distribution of World Bank Funding for Transport (1947–1994) 53
5.1 Change in Distance Travelled by a Selection of British Imports 63
5.2 Freight Traffic Trends in European Countries 64
5.3 Time Taken to Travel between London and Edinburgh (1750–1990) 72
5.4 The Spatial Reorganisation Process in Response to Transport Improvements 74
6.1 International Tourist Arrivals (1950–1990) 77
6.2 Percentage Share of Tourist Arrivals (1950–1990) 78
6.3 Percentage Share of Tourist Arrivals (1950–1990 in the Americas) 79
6.4 Index of Tourist Arrivals to Thailand 82
9.1 How Fast Must Grandma Run?
11.1 Electric Vehicle Life-cycle Greenhouse Gas Emissions 185
11.2 Life-cycle Greenhouse Gas Emissions for Alternative-Fuel Cars 186
12.1 Italian Ham 209
12.2 The Potential for Road/Rail Intermodalism (Stage 1) 213
12.3 Comparison of Strong Sustainability Scenarios (CO_2 Reduction) with UK Business as Usual Scenarios 215

Preface

This book has taken over two years to write. These two years have seen a considerable amount of change in UK transport policy as well as in transport policy in most other developed countries. Most countries now accept that for a variety of reasons it is no longer possible to continue to try to meet the growth in demand for motorised transport, with more roads and more parking. This dramatic shift in emphasis from the position adopted from the early 1960s through to the mid-1980s has still not reached the world of aviation which is now repeating the rhetoric and the mistakes made by the road industry and policy makers over the past three decades. The shift has also failed to inform global concerns. The growth in demand for car ownership in developing countries is accelerating at the same time as Western companies are expanding their production capacity in those countries.

Problems of health and environment and lack of sustainability are still severe even in those countries that have made an effort to reduce the supply of new infrastructure rather than try and keep up with demand. In the United States, Europe and Australia the car is still a dramatic intrusion into community and neighbourhood life but continues to enjoy considerable support amongst politicians and corporate decision makers.

This book is designed to lay bare the contradictions at the centre of this dependency on motorised transport and to point the way globally and locally towards economically and socially efficient transport policies that will also protect and enhance the environment as well as meet the demanding conditions for sustainable development.

The book was written in an unusual way. Three research students of the author at Lancaster University researched and wrote substantial sections for the first draft. Chris Goodacre wrote different parts of Chapters 5 and 6, Gary Haq wrote parts of Chapters 8 and 11 and Cathy McKenzie wrote parts of Chapters 7 and 9. All three contributions were then rewritten to produce a 'seamless web' or as near a seamless web as possible. The book then went through two more drafts. The opportunity to work with these three creative individuals was much appreciated and I apologise in advance for any damage that has been done to their insights and their prose through the process of rewriting.

I would also like to put on record my thanks to Sally Richardson, Robert Webb, Rachel Houghton and Pascal Desmond who all took me to task on those examples of my prose where enthusiasm ran ahead of clarity. As always, the remaining mistakes and patches of fog are entirely my own responsibility.

The book was written during an intensive bout of activity on a number of other projects and I would like to thank Sheila Hargreaves, Company Secretary of Eco-Logica Ltd, for keeping both this book and other projects on target under such demanding circumstances.

John Whitelegg
Lancaster
October 1996

CHAPTER 1

Perranporth and China

Introduction

In March 1995 over 100 people attended a one-day conference in Perranporth on the north coast of Cornwall. The conference was organised and attended largely by local people who were concerned about what was happening to Cornwall and what they saw as a misreading of the local situation by politicians and planners who were constructing a vision of Cornwall that did not correspond with their own.

> Cornwall is a rural county at the southwest extremity of England. It is a long way from the major centres of population in Britain and Europe and policy makers have decided that this is a problem and that the problem has a name – 'peripherality'. Every problem has to have a solution and the solution to the problem of peripherality is to build roads, reduce journey times, encourage more activity and more travel, stimulate tourism and, it is hoped, create jobs. All this becomes part of an even bigger solution to a problem that is never clearly specified, and this particular solution is called 'economic development'.

The significance of the Perranporth conference was clear from the very first discussion, where it became apparent that residents had a strong place identity with Cornwall. This perception is related to other factors that are seen to define quality of life: Cornwall has a dramatic, beautiful landscape and attractive culture and community and these intangibles interact to produce a powerful cocktail of identity, meaning, purpose, commitment and enthusiasm. Long-standing Cornish residents expressed deep suspicions of a process that focuses on more tourism, roads and 'better links with Europe'. They know from previous 'waves' of this process that it does not bring economic utopia but instead creates increased traffic and associated pollution; pushes up house prices so that local people are priced out of living in their own communities; brings a cultural homogeneity which strikes at what local people value as 'Cornishness'; and brings frequent and unrelenting proposals for new roads, new bypasses and the resultant damage to the countryside and landscape.

The official understanding of the Cornish 'problem' is that Cornwall is surrounded on three sides by water. Conversely the view expressed by local residents is that the so-called problem is better described as Cornwall having a land boundary on one side. The language and terminology used to articulate these different perceptions thus highlights a major discontinuity between the decision makers and politicians and the everyday experience of those who simply get on with life at a local level and spend time observing, understanding and relating to their local communities, their trees, their mountains, their culture and their view of nurturing and restoring rather than developing and exploiting.

Those expressing serious doubts about road building, tourist development and economic development are not oblivious to the social and economic needs of people who live in Cornwall. However, their view is deeply suspicious of economic development which is based on centralisation, long-distance movement and cost reduction, and acutely aware of the failure of past waves of economic growth and new infrastructure to deliver new and diverse jobs, and a strong local economy.

These arguments reflect a clash of paradigms. On the one hand the proponents of economic growth and new roads promise new jobs and implicitly prioritise economic aims and objectives over environmental considerations. Those who oppose new roads and other infrastructure are often and easily characterised as relatively wealthy, middle class and out of touch with real workers and the unemployed. This is a false dichotomy.

The choice is not one that has to be made between jobs or the environment. There is ample evidence that large numbers of jobs can be created in local economies as those economies adjust to supply more of their own basic goods and services, and where investment formerly going into roads and new infrastructure is channelled into making homes energy efficient, changing waste disposal practices, improving public transport and remediating past environmental damage. The residents of Cornwall who attended the Perranporth conference did not reject social and economic objectives; they merely affirmed the indivisibility of social and environmental justice and the importance of strong local communities based on strong local economies.

They also put very high priority on cultural identity and the links between culture, landscape and the environment. The threats to these priorities came from the land frontier on the back of economic development arguments and arguments in support of greater levels of accessibility to European markets. Residents said they were not convinced by the Euro-speak of cohesion, single markets and special attention to the periphery of Europe. These objectives destroy what they perceive to be important and replace the possibility of strong local economies and communities with a new concept based on one vast market, long-distance transport and hyper-mobility on new transport arteries.

Critical Mass

The Perranporth experience is being repeated throughout the world. For example, residents in Melbourne, Australia have been deprived of the quiet enjoyment of a fine nineteenth-century park (Albert Park) only to see an international grand prix racing circuit and adjacent car park put in its place. In the United States a 2,900 kilometre (km) 'superhighway' is being planned from the Great Lakes to the Rio Grande valley. This is seen as part of the changes that must take place to assist the functioning of the North American Free Trade Agreement (NAFTA) with more truck traffic linking the three countries concerned (the US, Canada and Mexico). In British Columbia in Canada a highway project is under construction which runs half the length of Vancouver Island from Victoria north to the Campbell River. The total cost of this will be £3 billion. The residents of Calcutta in India are battling to save a popular, low cost, socially and geographically accessible tram system which is threatened with closure to make more space available for cars. In many parts of Asia local authorities and politicians are making concerted attacks on rickshaws and bicycles as part of a modernisation and economic development push that will bring US levels of car use to societies with over two billion inhabitants. The Hungarian government, encouraged and bullied by the World Bank, is bent on closing railways and replacing them with motorways.

Here in Europe the European Union (EU) is desperately advancing its Napoleonic vision of Europe through major highways from Cork to Vladivostok, Madrid to Stockholm and Berlin to Moscow and Kiev, and the International Road Federation in Geneva is lobbying vigorously for its vision of a new Mediterranean rim motorway and a new highway which will be over 5,000km long from Finland to Greece.

Those who attended the Perranporth conference were not a self-selected group of latter-day anarchists, utopian visionaries and eco-fascists. Their gentle, caring and articulate vision of diversity, strong local communities, economic welfare rather than economic growth, and of a society that nurtures the health of its children and elderly and respects the views and status of women as well as men is being repeated wherever debate and choices are focused on transport issues. In January 1995 over 50 young people met at Eeklo, a small town in northern Belgium, to discuss transport, the economy and health in Europe. Participants came from Germany, Belgium,

Poland, Hungary, the Czech Republic, Lithuania, Latvia and Estonia and expressed concern about the rising tide of pollution from traffic, problems associated with being a pedestrian or a cyclist in a mobile and motorised society, and the decline of public transport and rail freight as motorway mania spreads across Europe.

The connection between Eeklo and Perranporth could not be clearer and the message has been reinforced time and again and at larger meetings, for example with local residents in Devizes and Salisbury (both in Wiltshire, England) during the 1994/95 period. Everywhere ordinary people have come together and identified the fundamental flaws in the logic of economic development and more roads, more jobs, more prosperity. They know it has not worked in the past and will not work at higher levels of intensity; they know it is unworkable on a local and global scale. At a local scale pollution levels are rising and the health of the population, particularly children, is apt to decline. Local facilities and services, for example, retailing, schooling and health, are also in decline as communities are pushed in the direction of bigger facilities which are further away and require more transport (and therefore more fossil fuel consumption) in order to get there. Longer distances mean higher levels of dependency on cars and lorries and less chance for feet and bikes. Even the bus cannot compete. More travel means less time for the local community, less local interaction, fewer local facilities, more roads and more pollution. Many realise that what is not sustainable at the local level certainly is not sustainable at the global level.

> The rising tide of criticism and social protest in the UK, Eastern Europe, Australia, India and North America represents the beginning of the end of an era dominated by fossil fuel consumption, auto-dependency and the reorganisation of space and time to service a society structured around mobility, spatial concentration of activities, environmental degradation and community disruption.

The same ideas, the same criticisms and the same deep dissatisfaction with the poverty of everyday life in increasingly sterile cities and socially deficient rural areas now amount to a worldwide recognition that the time for change has arrived and that change has to involve a transition from auto-dependency and all that goes with it to lower levels of car use and higher levels of accessibility and environmental quality. The growth and development of these ideas and critiques now amount to a 'critical mass' that is large enough to affect social change and bring about this transition.

The existence of such a critical mass, however, does not guarantee that this change will take place in the short term. It has taken 70 years to transform developed societies into spatial and economic structures that are dependent on high levels of mobility, the car, the movement of food products over long distances, and low levels of linkage between local production and local consumption. This spatial and energy transformation has been associated with a loss of local control (especially over the quantity and quality of employment opportunities) and its replacement by very large, distant, wealthy and non-accountable bodies which exercise control on a global scale.

On the other hand the development of a critical mass which embodies a clear set of alternatives to this arrangement does ensure the successful articulation of the arguments as well as a build up of the necessary impetus to change a situation which is currently reinforced by these global actors. Our local environments and community vitality are largely determined by transnational corporations, the World Bank, the EU and international financial institutions. These powerful actors are not immune to the process of change: slavery was abolished in the eighteenth century in response to a critical mass of argument and opposition that could no longer be resisted; nineteenth-century cities received massive investment to bring about improvements in sanitary conditions as a result of another rising tide of argument about conditions in cities. Likewise those in twentieth-century cities are now coming to realise that the car and the lorry are at least as a big a problem as the polluted water and sewage systems of the nineteenth century.

The critical mass of opinion and social change that has become evident in the last few years of the twentieth century will repeat the successes of the eighteenth and nineteenth centuries to produce a new set of arrangements of space, time and energy and a new relationship between people and places, and local action to determine local conditions.

The 'China Factor'

Problems at the global level are being brought into sharp focus by what is happening in China. What would happen if the high per capita energy consumption, grain consumption, meat consumption and carbon dioxide (CO_2) production of those in developed countries were adopted by the 1.2 billion people in China? Serious political and psychological problems would result if high levels of output and consumption were maintained in Europe or North America but not allowed to develop in China, Africa or India. In practice the global political and economic system has already swung into action. The global population of motorised vehicles in 1995 was approximately 500 million. The free market path being pursued in China and to be followed by India, the rest of South East Asia, Africa and Latin America will take this total well beyond 2 billion by 2020. China alone increased its vehicle population from 613,000 in 1970 to 5.8 million in 1990. The number of cars produced annually in China is expected to rise from 1.3 million in 1993 to 3 million in 2000. Major European and global car manufacturers are already in China ensuring that this will happen.

The combination of large increases in population – the equivalent of adding another Beijing every year – and huge increases in per capita incomes (40 per cent in the period 1991–1994 in China) is imposing environmental, social and health burdens that are larger than any previous period in history.

> There can be no doubt that the impact on local and global environments by this intensification of production and consumption will impose environmental burdens that exceed carrying capacity at all relevant geographical scales and threaten human health at local and global scales.

The impact of this 'China factor' (as the Worldwatch Institute in Washington in its 1995 *State of the World* report described it) will be to push up the consumption of all basic foods, materials and oil to levels that are very difficult to satisfy. China has eclipsed the US in total red meat consumption and faces the prospect of a massive grain deficit. The increased demand for basic food products and materials is taking place as farmland is converted into non-farm uses. Industrialisation, urbanisation and the demands for new transport infrastructure, particularly roads, will ensure that more and more has to be produced from less and less. Roads and parking needs are particularly greedy in their demand for more and more land, and with car ownership and use at a political premium and foremost of middle-class aspirations then the demand would seemingly be unstoppable.

And so to Salisbury, Devizes, Perranporth and Eeklo. The participants in these non-professional, citizen-organised events are designing solutions to their problems that could also provide solutions to China's dilemma. In fact, there can be no solution to China's dilemma without a solution to the Cornwall and Wiltshire dilemmas. The demands for a new central car park in Salisbury articulated by the controlling political groups prior to the May 1995 local elections (and subsequently cancelled) were in fact the direct equivalent of the demands in China for more roads, more industry, more jobs, more development and higher levels of consumption.

These citizen groups have seen that they must reduce their levels of consumption, development, pollution, land take and mobility because this is the route to a healthier society as understood in relation to community, economy and public health. They have seen that it is possible, and even desirable, to reduce mobility (which means increasing accessibility), to have stronger local economies (which means producing more things locally and eliminating damaging long-distance transport), and having healthier children (which means reduced healthcare bills). From this base it is possible to conduct a dialogue with China about equity, justice, development and sustainability. It is not possible to engage in a dialogue about who will control the increasingly inadequate resource base of the world from a base of more development, more consumption and, ultimately, more competition.

The central problem in many of the arguments involving transport and the environment is to find a solution that can take into account the concept of mutual self-interest. A car is very efficient indeed at providing high quality mobility when it is the only car in existence. When it has to share the road with millions of other cars the benefits are eroded at the local level (in terms of accessibility) and at the global level (in terms of greenhouse gases and climate change). Recognising the point of transition from benefit to disbenefit and the point at which the world would gain collectively from slightly reduced expectations about personal gain and personal satisfaction is the key to policy development and the identification of solutions.

If Salisbury and all the other Salisburys in the developed world were to keep piling on the concrete and tarmac in an (ultimately doomed) attempt to keep that little bit ahead of its neighbours in terms of jobs, shoppers and car access then all would lose out. This is the automobile equivalent of the arms race. Any lead is purely temporary as all other parties react to signals and intelligence to stop someone else getting ahead. If Salisbury had succeeded with its plans for an £8 million central car park it would have been unlikely that other retail centres within travelling range would have thrown in the towel and congratulated Salisbury on its achievement. In fact increasing competition would have likely resulted, with five or six retail centres probably springing up which would have all added to central car parking, and then to the road system which would be required to cope with the resulting demand.

China sees itself as poorly developed, and receives powerful reinforcement of this perception from the global economic community and its banks which are ever anxious to stimulate demand, increase profitability and globalise the Chinese economy. In such a globalised environment it is understandable that China's people should aspire to Western standards of living. Whatever sustainable development may actually mean (and this is discussed in full in Chapter 7), it is not surprising that the likes of China and India see this as an attempt to prevent them from following in the footsteps of the developed world and reaping the same perceived benefits – especially as the 'benefits' of a vibrant free market economy can always be used to improve the environment when development has reached a suitable level.

But China will lose out from pursuing the free market model of development just as will Salisbury and Cornwall. For this will mean more roads, more long-distance freight, less local economic benefit, more pollution, poor health and more loss of landscape. It will mean greater social inequalities as wealthy minorities exploit the advantages of this kind of economic system more successfully than the poorer majorities, as this discriminates against children, the elderly, women and the unemployed.

Institutional Obstacles to Delivering Change

The EU, China, the United Kingdom, Lancashire County Council and Cornwall County Council have all expressed their support for sustainable development and for environmentally well-informed policies. However, it is now the norm for public administrations at national and local level to proclaim their environmental credentials whilst destroying the environment. Most countries have signed the Climate Change Convention agreeing to bring about substantial reductions in greenhouse gas emissions but most find ways to avoid taking actions that can deliver on these pledges.

Comments made by the Worldwatch Institute on China's environmental policies are equally applicable to the EU, the United Kingdom and Lancashire County Council. Lancashire deserves special consideration. It has set up a high profile Environment Unit in its Planning Department and has won international prizes for its green audit, its Environment Forum and its 'LEAP' (Lancashire Environmental Action Programme). In the meantime Lancashire has enthusiastically progressed a large number of damaging road construction projects opposed by environmental groups and local communities alike. For instance, it has pursued a vigorous campaign to win governmental support for a new trans-Pennine motorway (the M65) across the nearest thing in the north of England to wilderness. It has pursued a new bypass, the Lancaster Western Bypass, which will destroy a large section of countryside which borders the Lune estuary. This will also destroy the livelihood of many farmers and their families that lie in its path. Sixty-seven per cent of those who took part in a consultation exercise around this project and run by the County Council opposed the bypass, and on its own figures the County Council say it will not relieve the city centre traffic problems of Lancaster.

The Lancaster problem is repeated at the European level. The EU has a well developed sustainable development policy in its Fifth Environmental Action Programme that clearly calls for a change in direction and policies that solve environmental problems at source rather than after they have begun. The policy also says that the environment is not a bolt-on extra that can be retro-fitted at some later date to some other policies, but is central to all policies and must be pursued as an integral part of other policies. Co-existing with this environmental emphasis and orchestrated within the same buildings is a massive assault on the environment of Europe. This assault comes from the agricultural policies of the EU, from cohesion policies that abhor the empty spaces on maps in Portugal, Spain, Greece and Ireland where there should be motorways, and from transport policies themselves that must be harnessed to a 1960s model of economic growth (characterised by a belief that the most important aspect of economic activity is to see Gross National Product increase, year on year, by a given percentage), more investment, more jobs and an end to the peripherality of places like Cornwall, Western Ireland and Andalucia. The EU plans to fund or stimulate private sector funds in a trans-European road network that involves 12,000 km of new roads, new high speed railway lines and new airports with new air traffic control systems and new airport links (road and rail).

The pursual of these contradictory policies is self-deluded and perpetuates the status quo. It is a 'business as usual' strategy dressed up to look acceptable to a superficial examination of environmental credentials. It is an obstacle to the solution of the Perranporth–China question simply because it denies there is a problem, and in the smoke-screen of environmental political correctness ensures that the old policies continue to gain ground within the protective umbrella of green labels and sustainability.

But the problem goes deeper than this. Lack of consistency and unwillingness to confront core environmental issues and their behavioural underpinnings take the world further in the direction of non-sustainability. China is unlikely to see any merit in a course of action that might reduce emissions and consumption if it observes the opposite tendency in developed countries. Similarly Lancashire and Cornwall are unlikely to implement genuinely sustainable development strategies as long as they fear that adjacent local authorities will take advantage of their 'weakness' and act to 'steal' their inward investment, their shoppers and their jobs.

Superficial and inconsistent policies also deny the possibility of fruitful cooperation with grassroots movements which are ready and willing to help, and, through experimentation, to identify the behavioural and structural changes necessary to put flesh on the concept of sustainability at the local and practical policy level. Effectively, local authorities and national governments are erecting a huge smoke-screen that will ultimately discredit the concept of sustainability and set in motion conflict with the very groups and individuals who are willing to devote energy to achieving sustainable development and a new model of economic welfare not driven by resource exploitation, pollution and damage to health.

The transport sector provides some very clear insights into why this policy inconsistency is so common at every level. Every politician and transport professional knows that walking and cycling are non-polluting, energy efficient, very cheap to provide for and very beneficial to health and fitness through the regular exercise they involve. In the UK 75 per cent of our trips are less than 8km in length and eminently suited to the bicycle for the vast majority of journey purposes. In spite of this information and awareness the majority of politicians and transport professionals pursue transport policies that work against walking and cycling. Public transport by bus and different kinds of rail (and everything in combination) can provide high quality services for rural and urban populations alike at much lower costs than a system devoted to private motorised transport and road expansion. Whilst public transport does better than walking and cycling (in terms of funds allocated) it is common for even its vigorous supporters in government and public administrations to allocate considerably more resources to private motorised transport than to the alternatives. Almost no attention is paid to the ways and means by which the demand for transport could be reduced by altering land use systems and influencing the spacing, timing, pattern and availability of those things that are at the destination of our trips.

The explanation for this neglect of the obvious and pursuit of policies that make things worse is the supremacy of the economic imperative interpreted in a traditional economic growth sense, with a strong belief system underlying the links between new roads, shorter journey times, inward investment and jobs.

This belief system is rock solid. There are very few local, national or European politicians prepared to question the dominant economic paradigm even though this dogma has failed to deliver its expected benefits over the last 40 years in Europe. Environmental goods (for example, clean air, clean water, lack of noise, lack of tarmac and concrete and devastation of the countryside on the scale seen at Twyford Down) are no less important than economic goods, even if the same economic goods could be guaranteed to provide increments in welfare, social justice, reduced inequality and community cohesion. Yet environmental goods are sacrificed in the political process that puts economic gains ahead of environmental gains. Transport problems, road building, road safety and community welfare cannot be understood until this economic policy leap-frogging is laid bare and held to account.

In Cornwall, Lancashire and the EU every environmental policy statement is valid only so long as it does not conflict with economic goals.

If environmental policies had real status then alternatives would be found to the construction of the M65 through Lancashire and to the road proposals that are intended to make Cornwall more accessible. If the environment was genuinely important then the EU would not be pursuing cheap and fast transport facilities in direct contradiction to its environmental policies, though on paper the EU has impressive credentials in the environmental area and it claims it would like transport to pay its full external costs and greenhouse gas reductions to be achieved through energy and CO_2 taxation. The EU has not, however, faced up to the deep policy contradictions suggested by its radical environmental stance in the Fifth Environmental Action Programme and its enthusiastic support of trans-European road networks. The former points in the direction of less traffic overall and more of it going by rail or waterway, and the latter points to much more traffic, the majority of which would travel by road. At best these two policies would cancel each other out. At worst there will be accelerated environmental deterioration.

Ironically both Lancashire and the EU have produced critiques of their own economic and transport policies which point out that, on balance, they will lead to a deterioration in environmental quality and a move away from the objectives of sustainable development. The EU's critique lies in an internal report ('"1992", The Environmental Dimension', Task Force Report on the Environment and the Internal Market) that was never published and Lancashire's critique lies in its Technical Report No 19 from the Structure Plan (Greening the Red Rose County) of 1994/95.

Both these critiques have failed to change the course adopted at both administrative levels which are still set on a non-sustainable trajectory.

Science, Logic and Perversity of Policy

Significant numbers of local residents throughout Europe have serious doubts about the economic advantages that are claimed flow from new or expanded roads. In Birmingham a proposal for a privately funded motorway around the eastern edge of the city is opposed by all local authorities, all the communities through which it passes and all the non-governmental organisations (NGOs) with an interest in transport and the environment. In Glasgow which, like Birmingham, has received more miles of urban motorway than most other UK cities, a new phase of urban motorway construction is now on offer which is also opposed by the local authority in Glasgow, NGOs and other community groups. In both cases the arguments in favour of the new roads are economic: Birmingham and Glasgow need these new roads as agents of economic regeneration. In both cases earlier waves of urban motorway have been followed by economic decline and it is local residents' groups and action groups which have demonstrated the flaws in the logic that promises economic gains from something which has already failed to provide such.

Liverpool has some of the best access conditions to the national motorway network of anywhere in Britain. It has a large and well-equipped port, high quality roads, a flyover right to the heart of the city and expensive tunnels under the Mersey. It also has massive unemployment, dereliction and social problems. The transformation of Liverpool from its nineteenth-century condition to a UK equivalent of Detroit in the US has been supported by planners, experts, scientists and large-scale state investment. All this has failed. Large investments in infrastructure have not regenerated Liverpool, have not created a strong, skilled, educated, confident labour force, and have not intensified social cohesion and a sense of well-being. Science, technology and the political system have failed Liverpool. Large public expenditure on new roads has accelerated the flight of jobs out of Liverpool. Market forces and deregulated economics have not regenerated the city and there are no new policy initiatives on the horizon to rescue the situation.

The Liverpool experience is wider and more significant than the transport issue in general but transport planning and transport failures have played a major role in the destruction of community and jobs in Liverpool and elsewhere. In some very important respects local communities and members of the public have been let down by the transport profession. Professionals working in civil engineering, economics, statistics and modelling, architecture and planning have subscribed to a scientific logic that assumes objectivity, independence and rigour. Their commitment to professional detachment and scientific objectivity has encouraged them to neglect people and communities with the result that many local environments are now seriously degraded.

The failure of science, like the failure of markets, is not an unusual phenomenon. It can be documented across a large number of subject areas. What is surprising is the constant reaffirmation of poor science as professionals either dilute or deny the traffic generation arguments and ignore their redistribution of job arguments. In transport one can see very clearly the activities of science underpinning the objectives of a larger political and social agenda and denying the observations of ordinary members of the public who have noticed the contradictions in the scientific position.

> Thirty years of traffic forecasting and statistical modelling have failed to incorporate the feedback mechanism that links new road construction to the generation of yet more new traffic.
>
> Thirty years of economic analysis and cost-benefit analysis have failed to notice that new roads and new transport infrastructure actually feed back into changed organisational and management strategies with the result that larger market areas can be supplied from a smaller number of production and distribution points.
>
> In the main new roads have not created new jobs; they have redistributed them, centralised them and in some cases actively contributed to their loss.
>
> Thirty years of transforming a society and a space economy to high levels of mobility and energy intensity have failed to notice the decline of community, the loss of people from the streets, and the increasing isolation of children, the elderly and women as the built environment fails them and through them fails the idea of community itself.

This is the significance of the Perranporth perception, the importance of the views of those consulted about Lancashire's new roads, and the importance of wider social protest about roads, airports and high speed trains. Large numbers of ordinary citizens have spotted the nakedness of the emperor in his supposed new clothes. They are complaining and they are articulating an alternative set of policies. They are the critical mass and they have produced an analysis and a solution that differs from the orthodoxy in transport and planning so effectively imposed on the world over the last 30 years.

Transport and road construction in particular demonstrate something very important about science and professionalism. The professionals are often wrong whilst those with local knowledge, acute powers of observation and a lack of peer group pressure that demands conformity are often right. This is not a universal law but an extraordinarily useful indicator of what could be achieved if professionals worked collaboratively with local residents rather than as the sole repository of expert knowledge that has to be forced on an unwilling and ignorant citizenry.

For the last 20 years transport professionals have denied the proposition that building new roads does not help to relieve congestion but adds to it by stimulating the development of new traffic. This proposition (traffic generation or induced traffic) has been advanced at numerous public inquiries into road schemes and by many organisations deeply concerned about a rash of road building that has failed to achieve its own objectives. In December 1994 the Standing Advisory Committee on Trunk Road Assessment (SACTRA), a UK governmental body charged with overseeing the methodology of evaluating road proposals, made its long awaited report on traffic generation.

The SACTRA report concluded that new roads generate additional traffic and that this new traffic can often exceed in total any relief that might be found elsewhere in the network by the new road. It concluded that this effect would lead to an exaggeration of the economic benefits of the new road because these roads depend on time savings which would be eroded if additional traffic enters the system to reduce speeds below the predicted level without traffic generation.

This report is very significant indeed and not only because it has given official credence to a matter of simple observation by those interested in watching their own localities. It has shown that a fundamental principle underlying road construction over the last 40 years that a new road will relieve congestion was false and that the conventional solutions to transport problems in fact makes them worse.

Traffic engineers and planners as a group could not have made this discovery unaided. It is a hallmark of professionalism, peer group opinion and promotion routines that radical ideas are suppressed and that a comfortable acceptance of an agreed body of knowledge and opinion is a preferable organisational strategy. The 'problem' with local residents and those with an interest in their communities is that they are not suppressed in this way.

Another rock solid belief which is now in the final stages of its life cycle is the idea that roads bring jobs – which is a central tenet of UK road building policy. Once again this is under attack from citizens' groups and non-professional observers who can take the risks associated with pointing out that the emperor really does not have any new clothes. The 1989 report from the UK Department of Transport that anticipated a major wave of new road building was given the title 'Roads for Prosperity'. The reason why Lancashire County Council wants to build the M65 across the Pennines and the Lancaster Western Bypass is the same – the stimulation of economic development. However, as mentioned before, there is no evidence that new roads bring new jobs but there is a large body of evidence which shows that economic prosperity, however measured, varies according to numerous factors, of which motorways and bypasses are a very small part.

If a high density road network was associated, even loosely, with higher rates of economic prosperity then Glasgow, Liverpool and Birmingham would be extremely prosperous, Edinburgh quite poor, and anywhere north of the Scottish lowlands or west of Cardiff and Shrewsbury an economic desert. On a larger scale, since Japan is peripheral to the European markets it serves so well it too should be quite poor. In addition, for everyone to be wealthy we should all live in a well-defined space–time enclave that ensures every consumer is as close as possible to every producer, and that every stage in every production process is as close as possible to every other stage. This would be incredibly efficient but incredibly boring and would require a concentration of activity so dense as to exclude the social, cultural and landscape elements that define the attractiveness and place loyalty associated with many of our regions and localities.

In the summer of 1994 Eco-Logica Ltd (Lancaster) carried out a research project for Greenpeace UK to gather reliable and rigorous data on proximity to motorways and dual carriageways in order to ascertain if those areas near to such high quality road links experienced an economic prosperity that was measurably better than those areas distant to such links. The question asked was very simple and the methodology crude – but then so was the rhetoric of the road builder and the economic development officer. If road building was matching the expectations of its supporters then it was thought it should be possible to identify a 'roads effect' of the kind the project was seeking.

The results of the analysis carried out in eight different areas in England and Wales was that there was no relationship between accessibility to the road system and economic prosperity. It was not possible to find a 'roads effect' where access to high quality roads had produced a measurable increment in levels of economic activity.

Support for road construction on economic grounds in the UK, like support for economic development and higher levels of motorisation in China and India, is not borne of rigorous analysis and careful choice but of a slavish adherence to a form of economic progress that is associated with raw material exploitation, pollution, social inequalities and increased consumption. It is this obsession and its manifestation as hyper-mobility and long-distance transport that damages the environment and damages communities. Sustainable development provides an alternative path and one willingly embraced by community groups and active citizens – though not by their local and central governments and their politicians.

So What is Sustainability?

The failure of transport policy and the love affair with motorisation is largely due to the false economics and false freedoms associated with mobility. These falsehoods are explored at various points in this book particularly with respect to time and space and the high level of externalities (health and pollution costs) associated with transport. Sustainable development offers a framework for reorienting the current vision of transport. It requires people to conserve and reduce (particularly energy and materials) not necessarily because this will save the planet but because this is central to preserving the welfare of present and future generations and reducing inequalities whilst improving quality of life. In fact sustainability is central to any shift from an energy and material greedy society to a conserving and renewing one.

Most citizens, when presented with a choice between a dirty, dangerous world which is unhealthy and congested, and one which is characterised by clean air, safety and security for children, healthy communities and healthy lungs, will opt for the latter. This choice accords fully with the policy direction subsumed within sustainable development. Mobility does not necessarily improve our access to things and the freedom to travel long distances to consume basic everyday goods and services denies us the freedom and choice to do this locally if we wish as well as the freedom of local communities to enjoy a rich social life based on high quality public space and local amenities.

Sustainable development also implies personal development. The critical mass referred to in this chapter is the social partner of sustainable development as a policy direction. The transfer of power from large corporations and public bodies to local communities and streets is more likely to assert a conserving and nurturing emphasis than is a bureaucratic emphasis on economic development imposed from Preston (Lancashire), London, Brussels or Washington. Large-scale state intervention like large-scale transnational intervention cannot respect local democracy or local self-determination. However, sustainable development can achieve these broader objectives and transport presents as clear a mirror and magnifying glass on these processes as one could wish.

The chapters that follow will explain the failures of transport policy, chart the insidious nature of policy failures to date and set down markers for a restructuring of space and time and local control that could achieve so much to improve quality of life and solve global and regional environmental problems.

These changes could bring about sustainable development and this achievement would be made more likely, if not certain, by the growth and vitality of citizen activity and citizen analysis, and by the attainment of the critical mass necessary to precipitate social change.

CHAPTER 2

A Faustian Bargain

Introduction

This chapter will consider the costs and benefits of private motorised transport. The car and the lorry are frequently described as bringers of freedom, progress, independence and economic growth. The advertising world supplies numerous images in support of this vision of freedom and mastery over nature. It is no accident that these images are based on speed, power, open roads, attractive scenery and sexuality. The attractiveness and seductiveness of the car is deeply embodied in our culture and in our psychology. In this it offers a great deal, but as shall be demonstrated in this chapter it actually delivers very few benefits and in fact a large number of disbenefits. In spite of the growth in our knowledge about the negative environmental, social and economic effects of private car use, the car still commands powerful support. Indeed, in his introduction to the fourth RAC (1992) report: 'Cars and the Environment: a view to the year 2020' the vice-chancellor of Cambridge University, Professor Sir David Williams, wrote: 'Few people are unaware of the immense benefits we gain from the ready availability of the car.'

The character of Faust is a major figure in Europe's literary heritage. In Marlowe and Goethe the image of a figure determined to increase his power and knowledge at whatever cost is a potent one. Faust's bargain with the devil to sell his soul in return for power and knowledge is a powerful metaphor for the forces that drive human wants and aspirations and for the strength of the inner self to defer any consideration of the final price that must be paid. The story of Faust does, of course, have two endings. In one the final price is paid and Faust is delivered to eternal damnation. In the other he escapes and is reconciled with the Creator.

The twentieth century's obsession with the car has many of the characteristics of this Faustian bargain. The car can liberate the self-imprisoned soul from its perceived boredom in a limited geographical area. It can confer strong feelings of power, external signs of material wealth, sexual mastery and status. These benefits are severely constrained by the extent to which the rest of the world shares the same degree of motorised affluence but, more importantly, are purchased at considerable expense. Consequences range from the destruction of health and community in local neighbourhoods to the destruction of planetary life support systems as a consequence of global warming. The ability to crave and enjoy the benefits and the inability to recognise the severity of the price that has to be paid is Faustian in character.

The final chapter of this book will return to the question of which ending to the story of Faust is more likely in the context of current obsessions with private motorised transport and hyper-mobility.

If it had been possible to carry out an assessment of the technology of motorised transport around the time that Messrs Daimler, Benz and Diesel were making rapid advances in engine and vehicle technology, and Henry Ford was converting the technology into a new organisational and social order, it is highly unlikely that it would have looked like good value for money.

The car is extremely efficient at creating ever deepening dependencies on itself and exterminating alternatives.

Henry Ford would have been acutely aware of the financial implications of this simple feedback loop. The car does not allow more contact with more things whilst holding constant the number of things that are available, but stimulates a new spatial order so that things are no longer as they were: they have reduced in number whilst increasing in size (for example, schools and hospitals), they have disappeared (for example, small grocery stores/corner shops) or they have become further away (for example, workplaces).

Henry Ford was obsessive about waste of time and waste of money. In *My Philosophy of Industry* published in 1929 he frequently returned to these ideas. The car has ensured that we all spend more time in transit, making more trips to increasingly distant things. The consequence of these longer trips and the greater amounts of time allocated to car travel is that more money must be spent on roads, car parking and all the associated infrastructure of dependency on motorised transport including the police and courts. Henry Ford would not have been impressed by the monster that he was instrumental in creating.

An Audit

A car consumes vast amounts of finite raw materials and resources in its manufacture, which in turn create the necessity for mining and quarrying activities and their associated spoil and water pollution. Raw materials include metals, glass, plastics and the energy used to manufacture one vehicle (1.77×10^4 kWh or 1.42 tonnes of oil equivalent) (Hill *et al*, 1995).

Although a car is only used for 5 per cent of the time, it requires as much energy each year as a home of approximately 80 square metres (m^2) living space, it requires parking space and road space that amounts to 180m^2, it is capable of speeds in excess of 150 kilometres per hour (kph) (but spends much of its time at speeds of less than 30kph), it has a passenger carrying capacity of four to five people (but most of the time carries only one person), and 75 per cent of car journeys are less than 8km in length.

A car threatens the life of children, the poor and non-white ethnic groups on every journey through a city and through residential areas. Non-white ethnic groups in European cities spend more time on the street than their white counterparts, thus exposing themselves to higher levels of risk from vehicles. Most of these vehicles most of the time are breaking the law. It is very rare for cars to observe speed limits on motorways or in residential areas, mechanical condition of vehicles (for example, brakes and tyres) is poor, while driving behaviour exhibits significant lack of concern for vulnerable road users, for example, child pedestrians, the elderly and cyclists, and for the hazards of drugs (alcoholic and non-alcoholic).

A lorry consumes several more times the mass of raw material than does a car. Typically, one vehicle kilometre in three is run empty and an unknown percentage of the partly and fully loaded journeys are engaged in what can be described as 'duplicated transport'. Duplicated transport describes the phenomenon of manufactured or partly manufactured products transported by lorry over distances of greater than 100km, passing intermediate sources of the same products (that is, nearer to the destination of the lorry trip) and passing other lorries en route heading in the opposite direction. Research at the Wuppertal Institute for Climate, Energy and the Environment in Germany has shown that each 150 gram (g) pot of strawberry yoghurt in Germany is responsible for moving one lorry 9.2 metres (m).

It is the nature of feedback loops in demand for both passenger and freight transport that, even if car and lorry totals remain static (which is highly unlikely), the total of vehicle kilometres will rise and so too associated pollution levels. This increase in distance travelled cancels out the time savings associated with the initial improvement in vehicles and roads. In effect people recognise the opportunities provided by the technology and adjust their behaviour accordingly so that the benefits of time saving are consumed by increasing the distance travelled. This ensures that we maintain a constant or rising time-budget and therefore avoid saving time.

Time is an important metric in an audit. Werner Brög (1996) of Socialdata (a private consultancy firm) in Munich has shown that the time spent travelling per person per day is remarkably constant across a large number of cultures and continents. Similarly the number of different activities undertaken per person per day is remarkably constant. This is illustrated in Figure 2.1.

Figure 2.1: Time Spent Travelling Per Day (number of trips per day and distance travelled)

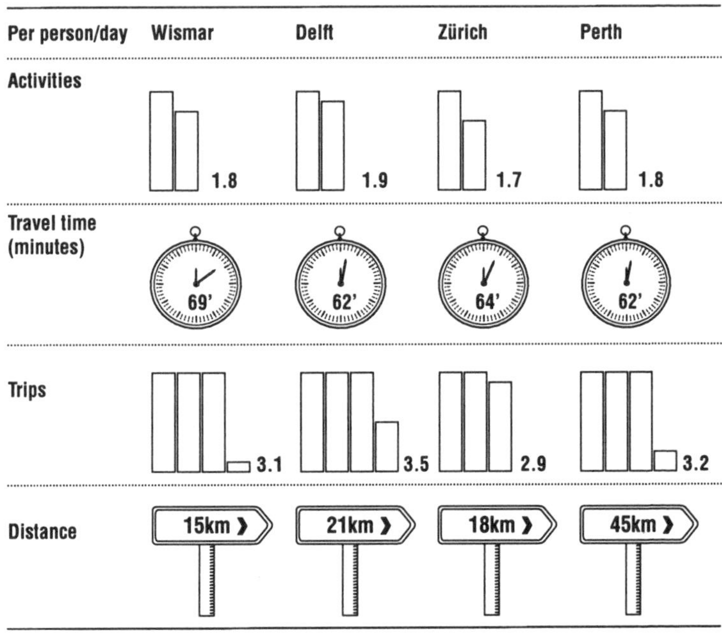

Per person/day
Wismar
Delft
Zürich
Perth
Activities
1.8
1.9
1.7
1.8
Travel time (minutes)
69'
62'
64'
62'
Trips
3.1
3.5
2.9
3.2
Distance
15km
21km
18km
45km

Source: Brög (1996).

Figure 2.1 shows very clearly that the citizens of Delft (Netherlands) and Perth (Australia) who live in very different worlds spend the same amount of time travelling each day to achieve almost identical activity rates. The difference lies in the distance travelled. Perth's citizens have to travel 45km to do what Delft's citizens do in 21km. The freedom and mobility of Perth's citizens boil down to the freedom to travel over longer distances to do things that could be done over much shorter distances. The long distances, moreover, translate directly into more fuel consumption, more pollution, more greenhouse gases and more difficult circumstances for community interaction and access for poorer groups and those without cars.

For lorries the effect is even more pronounced. Changes in the organisation of production and distribution have increased the length of haul and the distances covered by lorries. Road freight has adapted to the opportunities provided by the road system to substitute longer distance sourcing for shorter distance sources and to substitute national and international production and distribution strategies for regional strategies.

> The mass of goods carried in Europe has not increased by very much in the last 20 years but the distances over which they are moved has.
>
> The breakdown of local production–consumption links is the major factor in the growth of road freight, and not the loss of freight from rail to road.

Freight transport issues are central to the achievement of sustainable development objectives and are returned to in Chapters 5 and 12. The continuing growth of road freight transport across Europe at a rate that is in excess of growth in GDP is a potent source of environmental pollution and greenhouse gases. The decoupling of transport growth from economic growth and the substitution of regional systems of production and consumption by long-distance links are dealt with in a 1995 report for the World-Wide Fund for Nature (WWF) by Eco-Logica called: 'Freight Transport, Logistics and Sustainable Development' and by a special issue of *World Transport Policy and Practice*.

Both passenger and freight transport exhibit strong feedback mechanisms. If we add to the physical amount of high quality road space then we should expect higher levels of traffic and longer distance journeys for both passengers and freight. We should not expect a solution to traffic congestion problems, freely flowing traffic, and significant gains in time and productivity. The fact that these gains have not been achieved is due to feedback in a very dynamic system.

> The feedback mechanisms restructure time and space. They do this by offering the promise of time savings because of the convenience and efficiency of the motor vehicle and offering the convenience of more opportunities in a given amount of time for work, shop and residential activities. The feedback mechanism is multi-layered. By offering more possibilities for residential, job and shopping activities over a wider area more complex activity patterns are constructed involving geographically challenging travel patterns that cannot be satisfied on foot, bike or public transport. The consequence is a decline of these environmentally friendly alternatives and an increased dependence on motorised transport.

Time–space complexity produces a psychological inconsistency and contradiction in the transport debate at the level of the individual car user. In discussion with car users there is often a realisation of the disadvantages (personally and environmentally) of car use, but equally strong is the argument that the particular patterning of trips, the particular childcare responsibility, the particular need to carry bulky items and so on is such that car use is essential. This attachment to the car is understandable and is heavily supported by the strong lobbying forces in favour of the status quo and in favour of extending the so-called 'benefits' of car use to women. This means that sustainable transport policies are doomed if carried out within such a narrowly defined transport sector.

Sustainable transport is only achievable if space–time complexities can be unpacked, and if a strong element of local production–consumption links and of local services for local people in a high quality public and civic space that encourages walking, cycling and chatting can be restored. Policies aimed at transferring trips from car to trams/buses or from lorries to rail freight are unlikely to succeed if pursued in isolation from a wider strategy. This wider strategy should focus on land use systems, minimising distances, reducing the need to travel, and encouraging walking and cycling.

At a more detailed level (the level of the individual development proposals, for example shopping centres, leisure centres, business parks and muliplex cinemas) it is very clear indeed that policies aimed at improving bus, tram or rail access are frequently frustrated by the coexistence of road building, massive car parking and subsidised private transport policies. The Terminal 5 development at Heathrow airport provides a good example of the coexistence of ambitious plans for improving public transport with those for increasing the number of car parking places and road capacity. Manchester City Council has given a great deal of support to Metrolink, the new tram system, whilst encouraging maximum car accessibility to the city centre on the grounds that car access brings economic success. Most local authorities in the UK subscribe to a basic transport policy that recognises the environmental damage caused by cars – yet they pursue a policy which encourages cars to travel to the city centre, usually through road schemes and new car parking capacity.

Restructuring space–time relationships is not a new idea. 'Primitive' hunter–gatherer civilisations managed to work an average of three hours per day and filled the remainder with a rich mixture of social, leisure, cultural and ritual activities. The pace of these 'non-work' activities in a tightly defined space was part of the experience itself. Long distances, opportunities to do many things and machines to travel in do not necessarily equate with happiness, quality of life or satisfaction. The industrial revolution in Europe ushered in a major space–time restructuring so that leaving home and travelling to work became part of everyday life and mechanical, measured time became part of everyday consciousness. Schooling in the late nineteenth century took this trend one step further by providing another important journey purpose; another spatial separation that had to be overcome and another layer of spatial–temporal complexity in household life.

Schooling continues to provide a significant element of spatial–temporal complexity in late twentieth century Britain. More and more parents feel the need to transport their children by car to school.

Between 1970 and 1990 the proportion of nine to eleven year olds who were allowed to travel independently to school fell from nine in eleven to about one in eleven. In a very short period of time a major and largely unnoticed social revolution has deprived children of a significant element of independent learning, socialisation and environmental learning experience. As children are transported to school, this locks up the time of others, particularly women, and clogs up road space which leads to demands for more road space and levels of air pollution in cities that frequently exceed World Health Organisation (WHO) guidelines.

Escorting children in Britain in 1990 occupied 1,356 million hours of adult time. Much of this was female adult time thus imposing an additional time burden on women as a result of the inadequacies of the social environment and the transport system. Those that were able to escort their children to school by car were in their turn effecting a transfer of traffic danger to those who could not manage the motorised trip. Child pedestrians and pedestrians in general are far more vulnerable to road traffic accidents than car occupants. Additional car trips also expose children to health damaging pollutants but in this case the level of pollution was higher in the car than at pavement level. The final balance of disadvantage therefore remains unclear and is a function of total exposure of each child to in-car exposure, pavement exposure, playground exposure and indoor exposure (at home and at school). Since we do not measure individual exposure in this way the information is not available.

Schooling, whilst important in itself, is also an extremely good example of the interconnectedness of facility planning, location planning, traffic planning and the socio-psychological implications of planning failures. Travel to school illustrates the dramatic failure of our planning systems to protect elementary child freedom. This will surely have consequences on child development and maturation. This failure imposes burdens on women who are still seen as the primary carers in our society. Women are more likely to do the escorting and the ferrying of children than are men, and women will be subjected to the pressures of increasingly complex space–time activity patterns. This in its turn creates a new wave of demand for cars which has been exploited by the Automobile Association (AA) and by vehicle manufactures.

> The AA in its report 'Women and Cars', published in 1993, emphasises the importance of car ownership for women and points to the damage that would be done to women if car ownership and use were to be curtailed. Women are now seen as useful in the ideological struggle to justify extensions of car ownership and use whilst the exploitative systems that categorise women in the role that generates car use in the first place are ignored.

The arguments in favour of greater levels of car use focus on danger and the threat of physical violence to women if they should walk, cycle or use public transport. The implicit assumption is that these dangers are not present in car use and that all the measures that would improve public transport (for example, increased staff) and public space (for example, more people) are, for whatever reason, not available. At a deeper societal level it is even less likely that the assumptions casting women into these stereotyped roles will be questioned.

The use of gender arguments about women's safety to stimulate higher levels of car ownership and use effectively perpetuate the basic characteristics of a system that has always cast women as carers, escorters and shoppers. It also provides a rationale for avoiding the root causes of the problem, which are strongly associated with male violence, aggression and ego. The concept of sustainable transport provides an opportunity to tackle these root causes by downgrading the role of the car in supporting aggression (for example, by reducing the potential for speeding), violence and ego and by encouraging transport solutions that are more social, employ more staff and are more likely to encourage a social and friendly street than 30,000 cars per day. The technology and built environment associated with the car is inherently violent. The multi-storey car park is the modern equivalent of the gothic Frankenstein castle in popular culture – particularly film and television. Women and men know that the car is not a guarantee of safety and security. By emphasising the safety of women, male planners, male vehicle manufacturers, male advertisers and PR consultants transfer their own fears onto women and create a ghetto mentality by putting their trust in a technology that will actually lead to lower levels of safety and security.

Materials Intensity

It is clear from the work of the Wuppertal Institute that materials consumption and materials intensity is more important for sustainable development than energy intensity.

Transport is crucial in this respect. The mass of concrete, tarmac, metal, plastics, glass and composite materials that go into car production, lorry production, road construction and road maintenance is a serious cause for concern. Most materials have to be extracted and leave their mark on the ground in the form of waste or loss of agricultural land through quarrying. Energy is expended throughout the lifecycle of these materials as well as during the time the vehicle is in use, and the global exploitation of oil and oil products and its associated transport is both energy intensive and environmentally damaging.

Estimates of the materials usage of road, rail and air transport have been made by the European Commission as part of its Strategic Analysis in Science and Technology (SAST) programme (1992). Table 2.1 (overleaf) summarises the main results from the study of air and road transport.

These quantities of materials relate only to European inventories of vehicles and associated infrastructure from 1990 statistics. The vehicle totals are relatively small compared with global inventories. The road transport figures are based on 117 million cars (plus lorries) and the air transport figures on 4,255 aircraft. The growth of car numbers globally has enormous implications for materials intensity and for the land take implications of materials extraction, waste and new infrastructure. This issue, like the social impact and child freedom concerns, is totally absent from the technological debate about transport. New fuels, catalytic converters and vehicle electronics will not solve the problems created by the demand for materials.

The growth, for instance, in China's car population will trigger global problems of materials scarcity and materials competitiveness. The Delors White Paper ('Growth, Competitiveness, Employment') from the President of the European Commission in 1993 was very clear that 'extrapolating current industrial consumption and production patterns to the entire world would require about 10 times the existing resources, which illustrates the scope for possible distribution tensions at global level if current tendencies are not curbed.'

Paradoxically the solution to China's growth imperative is the same as that required in Europe and the rest of the world. This is to redefine the current concept of growth and economic progress so that human expectations can be fulfilled at much lower levels of materials intensity, land take, energy consumption and pollution.

There is ample evidence that the things people value can be obtained at these lower levels of production and consumption, and it is abundantly clear that there can be no solution to global problems and no incentive for China to choose a different route if Europe and North America do nothing tangible to change their development path – other than fudge the issue with lots of environmental and sustainability rhetoric and play around with technology in a deliberate act of self-delusion.

Table 2.1: Estimates of Resource Usage of Air and Road Transport (in kilograms)

Material	(A) Disposal	(B)Construction
	Air Transport	
Iron and steel	7.01×10^5	1.59×10^6
Aluminium	4.42×10^6	1.00×10^7
Titanium	8.41×10^5	1.91×10^6
Composites	6.31×10^5	1.43×10^6
Other materials	4.21×10^5	9.56×10^5
	Road Transport	
Iron and steel	7.01×10^9	1.05×10^{10}
Aluminium	6.05×10^8	9.08×10^8
Lead	9.33×10^7	1.38×10^8
Copper	9.33×10^7	1.38×10^8
Plastics	4.71×10^8	6.98×10^8
Zinc	4.83×10^7	7.10×10^7
Rubber	5.00×10^8	7.47×10^8
Glass	2.86×10^8	4.22×10^8
Other vehicle materials	9.90×10^8	1.47×10^9
Road aggregate	1.49×10^{11}	2.65×10^{11}
Asphalt-concrete	8.74×10^{10}	1.56×10^{11}

A= Total materials disposed of annually
B= Total materials required annually for construction

Source: SAST (1992)

A Global Audit

An appreciation of the scale of the problem is sometimes a stimulus to finding a solution. Dieter Teufel and his colleagues (1995) at the Environment and Forecasting Institute in Heidelberg (Germany) carried out a detailed audit of the consequences of global motorisation (Teufel, 1995). The description that follows is based on this work.

The current global motor vehicle population is approximately 500 million and this is expected to increase by a factor of 4.5 to approximately 2.3 billion in 2030. Volkswagen alone intends to manufacture about 660,000 vehicles per annum in China by the year 2000, and is forecasting a vehicle population in China of about 456 million (this was the *global* vehicle population in 1991).

Fuel consumption is expected to rise from 650 million tonnes in 1995 to 1.3 billion tonnes in 2030 – even taking into account improved fuel efficiency standards. Cumulative oil consumption for the car fleet alone between 1995 and 2030 will amount to 41.6 billion tonnes. This should be compared with a world oil reserve figure in 1994 of 135.7 billion tonnes.

The manufacturing of the vehicle fleet in 2030 globally is expected to produce 200 billion tonnes of CO_2 and 3.5 billion tonnes of waste matter.

NO_x (see glossary) emissions are expected to rise globally from 14 million tonnes per annum in 1995 to 35 million tonnes per annum in 2030. This rise will take place in spite of the reductions that are expected to result from the spread of catalytic converters. Catalytic converters do not perform well over their lifetime and do not deliver significant reductions in pollutants in the first 10km of a journey (the 'cold start' problem). More importantly increases in vehicle kilometres will cancel out savings and many vehicles in Africa, India and China will not have the technology. NO_x is associated with ozone formation and summer smog, and is directly injurious to human health (see Chapter 10).

Carbon monoxide (CO) is also injurious to health. Emissions are expected to rise globally from about 55 million tonnes per annum in 1995 to 90 million tonnes per annum in 2030. Volatile organic compounds (VOCs) are expected to rise from about 8 million tonnes per annum to 14 million tonnes by 2030. VOCs (for example, benzene) are implicated in carcinogenics and traffic emissions and are the main source of pollution for urban residents.

The Heidelberg study (Teufel *et al.*, 1995) sums up all the emissions with global warming impact from all the stages of car manufacturing and use, and estimates that the carbon dioxide equivalent emissions in 1995 were 4.4 billion tonnes. It is estimated this will rise to over 10 billion tonnes in 2030. The implications for climate change of global motorisation on this scale are staggering.

In addition, road traffic accidents killed 420,000 people in 1990 and injured over 9 million globally. In 2030 it is estimated that deaths will rise to an annual total of 2.5 million and injuries to an annual total of 60 million people. Cumulatively the period 1995–2030 will see 50 million killed and 1.1 billion injured. Currently about 800,000 people injured in road traffic accidents each year are permanently disabled. This total is expected to rise to 5.7 million per annum by 2030. Cumulatively, we can expect 100 million disabled people by 2030 as a result of road traffic accidents worldwide.

Land allocated to road and parking uses in 1995 amounted to approximately 50,000km^2. This is expected to rise to 200,000km^2 by 2030. This increase will cause serious problems for agricultural production and on the basis that each person consumes the output of 2,500m^2 of land in agricultural production the total land allocated to roads and parking in 2030 will be enough to feed 80 million people across the world.

The Heidelberg study is remarkable for its global vision and for its painstaking research. Even so it has not taken into account health impacts from respiratory disease, health impacts from noise, the effects on children and the elderly arising from loss of freedom to move around without fear of a road traffic accident, effects on communities of severance when road schemes divide them, effects on plants and animals which are very rarely enumerated, effects on biodiversity, water run-off, water quality, and global effects through the mining and quarrying of finite materials to support the road construction and vehicle manufacturing industry.

An earlier Heidelberg study constructed a life-cycle analysis of a car. This analysis considers a 'middle-range' vehicle and assumes an average annual distance travelled of 13,000km over ten years. The result is a documentation of all the energy inputs and waste products of manufacturing, use and disposal of this vehicle. These results are summarised in Table 2.2.

One car can be seen to be responsible for the production of 59.7 tonnes of CO_2 and 26.5 tonnes of waste materials. This is a very high price to pay for the school run, the journey to work and the trip to the local supermarket.

The balance sheet for the private car shows an impressive catalogue of negatives and work still has to be done to work this out for road construction, road maintenance, lorries and aircraft.

If transport generates a large number of negatives (usually referred to as external costs) it is possible that there exist an equal number of positives or external benefits. Whilst it is clear that noise, air pollution, road traffic accidents and health damage to the respiratory tracts of children are clear examples of external costs it is not clear what the external benefits of transport would look like. They cannot include the benefits to the producer or the supplier of the transport service nor to others in the supply chain because they are all internal to the market process that is guiding the availability of transport service, its price and the relationship between price and the quality of the service offered. If transport improved health or employment in some way and third parties outside the buyer/seller pair benefited, then this would be an external benefit. This produces problems however. Cheap transport can be shown to centralise and concentrate economic activity and so lead to job loss in many of Europe's regions. Motorised transport also damages health. It is very hard to conceptualise a situation where passing streams of traffic in an urban area contribute to health improvements. The evidence from regional development analyses points to the complexity of transport and economic development links and on balance would seem to suggest that better transport/cheaper transport is just as likely to drain jobs away from a local economy as attract them. Indeed this was the conclusion of the UK-based Royal Commission on Environmental Pollution (1994) in its eighteenth report on Transport and the Environment.

Table 2.2: Summary of Energy Consumption and Emissions: Life-cycle Analysis (per car)

Primary energy	22.9t CEU[1]
CO_2	59.7 tonnes
SO_2	32.8kg
NO_x	89.5kg
Particles	4.2kg
CO	368.1kg
C_xH_y	62.9kg
Polluted air	2,040 million m^3
Benzol emissions	812.5g
Formaldehyde	203.1g
Road surface abrasion	17,500g
Tyre abrasion	750.0g
Brake abrasion	150.0g
Lead	85.8g
Chrome	0.2g
Copper	4.3g
Nickel	1.2g
Zinc	0.8g
Platinum	1.3mg
Crude oil in world oceans	13 litres
Total waste material	26.5 tonnes

Note: [1] t CEU = tonnes of Coal Equivalent Units

Source: Teufel *et al.* (1993)

ECOPLAN, a Swiss economic consultancy, examined the concept of external benefits in transport in 1993 and concluded that they were almost non-existent. In a rather forthright statement it concluded: 'this altogether shows that transport policy can forget about external benefits'. This sweeping statement was based on a substantial economic analysis – both theoretical and practical – of external benefits in transport and has been supported by Maddison and his colleagues (1996) in *The True Costs of Road Transport*. This publication concludes: 'the only external benefits that we can think of are benefits to individuals who enjoy car-spotting'. The authors of this provocative quotation go on to put the question 'Will we benefit if our neighbours drive more than they do already?' The answer, clearly, is 'no', just as in the case of costs the answer is 'yes'. If our neighbour doubles his or her amount of driving then we will suffer an increase in air pollution, noise, road danger and loss of freedoms associated with cycling and walking. Transport shows a clear dominance of external costs in the complete absence of external benefits.

Counting the Costs

Public transport, particularly in the UK, has long been the object of derision for its economic inefficiency and the degree to which it has been subsidised. The use of the word subsidy has strong negative associations which are almost exactly mirrored by use of words like investment when the discussion turns to new road infrastructure to support car and lorry transport. The reality in both cases is more complex, with substantial sums of public expenditure going to support road transport and the use of the car and substantial benefits to society as a whole flowing from a greater use of public transport, walking and cycling. A decline in car use and an increase in walking and cycling produces substantial gains for the whole population through cleaner air, less noise and improved road safety. Under these circumstances the use of words like subsidy and investment are at best confusing and at worst slogans to achieve a particular set of political objectives. Maddison and his colleagues (ibid) provide a thorough grounding in the economic analysis necessary to follow the debate about costs and benefits, and which mode pays the full costs that it imposes on society as a whole.

In addition, evidence from several countries summarised in 'Transport For a Sustainable Future' (Whitelegg, 1993) and in Maddison *et al.* (1996) shows very clearly that road transport is imposing costs that are substantially bigger than all the taxation income from road transport. This is important, first because it reveals a large flow of resources into what is essentially a very inefficient way of organising transport, and second because it stimulates a more positive debate about the alternatives. It is also both UK and EU policy 'to ensure that (transport) users pay the full social and environmental cost of their transport decisions, so improving the overall efficiency of those decisions for the economy as a whole' (Department of the Environment, 1994b). Bringing about this situation where car drivers and lorry owners pay the full costs is often referred to as 'internalising the external costs of transport'.

> The EU has accepted the case for internalising the external costs of transport. This means building into the taxation system at some suitable point the costs attributable to noise pollution, air pollution, road traffic accidents, road damage, and so forth. Weizsaecker at the Wuppertal Institute in Germany has advocated the same strategy for a number of years in his argument 'prices should tell the ecological truth'.

The logic is a simple restatement of the polluter pays principle, which is now incorporated into the EU's Fifth Environmental Action Programme. The principle is easy but the practice very difficult. By definition there are a large number of approaches and competing assumptions in the tricky task of putting a financial value on a unit of air pollution or a dead body. However, this has not stopped the UK government over the last 20 years in its efforts to put a value on time and a value on dead bodies – as long as they were killed in a road traffic accident. These time and life valuations have been a great support to the road building programme – both work to show the advantages of new roads in cutting time for journeys and reducing road traffic accidents – so it is not unreasonable to assume that valuing air quality and pedestrian waiting times might tip the balance the other way. A large monetary value on peace and quiet and on trees and unpolluted air might just be enough to see off a new road justified on some other difficult-to-calculate variable.

There are many objections to putting monetary valuations on things that are difficult to measure on a financial metric. First and foremost it is an unstable system. If we are worried about badgers and toads and the health of children we can estimate some matching financial values but it only takes a slight increase in the value of time savings for 200,000 journeys every day to swamp our badgers and babies. Financial valuations are no substitute for political judgements that set priorities. If slavery and the use of small boys and girls down coal mines had been left to a financial valuation then there would still be slaves, and small boys and girls would still be down the modern equivalent of coal mines. Both these dubious practices were outlawed because they were wrong, and this 'wrong' is a political judgement.

But putting prices on things is a popular activity in the mid-1990s. In this the Organisation for Economic Cooperation and Development (OECD) has grasped the nettle and the European Federation for Transport and the Environment (T&E) in Brussels has produced a very comprehensive guide under the title 'Getting the Prices Right' (Kågeson, 1993). Table 2.3 reproduces the T&E calculations for the UK.

Table 2.3: External Costs in the United Kingdom (1993)

	ECU per 1,000 tonnes and 1,000 passenger kilometres				
Mode of Transport	Air Pollution	CO_2	Noise	Accidents	Total
Freight					
Lorry	5.6	3.5	0.5	2.3	11.9
Train	0.6	2.9	0.2	3.8	7.5
Ro-ro[1]	6.0	0.6	0.0	0.1	6.7
Passenger					
Car	14.6	4.5	0.9	8.9	28.9
Train	0.9	2.2	0.2	3.8	7.1
Aircraft	7.3	9.2	1.2	0.2	17.9

Note: [1] Roll-on roll-off vehicle ferries

It is interesting that cars impose the greatest burden of external costs, followed by aircraft.

In the case of road transport specifically, Maddison *et al.* (1996) summarise studies of the total external costs of this activity in 18 countries. As a percentage of GDP these costs vary enormously, reflecting the methodological variations as much as the actual circumstances in each country. The average for 17 European countries was 4.2 per cent of GDP and the highest figure reported was for the US at 12.3 per cent. The UK figure for 1991 was approximately ECU30 billion (£24 billion), or 3.7 per cent of GDP. These costs do not include aviation and do not include a number of externalities related to social equity and loss of freedoms.

EU and national government action to take the data in Table 2.3 and incorporate it into taxation on fuels would go some way to reducing the demand for transport, revealing alternatives and ensuring that different modes of transport competed on roughly equivalent terms. What this internalisation of external costs would not do is solve the problem of growth in the demand for all forms of motorised transport and its associated societal impact.

Conclusion

The evidence concerning the negative social, environmental and economic effects of transport dependency is very strong indeed. Chapters 8 and 9 will return to some of these matters in more detail, particularly for road freight and aviation. What is clear from this preliminary assessment is that the magnitude of the damage and severity of the problem has not triggered an equally serious response and commitment from those charged with the responsibility of finding a solution. At the individual and the collective level we are still in the euphoric stage of the Faustian bargain. Power and knowledge are fine until the time comes to pay for the consequences of what, in historical terms, is a very brief and compressed period of hyper-mobility, social disintegration, fossil fuel dependence and environmental destruction.

CHAPTER 3

Free to Choose and Free to Grow

Introduction

Car travel and aviation expand freedom and choice for those able to capture a disproportionate amount of the commodity on offer, but demand grows in response to market signals (for example, cheap fuel) and to the availability of new infrastructure.

The expansion of these choices restricts other freedoms, particularly of vulnerable groups, for example, children and the poor. Women in developing countries and those who travel short distances are unlikely to benefit from strategies that encourage longer distance travel. A comparison between shopping in developed countries and the acquisition of food, water and fuel in developing countries reveals a great deal about freedom and whose freedoms are expanding as a consequence of the operation of global markets.

The demand for transport in developed countries does not follow some inexorable law of the universe. It is there, and growing fast, because of the forces that shape the major components of lifestyle and of consumption. Transport planning has traditionally focused on the supply side of the equation and not the demand side: if more people wish to travel by air then it appears very logical to supply the necessary runway and airport capacity. This is the central argument for the construction of a new terminal at Heathrow airport which will add an extra 30 million passengers per annum to a 1996 total of 54 million passengers per annum (see Chapter 6). If more people live further away from their work and use the car to commute and to shop then it appears only logical to supply the roads and bypasses that will make this increased travel possible. This supply side approach is very attractive. It allows decision makers and politicians to fall back on market forces, to extol the virtues of freedom and choice, and to pour scorn on those who suggest different arrangements which would reduce the demand for transport. Any suggestion of social engineering – telling people how they can travel, by what mode of transport and under what circumstances – is dismissed.

There are many inconsistencies in the supply side approach and with the advocacy of market forces and the rejection of social engineering. The most important inconsistency is that the whole idea of meeting demand is very partial from a public policy perspective. In the UK, as in most developed countries, there is a large homeless population, large numbers of children deprived of pre-school (kindergarten) facilities, large numbers without access to the kind of medical attention they need and large numbers of elderly with insufficient income to pay for basic energy needs in order that they may keep warm in the winter. It is quite clear in all these instances that the political process has decided not to meet demand. The demand is there, but resources have not been allocated to whatever needs to be done to meet that demand. A supply side solution has been adopted instead to reduce demand (or more accurately ignore it).

There were a number of conferences on aviation and the environment in the UK in 1994 and 1995. At these conferences many speakers advanced the idea that aviation was very damaging for the environment, was heavily subsidised and should be denied public funds for its expansion and subject to a tax on aviation fuel. These suggestions met with a robust response, and not only from within the aviation industry. To increase the price of air travel, it was argued, would be iniquitous because it would deny lower income groups the pleasures of such travel, and air travel broadens the mind and helps us to appreciate the world, and so on. Leaving aside for a moment issues of mass tourism and environmental damage, and the even more difficult issues, for instance sex tourism in Thailand, this robust defence of air travel sits very uncomfortably alongside the lack of such defence for housing, healthcare and life-saving winter heat for the elderly.

Transport represents a very clear example of 'special pleading' for relatively well-off groups in society who are in a position to take three or four holidays abroad each year and drive the family's new multi-purpose vehicle to the supermarket each week. A concern for basic equity within and between groups would lead us more in the direction of many more local facilities, car-free environments, increased walking, cycling and public transport, and a society where housing, warm homes, healthcare, and access to local jobs, schools and shops has priority over the longer distance alternatives.

Governmental and political confusion about choice, freedoms and markets is very pronounced and is currently wreaking havoc, for example, in eastern Europe where the 'choice' to use railways for freight and dense networks of urban public transport for passenger trips is being replaced by the 'choice' to use roads and private motorised transport. Governmental intervention structures the choice regime in favour of road transport and then reduces the overall amount of choice. The process of weighting the bias in favour of roads and privatised transport modes is supported by the rhetoric of the market and by specific liberalisation policies such as privatisation and deregulation.

The political bias in this process can best be understood by considering a hypothetical situation. It is illuminating to ponder the implications of a transfer in the UK of a high ranking health official to the Department of Transport and a similar transfer in the opposite direction. If both officials are faithful to the experience and world view of their 'home' department there would be a massive expansion in hospitals, numbers of nurses, number of intensive care beds, GPs and support workers. The transport official will have been promoted and gained experience within a culture where predictions of future demand are made and then facilities are put in place to meet that demand. The health official, on the other hand, has gained experience within a culture where demand has to be constrained by resource availability. This is why waiting lists are long and why there is frequent discussion about rationing, for example, no hip replacement joints if the patient is over 65 years old. The health official now at the Department of Transport would find many reasons for scrapping the road building budget, closing roads (very uneconomic, particularly in rural areas), cutting staff concerned with roads and ensuring that as many people as possible used the remaining roads as much as possible so as to increase their utilisation rate, reduce unit costs and use waiting lists (queues) as a rationing mechanism. This fantasy dramatically illustrates how different are the (hidden) ideologies underpinning the two departments in question.

Motorised transport, particularly cars, has successfully colonised key aspects of human psychology. People believe cars offer freedom, power, sexual fantasy and reinforcement of personal esteem and ego. The fact that most of this applies to men and not women has not gone unnoticed in the advertising world and the arcane world of motoring magazines. In March 1994 a motoring correspondent in *Top Gear*, a BBC magazine, thought it perfectly acceptable to refer to a new car model he was testing as capable of 'snapping knicker elastic at 50 paces'. An understanding of psychology is more important than a morbid fascination with the sexual fetishes of motoring correspondents. If cars can be sold on the basis of this nonsense and if the advertising industry works in the same way then society is in deep trouble. Sex, freedom and power score very highly as behavioural drivers and motivators. Going by bike, walking or catching the bus are not likely to conjure up anywhere near as powerful a cocktail. It is for these reasons that inducements to leave the car at home or use an alternative mode of transport have to be equally powerful and cover as many policy angles as it is possible to design.

But cars do not deliver the freedom that their advertisers spend hundreds of millions of pounds telling us that they do. Cars get stuck in traffic jams, they pollute their own occupants with health damaging VOCs, they are prone to being used for, and subject to, crime, and they confer no immunity from personal attack.

They also cost a lot of money and take up a lot of time in working to pay for them, fuel them and maintain them. A small car in Germany owned by a middle-income individual will take 470 hours of work to pay its yearly cost. If these hours are added to the calculation of average journey speeds over a year taking into account congested traffic conditions then a new average speed can be calculated. This works out at 17kph. This is further reduced to 13kph when the external costs (see Chapter 2) are taken into account.

Figure 3.1 shows for the bicycle, small car and large car average speeds as they would normally be calculated over a year. These are compared with average 'social' speeds when time taken to work to pay for the vehicle is taken into account. The car does not represent particularly good value for money when compared with the bicycle.

The car kills children – both child pedestrians and the children of parents who have supplied a car to their nearly adult offspring. There are very few adults or 17 year olds who have not had direct personal contact with friends and relatives who have lost a 17–21 year old in a car crash fatality. These immense personal tragedies are avoidable but not within the fantasy world created by the advertisers, the car manufactures and the media onslaught on adolescents that works tirelessly to prepare them for their role as hyper consumers.

Cars do not bring freedom of choice. They narrow choice. In heavily motorised societies like the US and Australia it is very difficult not to own a car and drive it on journeys as short as 100m. Walking is seen as a deviant activity (more in the US than in Australia), cycling is dangerous and fume sodden, and public transport sparse to non-existent. These relationships are not accidental. In the US during the 1920s and 1930s, combined efforts on the part of car manufactures, oil companies, tyre manufacturers and highway builders bought up and closed down public transport systems. This process is described in some detail in Glen Yago's (1984) *The Decline of Transit*. So active were the representatives of the automobile industry in undermining rail transit in the US during this period that they were investigated by the FBI. By the mid- to late-1950s the auto, rubber and oil companies had achieved their objectives and largely eliminated rail transit from US cities.

Every aspect of US government at local and national level worked towards the elimination of public transport use. Building and zoning codes and traffic and parking regulations combined to favour car transport at the expense of public transport. The creation of special government units for bridge building, highway plans and ultimately the coordination of all urban transportation served to promote highway transportation alone. In the period 1915–1957, US companies abandoned approximately 29,000km of rail track.

Figure 3.1: Average Social Speeds (taking into account the total amount of time spent in transport)

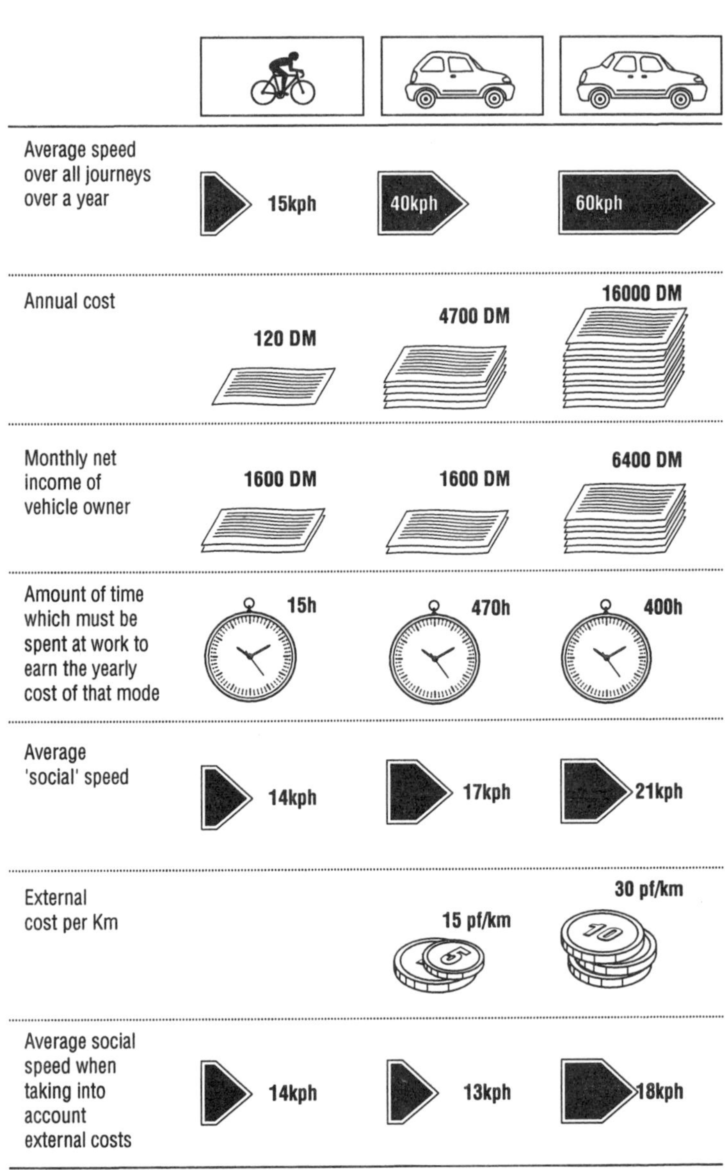

Source: Seifried (1990)

The Shopping Trip

Shopping takes up a lot of time, consumes a lot of energy and takes place in a way largely determined by the retail industry. This has metamorphosed over the last 20 years to present consumers with unparalleled choice, lots of car parking, long opening hours and a supply system that ensures an ever rising quantity of lorries on the roads and aircraft in the skies. The things that are actually bought on the shopping trip have less and less to do with local availability. Even if goods are available locally they will still be provided at the end of a very long supply chain involving numerous cross flows and many thousands of lorry kilometres. The sourcing of products, particularly food products, on a global basis has implications for the environment (at both the origin and the destination) and for the developing countries organised into this global logistic operation to ensure that a supermarket in a provincial town such as Basingstoke can stock New Zealand apples, Bangladeshi shrimps and green beans from Kenya. This has implications for energy consumption, the use of pesticides and ozone-depleting chemicals; and human health and transport are central components in this web of production, consumption and pollution.

Steffi Böge at the Wuppertal Institute has revealed the complexity and irrationality of the material flows that go into the production of yoghurt and chocolate puddings at a plant in Stuttgart, southern Germany. Each 150g pot of strawberry yoghurt is responsible for moving one lorry 9.2m. Her painstaking research (reproduced in figures 3.2, 3.3 and 3.4) accurately describes the spatial and transport impact of a representative group of basic food commodities.

The development of complex and spatially attenuated production–consumption relationships is aided by the economics of transport. Fuel is cheap and transport does not bear the external costs that it generates.

It is very cost effective, therefore, to source globally, stimulate consumer 'choice' and harness the productive capacity of African and Asian countries to supply the fruit and salad crops that we require. This provides choice – but at the expense of land and survival in origin countries, and at the expense of locally available food products. Britain, for example, is quite capable of supplying apples and in so doing supporting a healthy rural industry in the orchard business. Long distance substitutes wipe out local sourcing, necessitate more use of chemicals and consume much more energy.

In Kenya farmers have switched from growing potatoes, carrots, maize and cabbages for local consumption to producing luxury vegetables such as French beans or flowers to be flown to Europe. Exports of horticultural products have grown from less than 1,500

Figure 3.2: Transport Relationships: strawberry yogurt, 150g

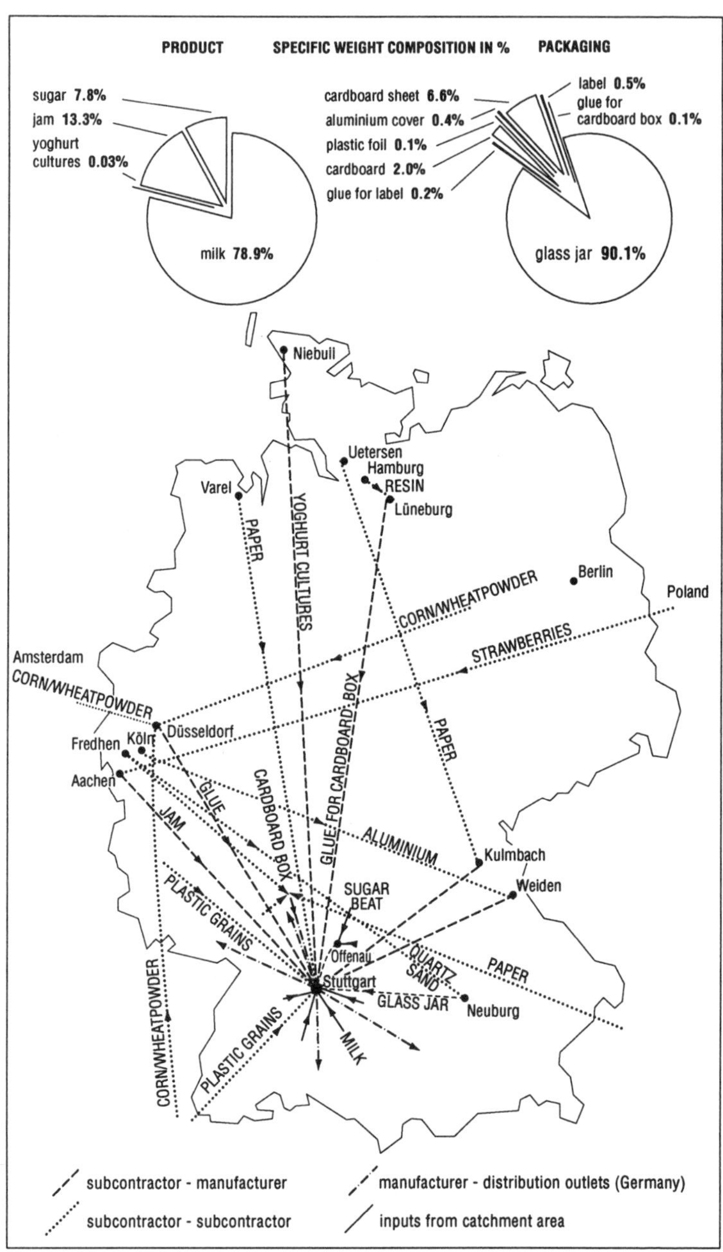

Source: Böge (1995)

Figure 3.3: Transport Relationships: strawberry yogurt, 500g

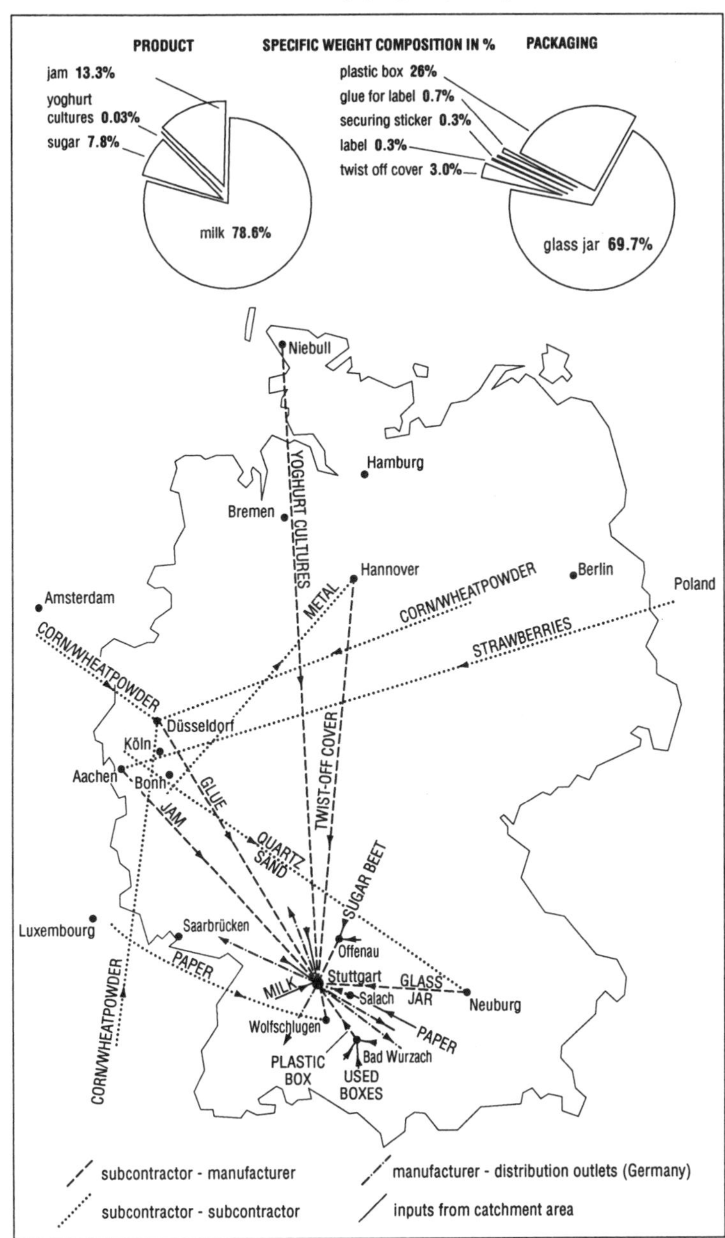

Source: Böge (1995)

Figure 3.4: Transport Relationships: chocolate pudding, 125g

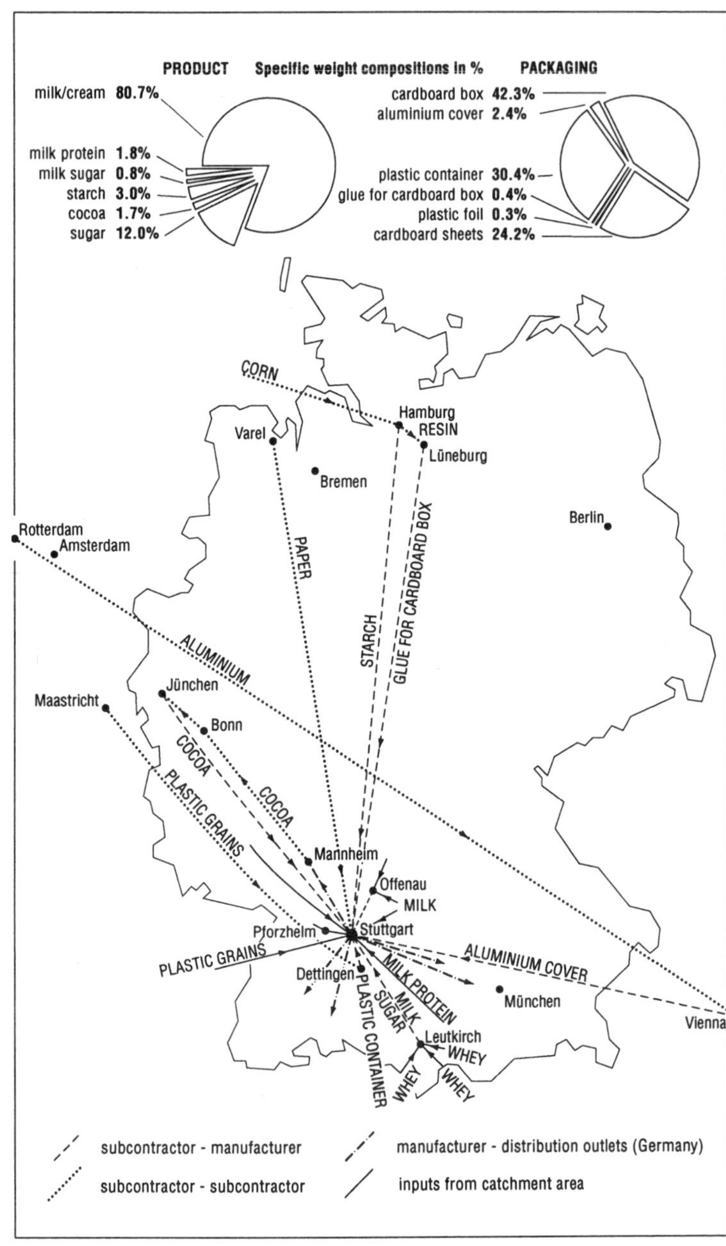

Source: Böge (1995)

tonnes in 1967 to 64,000 tonnes in 1993. Air transport of freight is extremely polluting. Each tonne-km of air freight will produce:

- 1,206g of CO_2
- 2.0g of CH_4
- 3.0g of VOCs
- 5.5g of NO_x
- 1.4g of CO

The energy required to air freight one tonne-km of cargo is 15,839 kilojoules (kj) which compares with road at 3,890kj, rail at 677kj and water at 423kj for the same amount of work.

> The availability of Kenyan beans or Latin American salad crops in supermarkets is defended as an increase in choice. It is only possible because of the expenditure of large amounts of energy which is under-priced, destroys local economies, replaces food production for local needs in source countries, and devastates their environment through intensive agricultural/horticultural practices, irrigation, water pollution and soil erosion.
>
> Transport very effectively links the devastation at both ends of the supply chain and in the middle, and once again is justified on the grounds of consumer choice, freedom to purchase and market forces.

Within the destination country the movement of food, drink and tobacco (these three are aggregated in statistical sources) is a major factor in the growth of road freight and the environmental impact of road transport. This impact also extends to the devastation of countryside for new motorway construction, as in the case of the M3 near Winchester (Twyford Down) and the M65 near Blackburn (Stanworth Valley). Over a third of the growth in overall tonne-km travelled by road freight in the UK over the past 15 years is attributable to the increase in transport of food, drink and tobacco which accounts for only 8.5 per cent of GDP. The sector accounted for more of the increase in tonne-km than for any other major commodity group.

Car drivers in the early 1990s accounted for 549km of travel each year for shopping trips (Department of Transport, 1994) compared with 424km for car passengers This amount of travel has been encouraged by the provision of large car parks at the edges of town and out-of-town supermarkets, and the development of stand-alone retailing facilities some distance from traditional town centres (for example, Merry Hill near Dudley in the UK). The car intensity of trips to retailing outlets matches the lorry intensity of supply systems and the air intensity of global sourcing. The sum total is an energy and pollution bill that puts a severe strain on sustainable development objectives and CO_2 reduction targets. In the case of Merry Hill and similar ventures elsewhere in Britain this high energy expenditure has devastated the adjacent city centres and added to the problems of those without cars whose search for basic foodstuffs has been made much more difficult as a result of the decline of the traditional centre and suburban shopping streets.

The combination of cheap fuel, aggressive corporate strategies to carve out new business opportunities, sophisticated planning and logistics, sophisticated advertising and peer group pressure, and a spiral of decay and decline in traditional retailing has produced a dramatic shift upwards in the demand for transport. This has put pressure on the global environment and damaged the social and food-producing systems for local needs in developing countries and increased the use of pesticides, herbicides, preservatives and packaging. It has damaged the health and welfare of the poor, the elderly and those without cars in Britain, and it has contributed to the pressure to build more roads and destroy more of Britain's countryside and woodland.

Two Worlds

The trip to the supermarket by car on a Saturday to pick and choose through the world's produce is very different to the everyday reality of two-thirds of the world's population who live in Africa, India, Bangladesh, South America and South East Asia. There are, of course, hundreds and possibly thousands of worlds. The daily experience of an unemployed single mother on a peripheral housing estate in Liverpool or in Moss Side in Manchester is a world apart from the suburban life of the multi-car family in Cheadle Hulme and Stockport to the south of Manchester. Spatial juxtaposition is a very poor guide to shared worlds and the extremes of Manchester and Liverpool are only shades different from the extremes of Bombay, Calcutta or Bangkok.

One of the problems with transport planning that makes life very difficult (and solutions impossible) is the tendency to ignore the rich variety of wealth, income, physical capability, childcare responsibility, attachment to place and altruism that characterises real populations. This is bad enough in the north of England or in Hackney in London, but on a global scale acts as a significant block to insight, creativity and problem solving in this area.

Shopping, or what passes for shopping, in some developing countries presents a very different picture to that in a developed country. Women in rural Tanzania spend about 1,800 hours a year in activities which are primarily transport related, for example, collecting water, collecting firewood, making journeys to the fields to tend crops and making trips to market. This equates to almost 5 hours a day, 365 days a year. Men, by comparison, spend about 500 hours on similar tasks. In rural Ghana a similar pattern emerges. Women spend about 1,000 hours on the same kinds of tasks as Tanzanian women, and men about 350 hours (Bryceson and Howe, 1992).

Transport in both countries for the vast majority of the rural population is a very local and very basic survival activity. Roads and vehicles are largely non-existent and the predominant activity is freight movement via the medium of head porterage. Loads are heavy and women are the main carriers. In a study carried out in Addis Ababa women on average carried a load per trip of 36.2kg (75 per cent of body weight).

Most travel in these rural communities was internal to the village or short-distance trips to neighbouring areas. In Ghana 0.6 per cent of trips were classified as long distance. In Tanzania 90 per cent of all trips, 80 per cent of time spent on transport and 95 per cent of the weight of goods was within and around the village. The amount of work done within the household is prodigious. In Ghana an average household of 11.4 members transported over 220 tonne-km per year, taking approximately 4,800 hours. In Tanzania less effort is expended. The average household size is 5.0 members and transport activities occupied about 2,500 hours per annum – that is, 48 hours per week. (The Tanzanian village had more difficult physical terrain and a more subsistence-based agricultural economy than the Ghanaian example.) (ibid).

These conditions of hard physical effort and women carrying out a disproportionately large proportion of transport-related tasks are very common and can be found throughout the Indian subcontinent as well as in Africa. The existence of such circumstances and the irrelevance of most contemporary transport planning to those circumstances is an important factor in arriving at a global perspective. Much of what currently goes on in India, Bangladesh, Africa and South America under the label transport planning and transport investment will not help the vast majority of the population who are poor and concerned with tasks related to daily living and survival. For 95 per cent of the population the prospect of car ownership is pure fantasy, and yet water and firewood have to be collected and produce taken to market.

Transport planning and traffic engineering as professional disciplines have very little to offer rural women in Africa. Their gender-specific tasks and their role in the social and economic structure of their countries confers a substantial burden upon them. Relieving this burden demands a broad social, economic and appropriate technology perspective which is very rare in highway engineering and traffic engineering. Transport planning and investment in Africa, as in Europe, is concerned with highways and bridges and only very rarely with transport technologies and designs that are appropriate to African women. Transport investment in Africa has failed to address the demand side of the equation. The parallels with Europe are dramatic. Transport solutions in Africa would involve giving attention to fresh drinking water supplies and to very simple and affordable technologies that would satisfy the requirements of domestic cooking. The solutions would address the problem of head porterage by finding ways of easing the burden on women and helping them to cope with the requirement of carrying young children at the same time. For instance, bicycle technologies appropriate to the particular geographical situation and journey purpose could be developed and implemented. Technologies appropriate to the circumstances of very local freight transport in terms of head porterage and bicycle devices should receive a high priority. The time of women would also be accorded a high priority so that solutions would have a further advantage of liberating time for productive work in the field to increase nutrition and improve health. The starting point is recognising women and their social and economic importance. This is likely to prove extremely difficult.

In Europe transport planners have similar problems with such 'invisible' people. If women and young children were 'visible' and the elderly were accorded some recognition then there would not be the depressing underpasses for pedestrians in cities such as Birmingham and Plymouth, and there would not be strong wire fences on central reservations blocking pedestrian flows in Slough and Hoddesdon. The products of transport planning in the form of surface existence for cars and an underground existence for pedestrians clearly indicates priorities. Standing at a pelican crossing on a wet day in Lancaster as the traffic flows past unimpeded gives the game away. Both African women and women in the north of England are receiving a very poor service from the vast amounts of money spent on traffic and transport systems each year.

> The invisibility of women around the world is matched by the invisibility of children and the elderly in transport planning and by the invisibility of pedestrians, cyclists, rickshaw pullers and any other group or technology that does not fit the technological and consumerist stereotype of the car.

There are approximately 700,000 rickshaws in Bangladesh. Approximately 1.25 million people are directly employed in the driving and maintenance of these and some 5 million people in total (4.5 per cent of the population) depend on them for their subsistence. In the mid-1980s rickshaws contributed 34 per cent of the total value added by the transport sector which was double the contribution of all motorised transport, 12 times the contribution of Bangladeshi railways and 12.5 times the contribution of the national airline. Every day about 7 million trips are made in Dhaka (the capital of Bangladesh) by rickshaw – double the output of London's Underground system.

Rickshaws did not exist in government planning in Bangladesh in the 1980s in the same way that bicycles did not exist in China. During the second Five Year Plan in Bangladesh (1980–85) not one transport project in 300 was connected with rickshaws. In the third Five Year Plan rickshaws were dismissed in a single sentence:

> Slow moving vehicles such as pedal-rickshaws, push and pull carts etc. should be gradually eliminated through development of automotive vehicles and training of existing operators for such vehicles (Gallagher, 1992).

This kind of dismissiveness and perpetuation of invisibility has been very much encouraged by the World Bank and other international lending institutions who have put in excess of 80 per cent of their funds into highway projects.

In the case of Dhaka and its rickshaws, the planners and politicians perceive a problem. Transport planners dislike large amounts of mixed traffic, each element of which has very different speed characteristics. The result of 40 years of expert opinion and Western training of traffic engineers is a strong desire to ease the flow of 'real' traffic, that is cars, and eliminate any traffic that 'slows down' motorised traffic. Likewise the planners in Delhi in India are clear that small motorised rickshaws (auto-rickshaws) are causing traffic problems and should be removed. In Manila the Philippines government banned 17,000 motorised tricycles from main roads on the grounds that they caused traffic delay and congestion. In Bombay auto-rickshaws have been banned. In Jakarta in Indonesia rickshaws ('becaks') have been banned though they still operate in the suburbs. In 1970 there were 150,000 becaks giving employment to 375,000 drivers and owners, approximately 23 per cent of the city's work force. Between 1980 and 1985 50,000 becaks were seized by the police and thrown into the sea.

The animosity towards two-wheeled vehicles, animal drawn transport and rickshaws is a reaction against things that are traditional (that is, not modern) and also a reaction to the enormous traffic jams and congestion in most cities in developing countries. Traditional modes of transport are slow, mix uneasily with cars, lorries and buses, and are also heavily involved in road traffic accidents.

The desire to modernise and the desire to clear the way for the private car have been the driving force behind this massive assault on a mode of transport that provides large-scale employment for hundreds of thousands of people, and services the basic access and mobility needs of cities well suited to this form of transport. A transport policy influenced by considerations other than consumption and the convenience of the wealthy would restrict cars in Jakarta, Dhaka and Bombay, provide technical assistance to make the rickshaw easier to pedal (or pull in the case of Calcutta), provide a social infrastructure for the pullers/pedallers that can supply healthcare, social insurance, re-training (where appropriate) and retirement provision, and incorporate rickshaws into environmental strategies to reduce air pollution. In the case of auto-rickshaws alternative technology would have to be found to polluting engines.

From Preston to Dhaka

Bangladesh is very concerned with broad national policies that will see per capita incomes rise, that will modernise traditional sectors of the economy, create jobs and give the country a progressive image. Investing in new roads is a key element in this strategy. In 1989 the president announced that another 7,400 miles of road were under construction. This would triple the existing network, and work was also in progress on 18 major bridges (Gallagher, 1992). Roads are seen as tangible, something that can be implemented quickly, with international aid, and are thought to create jobs. Similarly in Preston, Lancashire County Council (LCC) has an ambitious road building project (developed throughout the 1980s and 1990s and summarised in 'Greening the Red Rose County', 1994), sees the new roads (28 in total) as a key factor in the economic development of 'lagging' regions and expects to get government funds for their construction. Like Bangladeshi politicians, the LCC politicians prefer the quick fix solution of something very tangible – something that the electorate can see rather than something less tangible and slower, but possibly more effective.

Both Bangladesh and Lancashire have been around this circuit before and are still seeking the elusive economic utopia that new roads are expected to bring. Both are driven by the availability of external funds and a strong internal belief in the efficacy of new roads as an agent of economic development. Both have to deploy large amounts of scarce internal resources to keep up the momentum of planning and developing an improved highway system and this in its turn starves other sectors of funds and completely distorts the transport planning process so that it ignores people, local travel, the environment and social goals. The process creates invisible groups and invisible technologies in the pursuit of cars, lorries, tarmac and an economic nirvana that does not exist.

Conclusion

Widely varying needs and wants on a global scale provide some insight into the common problems of matching transport provision to basic needs. Both developing countries and developed countries largely fail to respond to basic transport needs and accessibility, preferring to invest in highway projects and higher levels of motorisation that cannot deliver socially just and equitable transport solutions. A commitment to traditional economic growth coupled with new infrastructure ignores the needs of the vast majority of the world's population and perpetuates a system of making choices that will eventually eliminate cycling, walking, low-cost transport and local production–consumption systems.

CHAPTER 4

A Word with the Driver

Introduction

The aggregate demand for transport is a function of large numbers of individual decisions but equally is determined by the actions of a very small number of key institutional players who are in a position to steer the development of the space economy and the market for transport services. It is a paradox of free market economics that these key players exist and can exploit the language of free markets to intervene strongly to shape those markets. Without exception, they work in the direction of increasing the demand for transport and the growth of the matching infrastructure

The Drivers

There are powerful institutional forces working towards higher levels of motorisation, car ownership and use, spatial mobility, road freight and traditional visions of economic growth based on consumption. These institutions include the World Bank and the European Bank for Reconstruction and Development (EBRD), the European Union and the European Investment Bank (EIB). They act as points of leverage in a complex global system and so are a legitimate part of thinking and policy development about new directions and sustainable transport. They are in no sense the cause of all environmental and social problems but they exert great influence and are capable of making things both a lot worse and a lot better.

These financial and governmental institutions are supported in their role by transnational corporations which, by definition, act on a global stage and campaign vigorously for new road transport infrastructure, the removal of any trade barriers and cheaper transport. In Europe these corporations have established the European Round Table of Industrialists (ERT) and have lobbied for new transport infrastructure including the Öresund link between Copenhagen and Malmö (in Sweden) and a link between Sicily and the Italian mainland across the Strait of Messina. These views on 'missing links' and the urgency of the need to pave Europe with high quality motorways has had a strong influence on the EU and its trans-European network strategy (TENs).

These institutions also act as barometers of ideas and concepts that inform the detail of planning and investment. It is clear, for example, that the World Bank is strongly influenced by a positive view of the private sector, private capital, privatisation and liberalisation of transport markets and a negative view of state control, state intervention, state monopolies and subsidy of transport systems. Both the positive and the negative views flow from deeper beliefs about efficiency, entrepreneurship, innovation and the management of change, and both are well insulated from direct experience from the failures of both models.

The World Bank, (1994) in 'Transport Sector Policy Review', states that 'poverty reduction is the ultimate objective of the Bank'. According to this review: 'Poverty reduction is facilitated by economic growth. Economic growth is facilitated by trade. Trade development, general productivity improvement, and social development associated with personal mobility are all critically dependent on the quality of transport provisions'.

If life were so simple there would be far less poverty. Sadly the experience of the last 40 years contradicts starkly the World Bank's basic premises. Economic growth has not reduced inequalities, nor has it helped the world's poorest groups. It has, in fact, made the situation worse. The World Health Organisation (WHO) in May 1995 reported that more than one-fifth of the world's population of 5.6 billion live in extreme poverty; almost one-third of the world's children are undernourished and half the globe's population lacks regular access to essential medicines. In addition, 12.2 million children under five die every year from lack of basic healthcare. Whatever international financial markets and the private sector are doing, the health of children in developing countries is deteriorating. This 1995 WHO report called *Bridging the Health Gap in Europe* (WHO 1995c) concludes that inequity in health is growing between countries, between well-off and disadvantaged groups within countries and between the sexes.

The World Bank's adherence to a basic premise that is fundamentally flawed does not augur well for the next 40 years. Healthcare organised on free market principles is not likely to deliver high quality services to those who have no purchasing power. The extermination of traditional forms of low cost transport in cities in the third world is not likely to help the urban poor, and the conversion of cities like Bangkok to freeways and car parks leads to a significant deterioration in air quality that damages the health of the urban poor. Poor people, children and pedestrians will continue to take the brunt of road traffic accidents and air pollution from the vehicles of the wealthy, as city administrations and governments deploy scarce resources to support car ownership and use, and neglect policies that improve accessibility for everyone.

The World Bank view is centred entirely on economics and makes only passing reference to social conditions, the poor and the environment. If poverty reduction is 'the ultimate objective of the Bank' then it has spent hundreds of billions of dollars in not achieving anything like its declared objective.

The Bank acknowledges that transport investments can cause problems, including the loss of homes, jobs and environmental deterioration (1994). It also acknowledges that trunk road infrastructure investments may yield little employment benefit to the poor and offer benefits to longer distance traffic 'which largely passes them by' (ibid). There are many parallels in developed countries with this analysis.

> Roads are justified on the grounds that they will bring jobs. This is a promise not fulfilled, and instead of jobs the local population get air and noise pollution.

The World Bank claim that a high quality environment can be purchased by the wealth created by economic growth is difficult to substantiate – particularly if that wealth is unevenly distributed and health is damaged. Indeed the view that we must generate wealth and then improve the environment is very difficult to reconcile with the principles of sustainable development. Sustainable development (see Chapter 7) is constructed around some key principles, particularly the precautionary principle, and definitions of environmental capacity. If capacity is exceeded through, for example, increases in greenhouse gases that precipitate climate change, then irreversible environmental and human damage is caused. The precautionary principle implies that these very serious threats can be anticipated and avoided by changes in policy and behaviour even in the absence of conclusive scientific proof. An accelerating rate of land take for transport infrastructure and an increasing amount of greenhouse gases associated with the growth in demand for transport threatens the key areas of national and international environmental protection. Under these circumstances it is prudent and rational to minimise the probabilities of environmental damage by shifting to systems of production and consumption that are less energy and materials intensive.

It is simply dangerous and unnecessarily risky to encourage economic growth and, by implication, pollution up until that point when real damage sets in, and only then to throttle back. There is currently not the information or expertise to practice this level of environmental and economic management. Neither is there the capability to ensure that such environmental damage as does occur is evenly distributed across income groups. To accept the Bank's logical sequence is also to deny the potential of high environmental quality as a more powerful engine of economic progress (and a more equitable source of progress) than the discredited models of economic growth that were pursued in the 1960s. The environment is an important commodity in its own right and it is illogical to demote it in preference to economic growth, as does the Bank.

Figure 4.1 shows how important highways are in the World Bank's activities. Highway spending now accounts for about 60 per cent of all transport lending and the Bank is committed to continue to lend for roads (ibid).

Figure 4.1: Modal Distribution of World Bank Funding for Transport (1947–1994)

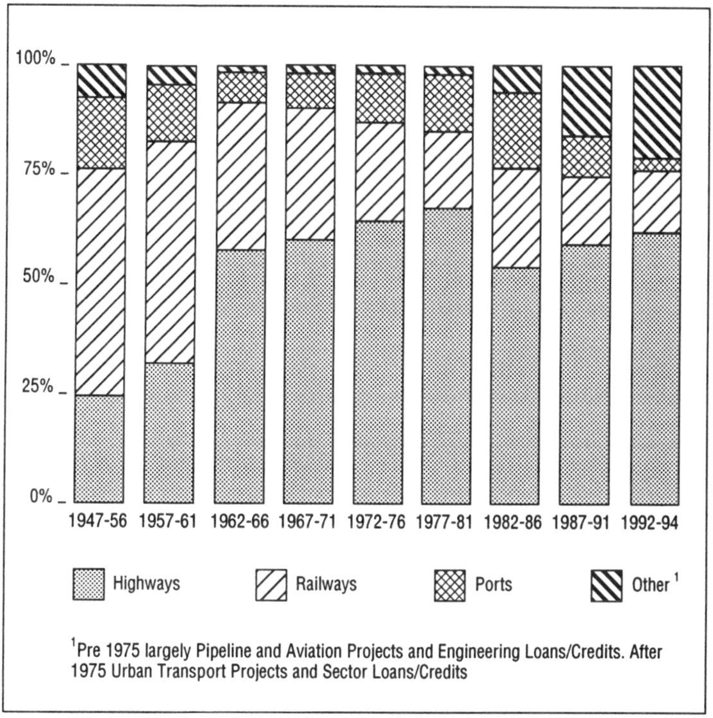

[1]Pre 1975 largely Pipeline and Aviation Projects and Engineering Loans/Credits. After 1975 Urban Transport Projects and Sector Loans/Credits

Source: World Bank (1994)

Paradoxically, there are signs of a different, more enlightened approach in 'Transport Sector Policy Review'. The Bank would like to define and achieve 'efficient and sustainable spatial structures capable of accommodating significant economic and population growth without excessive growth of private motorised mobility' (ibid). The Bank says it would like to give more emphasis to non-motorised transport (NMT) and to the informal sector 'which is important, particularly in Africa, both as a source of income for the poor and as a significant means of providing affordable basic transport service without subsidy' (ibid). The language used to support NMT is encouraging and the existence of Bank projects in the area of minibuses, jitneys and other examples of low-cost transport also encouraging, but the basic principles underlying the Bank's strategy cannot produce a significant shift in resources into low tech, small-scale, affordable personal transport. The prioritisation of economic objectives ahead of environmental objectives, and mitigation of the effects of investment on the poor rather than a fundamental restructuring of policy based on equity and social justice, lead inexorably to a continuation of the style of investment seen over the last 40 years with some minor excursions into NMT and the informal sector.

The International Institute for Energy Conservation (IIEC) has conducted a review of the transport policies of the multilateral lending banks, including the World Bank, the EBRD and the EIB. The report concludes that the policy of all three is heavily skewed in the direction of road investment, notwithstanding some examples of rail investment and reorganisation of public transport. The balance of policy initiatives in all three is in the direction of new highways and bypasses, rail closure and privatisation. The World Bank quotes bus deregulation in the UK as an example of successful transport policies introduced through privatisation and liberalisation. The experience of UK bus deregulation has seen the loss of over 25 per cent of urban passengers and considerable uncertainty and disorganisation about timings, connections and information. In the large UK cities, for example, Manchester, bus deregulation has introduced many more buses on key corridors, the majority of which are less than 10 per cent occupied and add greatly to air pollution.

Railways in both Poland and Hungary are being run down at the suggestion of the World Bank. In Hungary the proposal is to cut the rail system to half its present size. Coinciding with rail closure is the proposal to build 597km of new motorway in Hungary with Bank funds. The World Bank is also supporting motor vehicle manufacturing in Hungary and the Czech Republic. The Bank has supplied $34 million to support a Suzuki plant in Hungary and DM1.4 billion for a Skoda-Volkswagen plant in the Czech Republic.

The Bank supports motorway projects on the grounds that they will stimulate economic development in the 'transitional economies' of eastern Europe.

The EBRD has a documented environmental policy and is supporting both rail and road projects. It is contributing ECU48.7 million for the Berlin–Warsaw railway upgrading and a further ECU40 million for the A4 motorway between Krakow and Katowice in Poland and upgrading of the National Route 1 near Czestochowa. According to the EBRD these projects provide: 'an excellent opportunity to develop a continuous motorway serving the industrial conurbation centred on Katowice, the historic city of Krakow and linking Germany, Poland and the Ukraine'. (IIEC, 1995)

The combined effect of EBRD and World Bank discrimination against 'inefficient' rail and urban public transport and in favour of 'efficient' bypasses and motorways is to increase the rate at which motorisation increases and to add to greenhouse gas emissions and health-damaging pollutants. However, this is only a first stage effect. Following closely on the increased use of cars and lorries is the effect on spatial structures, market areas and local employment. Poland and Hungary will find themselves increasingly incorporated into a European market area stretching from Ireland to the Urals and Scandinavia to Greece serviced by sophisticated logistics, road-based transport and competitive pressures. These pressures will inevitably weaken the economies of these two countries. The best that can be hoped for in these countries is the occasional car plant or television/video manufacturing facility employing at best a few thousand workers. Whole other areas of the economy will be wiped out as local production is destroyed and communities without a viable employment base still have the motorways and the pollution.

The EIB is a long-standing provider of regional development funds and road, rail and port projects in the original European Community. It is now active in eastern Europe. In Poland the EIB is also involved with the A4 motorway and the upgrading of the railway from Berlin to Moscow via Warsaw. ECU200 million have been allocated for the railway project and ECU225 million for the A4 motorway. The funds will be used for a 56km section of new motorway between Opole and Gliwice as well as upgrading the road between Wroclaw and Gliwice to motorway standard. The EIB is also considering additional financing of up to ECU100 million for the A4 project at a later date. In these and in other projects the EIB is involved with implementing the trans-European road network.

In its 1996 (second quarter) information bulletin the EIB reported on its success in Portugal:

> About three quarters of the funds (ECU 6.4 billion) were devoted to strengthening basic infrastructure essential for the development of the country. Top of the list was the financing of roads (ECU 2 billion to BRISA and Junta Autonoma de

> Estradas), specifically the motorways serving Lisbon and Oporto and providing links with Spain and the other EU countries ... [T]he rail network's mainlines were modernised with EIB loans, totalling nearly ECU 400 million, going to CP and Nos Ferroviarios de Lisboa e Porto.

Further loans from the EIB went into car manufacturing at the Volkswagen/Ford plant at Setubal. The activities of the EIB are stimulating higher levels of personal mobility whether by train, air or road. The strategy (of the bank itself and of the governments it services) is not sensitive to the arguments in favour of a reduction in the demand for transport and in favour of increased social and economic welfare to be found in a sustainable development strategy.

Trans-European Road Networks

EU transport policy is dominated by thinking about new infrastructure. The trans-European networks covering road, combined transport, rail (conventional and high speed), air and waterways were an important feature of the Maastricht Treaty. The current shopping list runs to 140 road schemes, 11 rail links, 57 combined transport projects and 26 inland waterway links. The road network designated as 'Trans-European' is 65,000km in length of which 15,000km are completely new build. All of these links have been approved by the member states concerned so that, even though these are European projects, by definition they are also national policies.

These trans-European links are costly and monuments to the worship of longer distance transport at the expense of shorter distance transport. The total cost of the transport links is expected to be ECU400–500 billion over the next 15 years. Most of the finance will have to come from national governments but EU expenditure will also be large and will probably ensure that the project goes ahead. EU funding cannot exceed 10 per cent of the total investment cost but is nevertheless budgeting ECU2,345 million over the 1995–99 period for this purpose.

Trans-European links will have a devastating effect on the environment – both locally and at larger geographical scales. The local devastation that can be expected from these links can already be seen where major motorway projects have proceeded in sensitive areas such as Twyford Down in England and the Aspe valley in the Pyrennees. More generally, CO_2 emissions will rise by a predicted 15–18 per cent above the existing forecast and cause serious difficulties for meeting greenhouse gas reduction targets. The support for aviation, for example, Milan Malpensa, Sparta (Athens) and Berlin, brings with it even more serious problems for global atmosphere and local traffic pollution.

The EU has failed to integrate environmental policies into its transport thinking and is now one of the primary agents of non-sustainability in Europe.

The EU's Common Transport Policy Action Programme 1995–2000 reiterates the central belief in transport efficiency as a way to achieve competitiveness and job creation. Transport efficiency means more transport infrastructure and cheaper transport. It means higher levels of mobility, more freight transported longer distances by road and more passengers flying longer distances. Nowhere does EU policy address the underlying rationale and value of all this extra transport, and nowhere does it ask if our economic and social objectives can be served through the use of less tarmac, less concrete and less fossil fuel consumption. Social concerns are absent, as are visions about the future of the city, community, walking and cycling. This is a crude misrepresentation of transport policy and a narrow interpretation of the role of transport in creating healthy environments and healthy children, lively communities and strong local economies. Transport policy has never been well thought out in EU policy. It is a great pity that in its new post-Maastricht incarnation the EU has retreated to a 1960s view of transport and economic development based on the flawed logic that tarmac and concrete equal jobs. This also demotes environmental concerns to the lowly status from which they cannot challenge the search for international competitiveness. We are all the losers for this narrowness of scope and content.

Conclusion

A fundamental problem with the EU and international banking organisations is that they have a very fixed view of what transport policy and transport investment should look like in order for it to deliver economic growth within a free market model. This view has a very poor level of awareness of social justice, equity and accessibility issues, and is more likely to produce increases in the demand for transport than to develop accessibility objectives and reduce the demand for motorised transport.

Large institutional drivers also have a poor appreciation of policy interconnectedness. Policies in sectors of the economy other than transport will have an effect on the demand for transport. The activities of banks in agricultural, industrial, housing, land use and energy sectors all have the possibility to increase or reduce the demand for transport. Taking demand as given and then trying to sort it out with a transport policy constitutes a very reactive and intellectually defective approach.

If the World Bank has an ultimate objective of reducing poverty then it could get there relatively quickly by ensuring that the poorest have access to enough land to support themselves, that they have high quality healthcare supported by fresh water and sanitation, that transport policies and investments match the scale and location of affordable housing and that the informal, non-motorised sector in developing countries gets the lion's share of investment. Most importantly, they could ensure that 95 per cent of investment funds are not steered in the direction of the 5 per cent of the population who are in a position to drive themselves around and carry freight by truck. Any industrial or agricultural investment could be evaluated on its traffic generation impact and against the alternative of more local, smaller scale alternatives involving less travel for people and goods.

Tragically, there are no ideas of this kind in the World Bank's 'Transport Sector Policy Review', the EIB's documents or the reports of the EBRD.

CHAPTER 5

What Time is This Place?

Introduction

The experience of travel and transport has shifted over the last 100 years from one involving large expenditures of time for relatively short distances, to the reverse relationship. The friction of distance, much loved by geographers and spatial modellers, has been lubricated to such a degree that long-distance travel to exotic destinations for holiday purposes is the norm and most goods and services consumed by households are sourced at some distance from the local region. In Europe Marks and Spencer, in their heavily packaged offerings of fresh vegetables, proudly declare that runner beans and mange tout have been specially flown in from Kenya or Nicaragua. In the US 99 per cent of all shopping trips are made by car.

This chapter will explore the way that time savings have come to dominate thinking in transport and how transport systems are shaped by this single objective. The shift to faster and faster methods of transport to save time has the effect of increasing environmental pollution whilst spreading the range of activities and demands on goods and services so that they are global – even for the most mundane and widely available products.

Time, Distance and Lifestyle

Increasing dependence on transport, year on year, increases miles travelled for all journey purposes. The erosion of the friction of distance is expensive and it changes perceptions and psychology; it fundamentally alters lifestyles and expectations and creates land use patterns and spatial structures that require even greater inputs of distance and energy to sustain them. We are effectively consumers of distance, and distance has become a commodity. Unlike some other commodities, distance establishes its own logic on spatial structures and behaviour so that it becomes impossible or very difficult for individual consumers to exercise choice and reduce their level of consumption.

In a subtle and pervasive way higher levels of consumption negate the concept of free choice and we are imprisoned in a distance-intensive world.

This distance-intensive world is energy intensive and produces large amounts of greenhouse gas emissions and a number of health damaging pollutants. Faster and faster travel opportunities effectively destroy the friction of time. This alters the nature of place. If we live a spatially dispersed lifestyle then our home base or place consciousness is likely to become diluted. Daily activity patterns are more likely to be snatched glimpses of a large number of places shared fleetingly with other transients. Whilst temporarily immobile (in a space–time coordinate sense) we can of course consume large amounts of energy, food, entertainment or sex (or just go shopping) before embarking on another bout of air, car or high speed train travel to the next point of consumption and the next bout of frantic time-filling at some distant location.

The friction of distance imposed through time penalties generates and sustains place distinctiveness. High speed travel, exotic tourism and the reduction in the amount of time available to spend in a home locality effectively converts places into various shades of a general place identity. The shops, restaurants, goods available, food crops, culture and artistic life will eventually come to resemble that of all other areas. Time penalties, traditionally seen as a problem or as something to be overcome, could also therefore be seen as conferring a protection on distinctiveness. One can assume, for example, that when thousands of Volvo-owning British tourists migrate to Tuscany or the Dordogne every summer they are in search of some place identity which has resisted the ravages of space–time homogenisation – until the arrival of the tourists that is.

A lifestyle defined in terms of hyper-mobility and high levels of consumption exchanges time formerly spent locally in neighbourhood and household activities with activities spent at a large number of widely dispersed locations.

This shift from low distance intensity to high distance intensity is one of the roots of contemporary environmental problems and non-sustainability.

It carries a double penalty. There is no time available for local activities that take up time, for example, community involvement, discussions and actions with neighbours about traffic, local schooling, healthcare, priorities of local politicians and so on. This community deficit contributes to rundown of public services, public spaces and environmental degradation. There is no one looking after the store. The other penalty is the energy and raw material penalty. It takes a lot of energy and creates a lot of pollution to support frantic bouts of dispersed activity.

> The intensified consumption of distance that is made possible by the destruction of time is fundamentally non-sustainable.

If the intensified consumption of distance were adopted on a global scale it would wipe out a large proportion of raw materials and energy sources and lead to pollution levels that would make many world cities uninhabitable. If it can be accessed by only one-quarter or less of the world's population it fails the equity test of sustainability (see Chapter 7). And if it leads to depleted resources or heavily polluted cities it fails the inter-generational test of sustainability. In the UK John Gummer, the former Secretary of State for the Environment, put the inter-generational test very succinctly when he declared that 'we must not cheat on our children'.

On a more practical level, time (or a radical distortion of time) is implicated in environmental destruction. Destructive projects, such as the M3 motorway near Winchester (Twyford Down), have been constructed to save a few minutes on the journey from London to Southampton. Similar projects are in the pipeline for the A34 (Bristol to Southampton) and for a south coast motorway to link Brighton with Portsmouth. Time savings are formally incorporated into the cost-benefit analysis which is used to justify roads and these time savings are likely to be higher if the existing road system is congested. This is the case around Birmingham where a Birmingham northern relief road is proposed for the eastern side of the conurbation and a western orbital road is proposed for the west. The arguments for both roads are couched in terms of time savings on the existing crowded motorway system. The time savings themselves are individually too small to amount to much in the way of usefully reallocated time.

Road construction in the UK is justified on grounds of saving time. The additional road space which is being continually added to an overcrowded system will ensue that more car trips and lorry trips are added which will eliminate time savings by perpetuating congestion.

More importantly, the land use system is pushed further in the direction of dispersal, loss of local facilities, development of edge-of-town and out-of-town shopping facilities and business parks, and hence higher still levels of car use. The non-sustainable trajectory is given a strong boost by the urge to save time, while all the time we spend more time reaching those destinations that were once nearer.

If changes in transport over time are explored it becomes apparent that the advantages of faster and more frequent travel have not been equitable.

There are key areas in which transport has affected the way we perceive – and use – our global environment. Temporal changes in transportation technology at the local scale show, with intra-urban journeys as an example, how the nature and size of urban areas have changed as a direct result of the friction of distance being reduced.

This has led to progressively longer journeys being undertaken on a daily basis. Transportation between cities has also changed dramatically at both the national and international level. In both cases the concept of time–space convergence (a shrinking world) and cumulative linkage advantage (better accessibility) have been introduced to illustrate how greater demand for interaction between places leads to the development of high priority transport corridors that can exclude other places along a route. A direct result of this is that these excluded places may be more disadvantaged than places connected by the high priority corridor.

Finally, advances in air travel technology have effectively altered the relationship between distance and time at the global scale, distorting and stretching these variables as if the earth's surface was a sheet of flexible material. A direct result of these distortions – brought about by cheaper and more frequent air travel – has been an increase in global tourism to more and more remote areas. Though the arrival of large numbers of tourists can be thought of as beneficial to an area by shifting its economy from, for instance, subsistence farming to one based on cash, this chapter considers that in many cases the negative effects of a rapid and large increase in tourists have been greater than positive gains.

The Nature of Transportation Change

Human civilisations have constantly struggled to overcome the difficulties imposed on their economic and cultural development by the need to move goods and people from place to place – though in many ways this is the lifeblood of an economic system. Accordingly, this fact has resulted in innovations in transport technologies in an effort to move both goods and people more quickly and as cheaply as possible. The net result of these changes has been a progressive reduction in the time–space dimension of our global environment.

Throughout history civilisations have established massive trading areas over much of the known world. Yet the speed of communication or the quantity of goods traded was limited by the transport technology of the day. Thus, innovations which improved either (or both) of these variables, spread rapidly. The invention and expansion of wheeled vehicle technology was so important that its utilisation by other cultures was very rapid. Within approximately two millennia its use had spread from what is now Iran and Iraq to virtually all of Europe, India and China. The introduction of wagons to carry goods and people as opposed to animals did not initially increase the speed at which these commodities travelled, but it nevertheless increased the amount that could be carried, thus the draught-drawn wagon effected a significant reduction in the cost of transportation.

Although innovations in transport modes have occurred at all stages throughout history, it is in the industrial age that these advances have brought about the biggest changes to global society. As well as increasing both the volume and the speed at which goods and people could be carried, early innovations such as steam power, iron boats and railways, also dramatically increased the range over which commodities could be moved in a given unit of time and at a given cost. Figure 5.1 illustrates this effect by looking at the expansion of a selection of British agricultural import zones over the period 1831–1913. During the 1831–35 period no significant amounts of fruit and vegetables were imported into Britain. By 1909–13, however, the average distance these commodities were imported from was 3,200 miles. Similarly for butter, cheese and eggs over the period there was a ten-fold increase in distance travelled.

Figure 5.1: Change in Distance Travelled by a Selection of British Imports

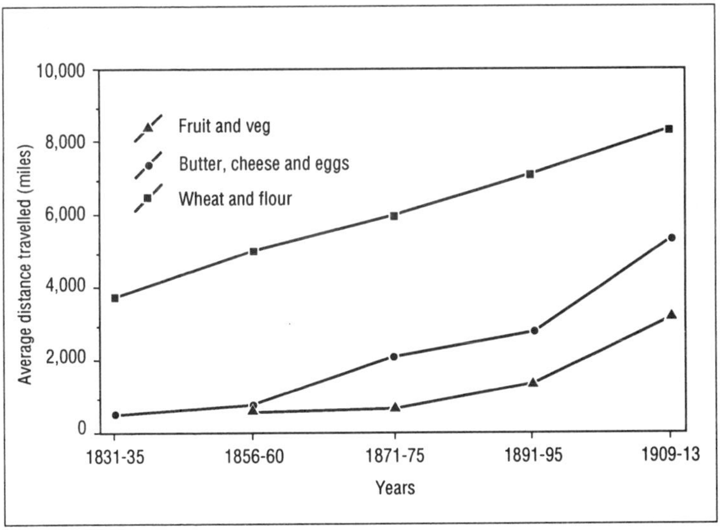

Source: Dicken and Lloyd (1990)

This increase in the physical range of products in the nineteenth and early twentieth centuries was accomplished through technological development in rail and ship transport. In more contemporary times the transport revolution has been centred on greater use of road vehicles, aircraft and pipelines. In western Europe, for example, over the period 1970–90 inland freight carried (measured in thousand million tonne-km) by these modes increased by annual rates of 4.04 per cent, 9.31 per cent and 3.06 per cent respectively, whereas freight carried by rail decreased at an annual rate of 0.38 per cent. In terms of percentage modal share of inland freight, in 1990 road carried two-thirds (66 per cent), whereas rail's share dropped from nearly 30 per cent in 1970 to just over 16 per cent in 1990. If these changes are considered over a longer time scale an even greater shift to road transport is apparent. In Great Britain over the 40 years between 1952 and 1992 road transport increased its share of freight moved from 35.2 per cent to 61 per cent, whereas rail saw a decrease from 42 per cent to just over 7 per cent.

Figure 5.2: Freight Traffic Trends in European Countries

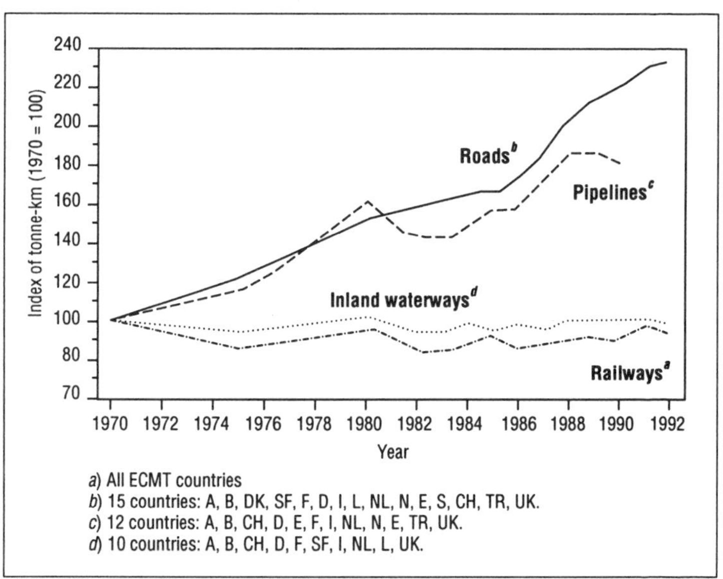

Source: ECMT (1995)

Trends in freight transport are shown in Figure 5.2. Road haulage is expected to increase by 42 per cent between 1990 and 2010 presenting a number of serious environmental difficulties and policy conflicts in Europe between those policies intended to make transport easier (for example, new international road links) and those intended to reduce impacts (for example, infrastructure charging and energy/carbon taxes).

These changes in freight transport have been driven by a dramatic increase in the need to move food, drink and tobacco by road (up 51 per cent during the period 1979–1994) and by the increase in the distance travelled by the average road freight journey. This was 54 miles (86km) in 1994 compared with 52 miles (84km) in 1993 and 43 miles (70km) in 1979. Road freight trends represent fundamental changes in the location and organisation of industry and all economic activities. Local saving and local employment are eroded by the concentration of economic activity at fewer points and the increasing distance intensity of production.

These supply side changes are in turn mirrored by changes in lifestyle on the part of households and individuals who spend more time travelling over longer distances to more destinations than they would if local facilities were available.

What factors have contributed to this dramatic change in the nature of freight transportation and associated lifestyle characteristics? Whilst it is tempting to answer this question by continuing with the theme of technological change, this is not in itself a satisfactory explanation. Transport innovations such as greater fuel efficiency, better roads, faster speeds, and larger payloads have played a central role in enabling change to occur. Innovation and technical change provide the right conditions for social and organisational change but cannot bring about that change in the absence of other factors.

For example, high land values and rents at traditional manufacturing sites have contributed to the dispersal of this sector to greenfield sites away from urban areas, or at infill sites at the urban periphery. Typically, these new areas of economic activity are not served by fixed route transport corridors such as railways or waterways. These forms of transport cannot therefore provide industry with the flexible, low-cost and controlled transport services that it requires.

In the case of freight transport there has been a pronounced trend towards higher levels of manufacturing and processing (involving large investments in new plant and equipment), concentration at fewer sites to reap economies of scale, higher levels of energy consumption, greater transport intensity and higher consumption of materials in packaging. This process has been made possible by improved transport technology but larger scale social and economic processes have played a major part. These include changes in lifestyle of individual households in the direction of more convenience food, larger disposable incomes and the development of a corporate culture heavily influenced by the desire to create new tastes and fashions through heavy advertising and large marketing budgets.

In *My Philosophy of Industry* (1929) Henry Ford wrote about much more than industry. He identified social change, rising aspirations, modernisation, time savings and the desire to be free of the drudgery and dullness he associated with farming in the American midwest up to the 1920s as key factors which increased the demand for consumer products and liberated the population. Even though he overlooked the drudgery and unremitting dullness of the production lines which he established, his comments still hold today with regard to his assessment of the place of mobility and distance intensity in lifestyle aspirations. Changes to distance intensity and mobility will involve a fundamental restructuring of lifestyle aspirations as dramatic as the restructuring that took place in the US in the 30 years after Henry Ford's perceptive assessment.

Culture and Technology

Technological change opens up new possibilities but is borne of the vision that first sees those possibilities and the potential that can be exploited. Freight transport and its development over the last 25 years reveals a great deal about the way technology moves in close harmony with cultural change. Freight transport has both responded to, and stimulated, changes in methods of industrial production and organisation. The growth of large centralised production units with their associated large transport requirements in order to serve distant markets is a basic engine in the growth of freight transport. The growth in that demand under strong competitive pressures and the realisation on the part of manufacturers that they can save a great deal of money by reducing stocks of materials or inventories to almost nothing has spawned a new organisational culture and one based on the sophisticated management of time. This is the world of logistics and 'just-in-time' transport.

'Just-in-time' transport, or JIT, started in the US and Japan and is now the dominant organisational form within the world of freight transport. A manufacturer or distributor now requires raw materials or intermediate products to be made available at a precise time and location to fit in with a production schedule that reduces the need for storage and warehousing and uses the road system as a conveyor belt.

This represents more than just technical change. The whole culture of production has had to adapt to the new regime and to strict contractual conditions about delivery times and schedules. This increases the number of lorries on the roads and reduces the number of circumstances (under current organisational and technical conditions) where rail can perform as well as road. As JIT becomes an industry-wide standard, so locational decisions are made to fit in with the world of logistics, and the demand for transport over longer distances continues to rise. Unpicking this complex mass of mutually reinforcing trends and cost-driven principles will require far more than increasing the costs of road transport and promoting rail transport. The technology and the culture have intertwined to produce a dominant spatial and organisational form which is, in its turn, reflected in the lifestyle aspirations of those who choose to consume products from all over the world and expect producers from Australia and New Zealand to sell produce at prices lower than their UK competitors in UK supermarkets.

JIT delivery based on splitting loads into smaller batches can (in theory) reduce inventory levels to zero. McDonnell Douglas (a UK aerospace company) switched from a conventional manufacturing system to JIT in the mid-1980s and was able to relieve one-third of shopfloor work space that had been used for 'kitting' in the traditional system. They were also able to reduce the value of work-in-progress from £2.2 million to just £0.8 million. Clearly, JIT can bring significant cost saving to companies. Accordingly, it is seen by many as one of the most important and successful innovations in logistics in recent times. However, the environmental costs are equally as significant.

Instead of one large vehicle delivering goods once a week JIT means that smaller vehicles will deliver daily, or in some cases several times a day. A result of this is an increase in fuel consumption for a similar amount of goods moved.

For example, if one vehicle carries 25 tonnes for 100km it uses approximately 49 litres (l) of fuel, whereas five smaller vehicles carrying 5 tonnes each consume over three times this at 165 litres. In addition to being less energy efficient the use of more vehicles increases noise disturbance and intrudes visually, as well as increasing the demand for more road space. Since rail is presently ill-equipped to match the performance of JIT an industry-wide dependence on JIT will impact on the prossibility of change in the rail sector.

Transport intensity – defined as the physical amount of transport used in the production of a given unit of a given product – is increasing. The UK Royal Commission on Environmental Pollution, reporting in 1994, explained that transport intensity in the period 1952–1992 increased by more than 25 per cent. This means that it took 25 per cent more transport activity in 1992 for each £ GDP than it did in 1952. Part of the explanation for this increase is the very low cost of transport as a proportion of total costs; and the very large savings that can be made by manufacturers who use long-distance sourcing and inter-plant transfers to benefit from wage rate differentials, economies of scale, and variations in grants and subsidies to manufacturers who claim, and appear, to be creating jobs by moving them around.

The erosion of space–time constraints has had a dramatic effect on the way in which urban and rural environments are used. Advances in transport technology mean that businesses now attach little value to the advantages of clustering economic activity, or 'agglomerating' in a single area. Also, modern transport technology has lifted the constraint on many firms to locate close to a source of raw material or the marketplace. Rather, in a shrinking world where transportation costs are relatively low and travel time fast, the marketplace or the source of materials could be on the opposite side of the world. Due to the removal of these constraints other factors, such as cheap labour, cheaper land costs, and the availability of economic incentives such as grant aid, are now seen as being more important locational considerations. Benefits thus acrue to firms in the form of greater profitability and have been bought at the expense of greater damage to people and the environment because of the need to transport raw materials and finished goods greater distances. Current consumption patterns are thus maintained at a high cost in terms of energy use, carbon dioxide emissions and health damaging exhaust emissions. This alters the physical structure of cities and regions so that higher levels of dependence on cars and lorries are necessary. It also destroys beauty.

Similarly, the need for employees to live close to their source of employment is no longer necessary. Cheaper and faster forms of transportation have given workers and shoppers greater levels of mobility enabling them to increase the distances that separate work, home, shops, schools and leisure facilities.

Transportation Changes in the City

Generally speaking the major growth phases of individual cities have been governed by the movement of labour and capital into these areas. This has stimulated the necessity to build more housing to accommodate additional workers needed by the growing industries, and the result of this is that zonal and sectoral patterns of cities have developed over a long period of time. However, the single most important determinant of urban morphology and residential differentiation has been changes to systems of transportation. This process has advanced at markedly different rates in different parts of the world. Rising affluence and mass consumerism in the US, Canada and Australia ensured that cities in these countries changed their morphology to suit the needs of the car much earlier than in Europe. The large-scale expansion of relatively featureless suburbs and the increasing distances that have to be traversed to connect homes, workplaces and social activities are both a response to the availability of the car and a cause of increasing car dependency.

Cities that have experienced these developments are much more energy intensive than cities that have retained a compact shape and have maintained smaller distances between activities.

The development of different urban transport systems and the resultant phases in city growth can be divided into three distinct periods. These are:

- the walking city; pre- mid-nineteenth century;
- the public transport city; mid-nineteenth century to mid-twentieth century;
- the car city; post World War II.

Typically, walking cities were characterised by their compactness. London in the early part of the nineteenth century housed approximately two million people yet extended not much further than what is now the City and West End. Though horse-drawn carts brought goods into and out of these areas, the principal mode of transport was by foot. This limited the functional size of the city to a radius of approximately 5km (the distance a person could walk in one hour). A direct result of this constraint was that the city exhibited an urban population density gradient which declined sharply with increasing distance from the centre and then abruptly stopped at the edge of the city.

The public transport city phase can be divided into 'early' and 'late' periods that correspond to the development of horse-drawn systems and then the emergence of steam and electrically powered trains.

The shift away from walking as the principal mode of transport was essentially a response to the development of railway technology, in particular the manufacturing of steel wheels and rails. Although the Stockton to Darlington railway had been in operation since 1826, the use of railways was not initially seen as being applicable to the mass movement of people over relatively short distances due to the slow acceleration and deceleration rates of these early steam engines. Rather, this technology was seen as a method to transport goods and people on inter-urban journeys. In the mid-nineteenth century the first horse-drawn tracers (a passenger wagon on steel rails) and the omnibus (a simple passenger wagon drawn by a horse) appeared. These early examples of mass transport systems, together with steam-powered versions developed later, enabled the already strained cities to expand further into the surrounding open country by reducing the friction of distance – in that, though still slow by modern standards, they nevertheless enabled the daily travel range of workers to be extended by up to a factor of two to approximately 10km.

The later public transport phase began with the application of electricity to the tramcar networks and commuter railways. This further revolutionised the mass transportation of people because of two fundamental differences: efficiency and cheapness.

Electric trams were more efficient than horse-drawn systems (they could carry more people) because of an increased power to weight ratio, and could travel twice as fast. Due to its increased efficiency the electric tram effectively made the cost per passenger kilometre much cheaper, thereby allowing a policy of low fares which attracted a high volume of passengers. It has been estimated that the move to electrically operated systems reduced the real cost to passengers by as much as 50 per cent in the UK. More importantly, the increased speed of the trams increased the range of commuters four-fold.

The development of electric trams changed dramatically the urban form of many cities. For example, much of the early housing developments took the form of discontinuous ribbons along major routes. As commuter distance increased, these ribbon developments were also extended (in some cases speculative developers working in conjunction with tram companies) to promote suburban developments.

Transport has had a well-documented effect on the social geography of cities in the developed world. The ability to purchase distance, like the ability to purchase space, (both internal and external to the dwelling) has made a distinctive contribution to urban and social segregation in terms of income, class and ethnicity. In practice, reality is more complex than can be encompassed in explanations based on land values, transport costs or transport technology. Many European cities have wealthy individuals living in high density city centre areas not far from ethnic enclaves (for example, Wedding and Kreuzberg in Berlin and the New Town in Edinburgh). British cities are frequently characterised by concentrations of poor quality housing in peripheral greenfield sites developed by public bodies without adequate attention to social infrastructure and basic facilities. In many cases the affluent live in rural areas many miles from the city.

The explanation for the complexities (and failures) of both market forces and the planning system goes much deeper than a mechanistic model of transport choice and housing price or supply. The built environment in all its space–time complexity can only reflect the inequalities and structural imbalances in the distribution of wealth and income. Transport policies cannot resolve fundamental inequalities in society and cannot eradicate poverty. Transport policies can provide high quality access at low cost to basic goods and services, and by improving access can stimulate the development of denser patterns of local facilities (for example, shops, schools and healthcare facilities). They can also improve air quality and health (see Chapter 10). In this sense, transport policies have the potential to deliver significant improvements in quality of life to low income and no income groups. In the main, these opportunities are not exploited and the reverse situation is more common. Low income or no income groups living in degraded inner city environments often have to endure the noise, traffic danger and pollution from the vehicles of the relatively wealthy as they journey to work, the shops or to pursue leisure.

The increase in the use of cars cannot be accounted for by the decline in the amount of bus use, cycling and walking. There has not been a transfer of travel activity from these latter three modes to the car, rather there has been a dramatic increase in the amount of travelling we do to a larger number of destinations over a much wider geographical area. Whilst this gives the illusion that we are in some way better off (through more choice) it also means that a great deal of money is spent to maintain this level of mobility as well as more time travelling on our own behalf and ferrying children around. It also means that a new class of 'access poor' has been created. As local facilities decline in number so accessibility for those without cars deteriorates. There is no mechanism in existence to compensate for the loss of local grocery shops, local schools and local leisure facilities.

Has this modal shift and subsequent move to a more polycentric urban morphology been beneficial to cities and their inhabitants? Cities such as London, New York, Paris and Tokyo have retained the importance of their central areas in terms of employment. This has enforced a form of rail dependency due to the fact that it is only rail systems that can handle the peak rush hour flows of up to 40,000 per hour on a single corridor or track. The more peripheral areas of these cities are increasingly becoming car dependent. Furthermore, other smaller urban areas such as Manchester, Brussels or Frankfurt have lost some of this centrality and have taken on a more multi-centred morphology.

In theory, the development of many different and competing centres for shopping, employment and recreation should increase choice and reduce distances travelled. In practice, distances travelled go up. Changes in job, the requirements of two-career families and changes in individual lifestyles over time (for example, from living alone to sharing with a partner, to having young children and children finally leaving home) all work to reduce the probability of short-distance links between residential location and other activities.

Transportation Changes Between Cities

The previous section focused on intra-urban transportation change where the vast majority of everyday interaction takes place. At the inter-urban level there have been equally dramatic changes which have redefined the nature of local and regional economies and made possible much of the contemporary concentration and specialisation of employment. Figure 5.3, for example, shows that improvements in passenger transport infrastructure between London and Edinburgh have caused an exponential decline in the relationship between time and distance between these cities. In the 1750s the only mode of transport available to people was the horse-drawn coach, and the journey (629km) took approximately ten days (14,400 minutes). Successive waves of improvements to the type of transport system used has reduced the time taken for this journey by a factor of 68 (Intercity 225 high speed train; 211 minutes). Further, this example has only considered terrestrial modes of transport. If the time taken for a modern jet airliner to travel between these two destinations is considered (approximately 60 minutes) then, since the beginning of the industrial revolution, the friction of distance has been reduced by a factor of 240.

Figure 5.3: Time Taken to Travel Between London and Edinburgh (1750–1990)

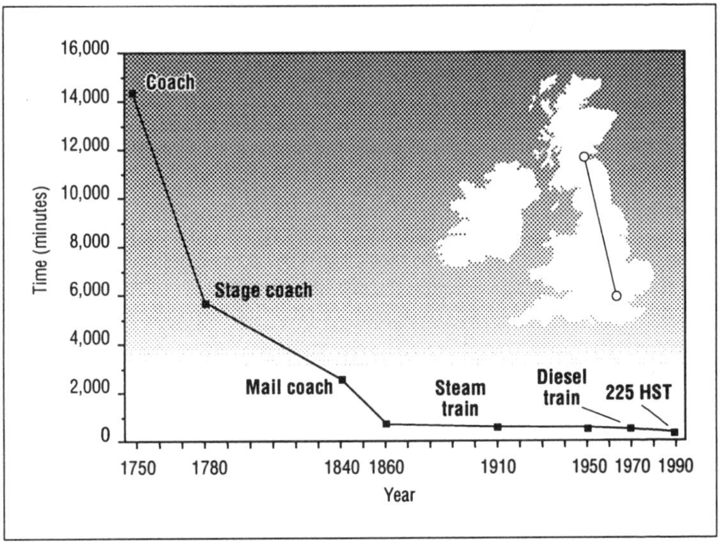

If one considers these changes on a global scale, particularly for communication, they are even greater. Prior to the development of the telegraph, Australia was three to four months sailing from the UK. The telegraph reduced this time to approximately 10 hours. Today satellite telecommunications can connect the UK to Australia in a matter of seconds.

In the field of physical transport, change at the global scale has not been as dramatic. Nevertheless, the decrease in time needed to travel between different points on the globe has been reduced considerably. Over the past 40 years, improvements in the speed of aeroplanes, and the ability to fly greater distances between refuelling stops, has considerably increased the volume of passengers and freight moved by this mode. In 1950, the fastest aircraft (the DC7) travelled at approximately 350 mph (560kph). Thus most cities in Europe could be reached from, say, Paris, in about two hours, while flights to eastern North America took seven hours. Due to refuelling stops, it took nearly 24 hours to reach cities half way around the world. The Boeing 747 jumbo jet introduced in the late 1960s reduced these times considerably. Flying at 640mph (1,024kph), northern South America, central Africa, southern Asia and central North America could be reached within about six hours from Paris. The Concorde, introduced in 1976, reduced these travel times by about one half. Travelling at 1,350mph (2,160kph) New York, Caracas, Lagos and New Delhi are within four hours from Paris, and Sydney and Buenos Aires within seven hours.

This ability to travel further for the same amount of time has in effect increased accessibility at the global scale. Accessibility has not fared as well at the regional scale. Some journeys by rail in countries like Britain and Germany can now take longer than they did in the nineteenth century. This is usually the case away from inter-city lines. In the north of England the journey from Bradford (Yorkshire) to Morecambe (Lancashire) took 90 minutes in 1910. In 1996 it took 136 minutes. Improvements in accessibility over the last 50 years have usually benefited larger urban centres and the main routes to capital cities and other large centres. This reflects a prioritisation of longer distances over shorter distances and of larger centres over smaller centres. The prioritisation stretches to the directional, particularly in the UK. Train services on one of the UK's main lines, the West Coast Main Line, are geared to London-bound journeys in the morning and trains out of London later in the day. This directional discrimination can be seen at its most severe if the traveller wants a train south from Carlisle in the evening: they do not exist.

Changes in accessibility over time and between regions and cities redefine who gains and who loses in an urban regional system. This is one reason why there is so much competition for high speed rail station stops in France and Belgium. Cities with better transport links are often thought to be in a better competitive position than those without good links, though this rather naive determinism is difficult to demonstrate in practice. Donald Janelle's 1969 paper 'Spatial reorganisation: a model and a concept' was the

Figure 5.4: The Spatial Reorganisation Process in Response to Transport Improvements

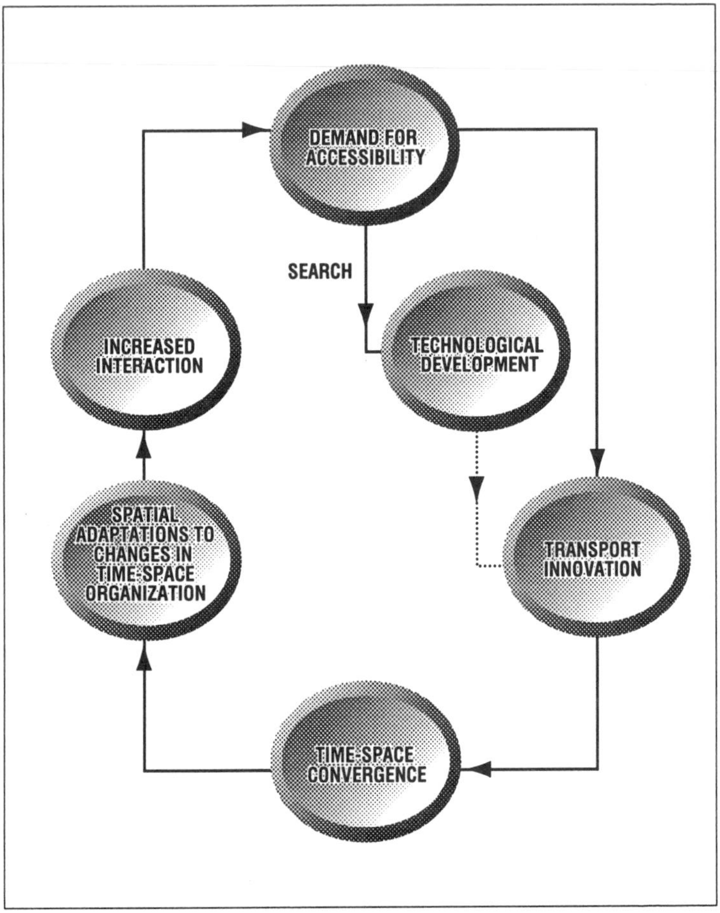

DEMAND FOR ACCESSIBILITY

SEARCH

TECHNOLOGICAL DEVELOPMENT

TRANSPORT INNOVATION

TIME-SPACE CONVERGENCE

SPATIAL ADAPTATIONS TO CHANGES IN TIME-SPACE ORGANIZATION

INCREASED INTERACTION

first to try and explain the phenomenon that he called space–time convergence. Figure 5.4 is a diagrammatic representation of Janelle's proposal in which the process of cumulative linkage advantage (better accessibility) is triggered by greater demand for accessibility from some part of the economic system, for example, a pair of cities or individual businesses. If demand is sufficiently high, this leads to an early search for technological developments that result in transport innovation in the form of either a complete new mode, for example railways over horse-drawn wagons and waterways in eighteenth-century Britain, or improvements to existing systems, for example motorways over single carriage roads. The effect of these innovations is a time–space convergence by increasing the speed of travel between centres, or by enabling the movement of larger volumes of traffic. The net result is a reduction in the real cost of moving from place to place, leading to the development of high priority corridors along which greater interaction occurs. Thus the benefits of better transport and communication linkages between larger cities has been, in effect, to draw these areas closer together, whilst those towns or cities where innovation has been retarded have remained at a similar or increasing distance away from each other.

Janelle's one-dimensional formulation takes no account of the heavy resource costs of intensified interaction over longer distances, nor of the damaging consequences for intervening areas and local production by heightened competition from outside the area brought in with improved infrastructure. There is a central paradox here. Improved communications can produce more interaction and more traffic but this can actually damage local economies as their employment and economic structures are destroyed by competition from afar. Poor physical communications may well 'shield' a local economy and stimulate local production, innovation and marketing strategies.

Conclusion

This chapter has questioned the social, economic and psychological impact of speed, time compression and space expansion. The impacts are wide-ranging and fundamental, and they redefine the meaning of place and the linkages between people and places. This is important because it is purchased at an enormous cost in terms of energy, physical and financial resources, and environmental destruction. It is also pursued on the assumption that it must be a good thing even though there is very little evidence to support the contention that travelling further, sourcing goods and services over longer distances and having a global range for tourism has produced gains in income, welfare, air quality, community cohesion or security. The prioritisation in investment decisions and in the psychology and status of distant things is intimately bound up with the loss of high quality, rich and diverse local neighbourhoods. If anything, this process has intensified during the 1980s and 1990s so that most places now struggle to maintain their environmental, economic and psychological integrity. This obsession with speed and saving time has almost destroyed place.

CHAPTER 6

What Place is This Time?

Introduction

Distance has been transformed into a commodity that is consumed at an increasing rate. This consumption is made possible by the allocation of large amounts of energy and large amounts of public expenditure – both direct in the provision of infrastructure and indirect (or defensive) in coping with the damaging effects of speed, pollution, community dislocation, road traffic accidents and poor health.

The drive to consume large distances (as part of the search for experience) reaches its apogee in global tourism and air travel. No other aspect of human behaviour pursues long-distance travel and time-compressed experiences in the virtual reality of an exotic location, often in a developing country. Global tourism colonises spaces and redefines experiences for both the traveller and the permanent residents of, for example, Goa, the Seychelles and the Kalahari. It is fuelled by time compression but wreaks havoc on places through the disfigurement of coastline with buildings, loss of habitat, pollution of coastal waters with sewage, over-consumption of available water supplies and cultural damage. Global tourism, made possible by the development of cheap air travel, is an extreme example of the ways in which hyper-mobility and the consumption of distance destroy place identity, and the deep cultural and psychological meanings which are attached to place.

Global Tourism and Increased Air Travel

Air travel and tourism currently exhibit strong growth tendencies (a predicted doubling of passenger kilometres by air in the next 12 years), with no consideration given to sustainable development principles, environmental capacity constraints, or the need to manage demand. The impact of this form of consumption of space and time in the twenty-first century will be dramatic in terms of damage to the atmosphere (ozone layer depletion), greenhouse gas emissions, loss of biodiversity, cultural and social damage at tourist destinations and health damage from air and noise pollution at the epicentres of global tourism (for example, at Heathrow, Manchester,

Frankfurt , Paris Charles de Gaulle (CDG) and Schipol Amsterdam airports).

One of the most important areas in which global air travel has effected massive social and economic change has been that of increasing the accessibility of remote and fragile areas to the global tourist. This increase in accessibility, coupled with higher levels of disposable income, more leisure time and better education have promoted the demand for foreign holidays; furthermore, this increase in demand has enabled tour operators to keep prices low, thereby satisfying this demand with offers of relatively cheap package tours and charter flights to more remote and exotic locations.

Before illustrating these changes with data, we should first define what a tourist is. According to the World Tourism Organisation (WTO), a tourist is a temporary visitor staying at least 24 hours in any country that is not normally his/her place of residence. However, this is a very broad definition and can include many different types of travellers. Furthermore, a traveller may combine several different types of journey purpose in the course of a single trip. For example, a person on a business trip may well include some form of leisure excursion.

Figure 6.1: International Tourist Arrivals (1950–1990)

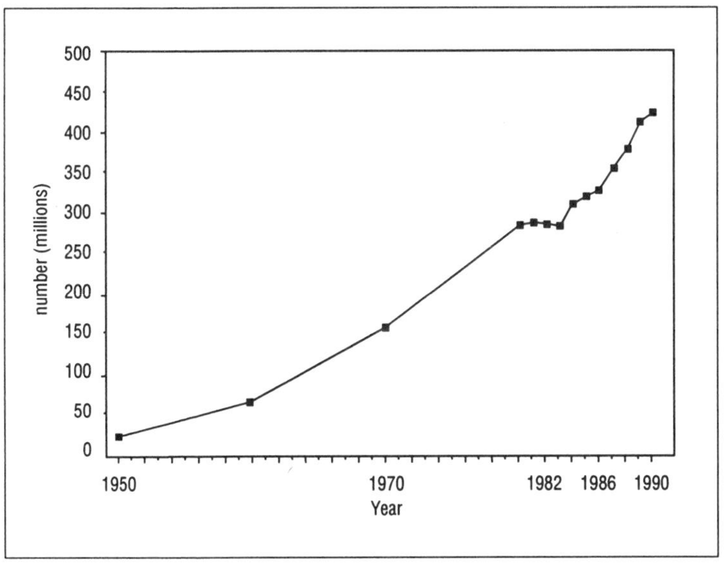

Source: WTO (1992)

Figures from the WTO (figure 6.1) show that over the 1950–1990 period tourist arrivals (excluding day trippers) increased nearly 17-fold. The exponential shape of the curve also shows that with the exception of the 1980–83 period, annual growth rates of tourist arrivals also increased. In terms of cash flows WTO data shows that global tourist receipts rose from US$2.1 billion in 1950 to US$209.2 billion in 1989.

Tourists generally come from the developed world. In 1988 the US, Germany, Japan and the UK generated one-half of total international tourism expenditure, even though their combined population is less than 10 per cent of the world total.

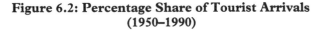

Figure 6.2: Percentage Share of Tourist Arrivals (1950–1990)

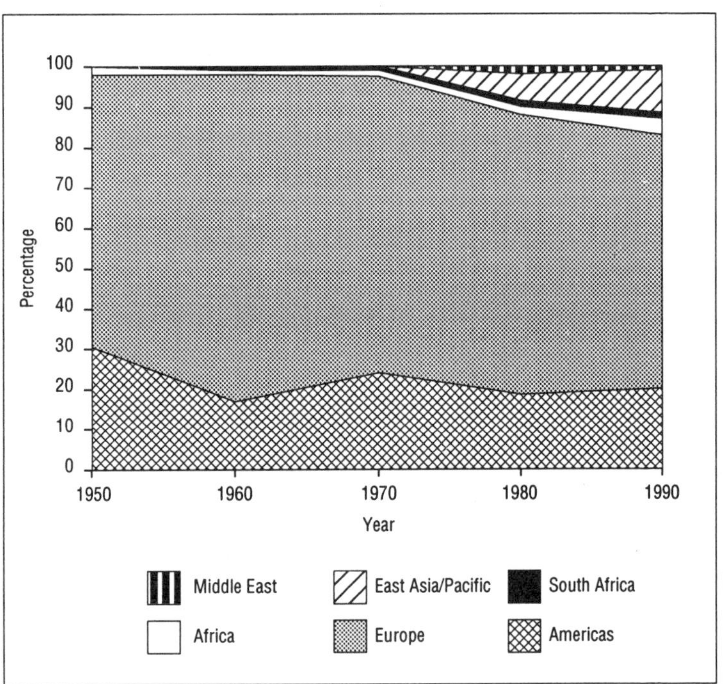

Source: WTO (1992)

Though Europe and North America remain the most popular places to visit, over this 40 year period there has been a continuing shift away from these countries to more exotic and remote locations. Figure 6.2 shows that, whereas in 1950 Europe and the US accounted for 96 per cent of world tourist arrivals, in 1990 this figure had dropped to 84 per cent. In contrast, by 1990 East Asia and the Pacific region had increased its share of world tourists to 11 per cent (46.5 million arrivals).

The above data show at a global scale that there has been a significant shift away from established tourist destinations, typically in developed countries, to those in less developed areas. At a more regional level this trend can also be seen. Whilst Figure 6.2 shows that the Americas as a whole has witnessed a 10 per cent decline in tourist arrivals over the 1950–1990 period, Figure 6.3 shows that this has not been evenly distributed; the US & Canada have experienced a 16.7 per cent reduction in tourist arrivals whereas the region's less developed areas (the Caribbean, Central America and South America) have seen tourist arrivals increase by 6.8 per cent, 5 per cent and 4.9 per cent respectively. These increases represent in effect a doubling of the number of tourists visiting these areas over the 40 year period. The root cause of this shift is the search for ever cheaper tourist locations. Cheaper, faster and more frequent air travel makes these distant places more accessible.

Figure 6.3: Percentage Share of Tourist Arrivals (1950–1990 in the Americas)

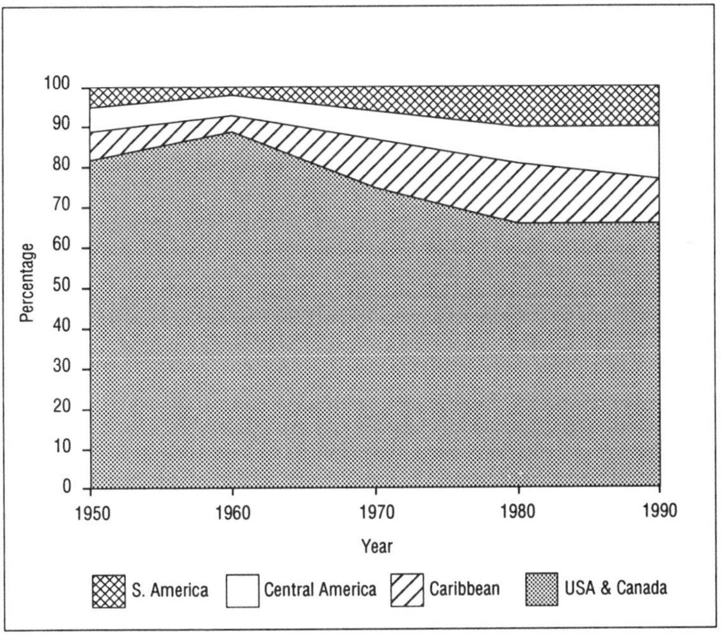

Source: WTO (1992)

Social and Cultural Effects of Tourism

The arrival of large groups of people to an area with poor infrastructure and fragile environments has, in the past, put increased pressure on a country's scarce natural and economic resources. Some commentators have considered tourism to be analogous with prostitution in that poor countries, with few development alternatives, must sell their beauty for foreign currency, and are psychologically 'penetrated' by tourists from developed nations. Certainly tourists travel to a particular country because of the attractive power of some individual or collection of resources contained within that country. These can be natural in origin, such as beautiful scenery and wildlife, or cultural in origin, such as historical or contemporary artefacts. Whatever these primary resources are, the influx of tourists into an area stimulates the building of secondary resources, for example, accommodation, transport facilities and service infrastructure. These pressures to 'modernise' an often closely knit society, where culture and tradition have historically dictated the pace of life, have had a profound effect on the development of these societies. Not only does tourism alter radically the local built environment through the erection of guesthouses and hotels, frequently unsympathetic to local building practices and materials, but it also puts increased stress on often inadequate or non-existent systems of waste disposal causing problems of polluted water courses and disease.

David Harrison (1992) illustrates this in his book *International Tourism and the Less Developed Countries* with reference to Boracay, a tiny island in the Philippines. Until its 'discovery' in the 1980s the island's economy centred around farming and fishing. Increased numbers of tourists have since put intense pressure on the island's infrastructure leading to the installation of electricity, and a better water supply. With electricity came neon lights and discos; villages began to sell souvenirs and rented out cottages instead of growing crops or fishing, and, due to the shortage of accommodation, hotels were built and land values increased substantially.

Clearly the local inhabitants may have benefited from some of these 'improvements' which have made life easier due to better infrastructure and extra income generated by tourism. Increased employment opportunities have enabled greater numbers of young people to remain on the island, or indeed return from the cities to be with their family. Accordingly, many Boracanese view the increase in tourists to their island as positive. However, tourism has also brought drunkenness, narcotics and prostitution, together with the 'near idolisation' of Westerners and their values by the young, which has led to a rejection of traditional island life. Furthermore, in 1988, the Filipino government was having to decide whether it could provide extra funds for an urgently needed sewage treatment plant, a refuse disposal system and an upgrading of the water system because of increased tourist pressure.

The case of Boracay illustrates many of the social and cultural tensions that can arise from an unrestrained increase in tourist numbers to less developed countries. One of the major worries only briefly mentioned above, but which causes considerable concern at the moment due to the rise in the incidence of AIDS related diseases, is sex tourism and prostitution, particularly in developing South East Asian countries where cost differentials for sexual services have proven to be immensely attractive to male tourists from developed countries. Though tourists from industrialised countries are not necessarily the root cause of this trade in sex, they have nonetheless stimulated a dramatic increase in prostitution and so indirectly contributed to the decline of rural economies in Thailand.

Thailand provides an excellent example of this problem. Traditional attitudes to women have created a ready-made framework within which sex tourism can thrive. Reasons for this expansion need no more explanation than the answers given by Japanese men to a survey conducted in Bangkok in 1991 by the Japanese Men's Group Against Prostitution. 'I come here because Thai girls are pretty and gentle' ... 'Girls here are much cheaper than in Japan: they are poor, that's why they need customers, isn't it?' ... 'I don't feel immoral to come here, because I'm sort of contributing to the Thai economy'. Indeed, sex tourism is so big in Japan that books such as the international guide book *A Man Travels Alone to Pleasure Spots in South-east Asia* with the subtitle *'Please enjoy vice'* are best sellers.

Figure 6.4 shows that during the late 1980s international tourist arrivals to Thailand expanded rapidly, out-stripping rates to other Asian and Pacific countries by a significant amount. It must be stressed, however, that not all prostitutes cater for foreign tourists, or all tourists travel to this country because of the sex industry. Rather, those tourists who arrive in the country with the specific intention to visit massage parlours and sex shows have induced a demand for prostitutes, which in turn has created an available supply. In Thai society women historically have played an important role in trade and small business enterprise. Accordingly, girls from the economically marginal provinces of the northeast and north of the country who are recruited by employment agents into Bangkok's massage parlours are in fact performing the expected daughterly duty of providing support to their families. Unfortunately, the pattern of development has changed the circumstances in which they can fulfil this role: they sell sex, and send money home.

Figure 6.4: Index of Tourist Arrivals to Thailand

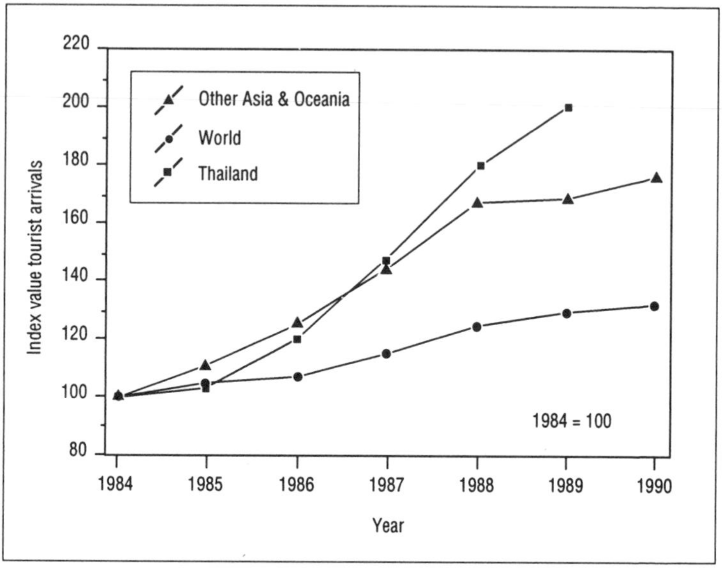

Source: WTO (1992)

In spite of the fact that prostitution has been illegal in Thailand since 1960 the government has done little to curtail the country's sex trade as it is seen by many officials as an integral part of services offered to tourists. In 1989 tourism expenditure amounted to US$3.75 billion, or over 5 per cent of GDP. Due to this the Thai government continues to place great emphasis on the promotion of tourism to the country because of the foreign exchange earned. Indeed, in 1985 the Thai vice-premier informed provincial governors that the sexual entertainment of tourists was necessary for the creation of jobs. The number of women involved in sex tourism has continued to rise. In the late 1950s there were about 20,000 female prostitutes; by 1990 this figure was estimated to be somewhere between 500,000 and one million. Furthermore, the current rise in child prostitution is causing national and international concern.

Environmental Effect of Tourism

Environmental destruction occurs at the same time as social damage. The combined effect of increased social and environmental pressures presents sensitive areas, fragile ecosystems and finely balanced cultures with very real threats. Paradoxically, tourist pressures and the changes induced by tourism often alter and destroy those features of landscape, society and culture that triggered the original tourist interest. In a very real sense the place identity of target areas is sacrificed to the needs of the global tourist.

The demands of tourism siphon off scarce public expenditure and foreign exchange to support cars, fuel imports, concrete and tarmac and the construction of new hotels. These funds are subsequently unavailable for more important but more basic needs – such as health, education and agricultural infrastructure.

Major tour operators now offer package holidays to more remote locations alongside those areas which have already sunk beneath a blanket of hotels and entertainment facilities – such as the Spanish 'Costas' and some of the Greek islands. In addition to these major actors there are now a substantial number of minor players offering specialised adventure holidays away from the crowds, and, by definition, into even more remote and fragile areas. The most spectacular of these tours are to Antarctica and the South Pole – the remotest and most untouched continent left on the earth.

Currently, about 6,000 tourists per annum make the journey to Antarctica which is in the vanguard of the new wave of exotic destinations. The problems faced by Antarctica from this influx are similar to those of the Kalahari (Namibia) or Sinai (Egypt) deserts. These are especially sensitive regions with no basic infrastructure to support tourism. Indeed the provision of that infrastructure fundamentally affects the wilderness character and the habitat for plant and animal life. The consumption of distant spaces and experiences knows no bounds. In this sense young girls and boys from rural Thailand are just as much at risk as the fauna and flora of the world's remaining wilderness areas. The picture is completed by the environmental destruction of the atmosphere caused by the air travel that brings the tourist.

Ecological damage resulting from uncontrolled numbers of people visiting fragile areas is not confined to less developing countries. In the French Alps winter sports tourism, such as downhill skiing, has brought with it the building of resorts at altitudes well above normal settlement limits. These developments need access roads, provision of accommodation and the creation of ski-runs (pistes) and ski-lifts, all of which disrupt local ecosystems. For example, the construction of roads, ski-lifts and the large-scale movement of earth to improve ski-runs has compounded erosion problems by causing soil compaction, loss of vegetation and the alteration of drainage and run-off patterns. Tourists generally travel to these areas by road, thus compounding the environmental problems of tourism itself with vehicle exhaust emissions, noise and the run-off from 'salting' the roads. Finally, damage caused by winter tourism can reduce an area's attractiveness to summer tourists, a fact now being acknowledged in Austria and in the Cairngorms in

Scotland. The combined effects of vehicle pollution (including acid rain), provision for vehicles (roads and parking), hotels, waste and sewage disposal, litter and deforestation, amount to what Krippendorf (1987) calls 'landscape consumption'. The final act of consumption is the consumption of the place itself so that it is of no use to its original residents and of no further interest to tourists. This is the fate that potentially awaits all tourist destinations.

Of the less developed countries, perhaps the Kingdom of Nepal provides a classic example of problems that can arise from rapid and substantial increases in tourist arrivals to a delicate environment. Since the 1960s there has been rapid growth in the numbers of people visiting the kingdom. In 1962 tourist arrivals totalled 6,179; by 1986 this figure had risen to 223,331. Although nearly one-quarter of these were affluent Indians coming to escape the heat of the north India plain in April and May, or pilgrims to Hindu shrines, Nepal's tourist trade is dependent upon air routes from western Europe, Australia and North America (56 per cent).

The economic contribution of tourists to Nepal is significant. With Gross National Product (GNP) per capita at US$170 in 1990, Nepal is eleventh on the United Nation's list of 15 most impoverished landlocked countries. Accordingly, foreign tourism is actively encouraged by the Nepalese government as it brings in substantial amounts of foreign currency (US$63 million in 1990). Further, about 4,000 people are employed in tourist hotels – over half in Kathmandu – and it has been estimated that approximately 80,000 Nepalese are involved in some tourist-related employment.

With eight of the world's ten highest mountains, it is not surprising that mountain tourism – climbing and trekking – are the main reasons for the majority of (Western) tourist visits. In 1976 nearly 14,000 trekking permits (permission to trek in areas beyond the vicinity of main towns) were issued. In 1986 this figure had risen to almost 50,000. There are of course many benefits attached to this growth in mountain tourism. In Khumbu district (in which Everest lies) housing has been improved and a range of new facilities such as a school, piped water, a mini hydro-electric generation plant and solar water heaters, installed. In addition to these benefits, there is evidence to suggest that the previously high birth rate is falling and emigration has been reduced. Finally, the main trekking seasons (October–November and April–May) are at times when there is little work in the fields and tourism can be complementary to the agricultural way of life rather than destroying it. The impact of tourism has been to change the economy of the area from one based on subsistence to a cash economy in less than ten years.

There are also a number of strong negative effects. In the Annapurna region, the arrival of over 30,000 tourists per year has put immense pressure on the supply of fuelwood for cooking and heat. The average daily consumption of fuelwood per tourist has been estimated at 6.4kg. Multiplying this by the average size of the trekking group, it has been estimated that each uses as much fuelwood in two weeks as a local family uses in six months. Accordingly, the need to cut down more trees has promoted instability on the mountain slopes which has resulted in an increase in the incidence and scale of landslides and rock falls, in addition to soil erosion. The dumping of non-biodegradable waste and the need to dispose of significantly more amounts of human waste along the trekking routes has given rise to major concerns about the purity of essential water supplies in popular upland areas. Indeed, during the 1980s the Everest trek was renamed the 'Kleenex trail' because of the amount of toilet paper left by tourists.

Due to these problems, and the belief that a continuation of these trends will in fact deter tourism, the Nepalese government has been instrumental in attempting to integrate the twin goals of conservation and local development to achieve what has been termed 'sustainable tourist development'. In the Annapurna Conservation Area, local villagers have been brought into the decision making process over the future numbers of tourists to be allowed to visit the area, and the type of resources required to meet this demand. Also, village assemblies are involved in the banded pricing system that fixes charges for food and accommodation that reflect the portage required to carry goods further into the area. Environmental notices request that trekkers use appropriate toilet facilities, do not leave rubbish lying around and take only biodegradable materials into the area where possible. Finally, to reduce the pressure on the use of scarce fuelwood the organisation set up to administer the area, the Annapurna Conservation Area Project, has installed kerosene stoves in all guest houses and lodges and developed a portage system for the kerosene. For these facilities trekkers must purchase an entry permit. This allows the Nepalese to control the number of people in the area by limiting or even refusing to issue additional permits. In this way damage to the environment can at least be reduced whilst at the same time income is generated for further environmental improvements.

The Environmental Impact of Aviation

Global passenger air traffic for total scheduled services measured in terms of passenger kilometres is expected to increase from 1,834 billion kilometres in 1991 to 2,959 billion kilometers in 2000 and 4,729 billion kilometres in 2015. This is equivalent to an annual average growth rate of 5 per cent for the period 1991–2015. Some of the largest growth rates can be seen on trans-Pacific and Europe/Asia/Pacific route groups, with average annual growth rates of around 8 per cent for the 1991–2000 period moderating to around 6 per cent for the 2000–2015 period. These growth rates are shown in more detail in Table 6.1. The scale of this growth and its association with tourism as well as economic growth in 'Tiger' economies is a source of large-scale environmental damage.

In 1995 UK airlines carried 61 million passengers on international journeys and 14.3 million on domestic journeys. This meant a total of 1051 million aircraft kilometres flown. However, when all airlines are taken into account the total number of passengers using UK airports for international journeys in 1993 was 88 million. In comparision, in 1992 22 million UK residents made visits abroad by air. The number of UK residents not flying and the number of residents flying very frequently is not recorded in UK statistics. What is clear though is that flying is now a source of considerable growth in individual mobility and is firmly set on a rapid growth trajectory supported by large investments in airports, runways and road infrastructure.

Aviation has a considerable environmental impact. Aircraft provide the only source of pollution from human activity at the tropopause, which is the boundary layer between the lower atmosphere (the troposphere) and the upper atmosphere (the stratosphere). The injection of exhaust gases and water vapour into the atmosphere at 10–12km above the earth's surface and their impact on ozone layer depletion and global warming is one of the most important global environmental issues which requires attention. The impact of air transport on the ground is also a significant source of pollution, environmental damage and loss of habitat. Local impacts include the following:

- land take for airports, terminals and runways;
- noise;
- air pollution from aircraft, buildings and ground transport within the airport boundaries;
- air pollution, noise, loss of habitat and community disruption from roads and road transport serving the heavily car-dominated traffic flows generated by air transport;
- water pollution from airport activities, including de-icing;
- health impacts, particularly on susceptible groups.

Aviation in the UK and in Europe as a whole is experiencing dramatic increases in passenger and freight activity. The Association of European Airlines (AEA) has predicted a doubling of traffic over the next 12 years, a period of time that may well shorten with annual average growth rates in passenger traffic of above 12 per cent. In the year ending April 1995, the AEA reported a 19 per cent increase in North Atlantic traffic and a 16 per cent increase in European traffic.

Table 6.1: Global and Route Group Passenger Forecasts

	RPKs[+] 1991 (billions)	Average Growth Rates, per cent per annum 1991–2000	2000–2015	1991–2015
Global				
passenger-km	1,843.4	5.4	4.8	5.0
Route Groups				
International				
North Atlantic	176.3	4.5	4.5	4.5
South Atlantic	12.9	6.0	5.0	5.4
Mid Atlantic	12.7	6.0	5.0	5.4
Transpacific	111.8	8.0	6.2	6.9
Europe ↔ Asia/Pacific	71.1	8.2	6.4	7.1
Europe ↔ Africa	24.8	4.0	4.0	4.0
Europe ↔ Middle East	11.9	4.5	4.0	4.2
North America ↔ South America	17.5	5.5	5.0	5.2
North America ↔ Central America/Caribbean	29.1	6.5	5.0	5.6
Intra – Africa	3.4	4.2	4.5	4.4
Intra – Asia/Pacific	118.7	8.4	7.0	7.5
Intra – Europe	62.9	5.1	4.4	4.7
Intra – Latin America	6.9	5.5	5.0	5.2
Intra – Middle East	0.5	4.2	4.5	4.4
Intra – North America	14.3	4.5	3.8	4.1
Other International Routes	185.6	4.4	4.9	4.7
Total International	860.4	6.0	5.5	5.8
Domestic				
Africa	8.0	3.5	3.5	3.5
Asia/Pacific	122.3	8.1	6.5	7.1
Europe	260.4	3.5	3.5	3.5
Latin America	35.9	3.0	3.0	3.0
Middle East	8.5	3.5	3.5	3.5
North America	547.9	4.0	4.0	4.0
Total Domestic	983.0	4.3	4.3	4.3
Domestic Traffic in Individual States[*]				
China	23.7	9.0	7.5	8.2
France	15.8	–	–	3.0
Germany	4.5	5.0	3.9	4.3
Sweden	2.8	–	–	3.5
US	530.9	3.9	3.9	3.9

\+ RPK = Route Passenger kilometres.
* Forecasts provided by countries; for reference only.

Note: Europe includes Eastern Europe and the Russian Federation. North America includes the US and Canada, but not Mexico.

Source: ICAO (June 1995) Report of the databases and forecasting sub-group.

The response of the aviation industry, most national governments and the EU to these increases in demand has been to support increases in airport capacity. Aviation is an outstanding example of a commitment to the widely discredited 'predict and provide' philosophy that dominated road building discussions until the early 1990s. Individual airlines and airport operators are deeply committed to the year-on-year expansion of aviation without limit, and are prepared to invest large amounts of money to achieve this objective. Such a commitment to growth is fundamentally at odds with policy commitments to sustainable development. Aviation as a whole is non-sustainable and individual airport expansion plans are likely to breach local environmental capacities.

Aviation's commitment to expansion is taking place within a highly competitive environment where Heathrow airport is determined to capture the biggest market share and ensure that growth at Frankfurt, Schipol or Paris CDG airports does not challenge its dominant position. The same arguments (against Heathrow) are used in these non-UK airports and the result is that every location experiences expansion supported by nervous governments which have accepted flawed arguments about the economic gains to be had from aviation. Similar arguments exist within Britain where regional airports view each other as competitors. This has been extreme in the case of Manchester and Liverpool.

Aviation is highly subsidised. It is the only transport industry whose fuel is not taxed. Domestic and European travel by air is VAT exempt and airlines and airports earn substantial incomes from antiquated systems of retailing known as 'duty-free'. Infrastructure provision to support road access and air traffic control, emergency services and so forth represents another area of direct financial support by the state to an industry that, on a European scale, finds it very difficult to make a profit even under such favourable conditions.

Aviation and Global Warming

Exhaust emissions from aircraft have a much greater effect on global warming than similar quantities of pollutants released at ground level. The effect on climate is 30 times greater than for emissions from cars, homes and factories.

This is mainly the result of emissions of nitrogen oxides (NO_x) at 10–12km above the earth's surface where the gases react with sunlight to produce ozone, a greenhouse gas that traps heat and exacerbates global warming. This 'factor 30 effect' is crucial to the understanding of aviation and climate change and has a much greater impact than the actual percentage emission by aviation of nitrogen dioxide (about 3 per cent). Karl Otto Schallaböck (1993) of the Wuppertal Institute has calculated that by 2005 aviation in Germany will be responsible for about 50 per cent of all transport's CO_2 emissions. This calculation takes into account both the global warming impact of emissions at aircraft cruising levels and the air travel of all German citizens as long as their permanent residence is in Germany. Schallaböck's calculations are summarised in Table 6.2.

Table 6.2: Relative Importance of Different Modes of Transport in their Contribution to Global Warming

Source of Calculation	Mode			
	Rail	Road	Air	Water
CO_2 in 1987 from calculations by PROGNOS 1991[1]	4.6	90.1	3.9	1.4
CO_2 in 1988 from calculations by IFEU[2]	3.9	86.8	8.1	1.2
CO_2 1988 – Air transport taking into account all flying by German citizens[3]	3.6	80.3	15.0	1.1
Climate impact 1988[4]	3.2	69.9	26.0	0.9
Climate impact 2005: Extrapolation of annual average growth rate[5]	2.0	47.6	49.7	0.8

Source: Schallaböck (1993)

Notes:
1. Air travel percentage includes only the air travel within Germany's borders.
2. Air travel percentage includes flights from Germany to their first destination in a foreign country.
3. Air travel percentage includes secondary flights in the foreign country and flights back to Germany.
4. Air travel percentage includes global warming effect of NO_x and water vapour at the tropopause.
5. Includes pervious components and extrapolates to 2005.

The aviation industry devotes a great deal of energy to downplaying the size of its emissions and their contribution to global warming. British Airways claim that carbon dioxide from aviation accounts for 1–1.5 per cent of global warming. This estimate should be compared with Schallaböck's estimate of 50 per cent by 2005 which relates to air transport's share of total transport CO_2 emissions. The absence of fuel taxation for aviation fuel is a significant anomaly in the transport industry and is estimated to represent a subsidy to British Airways alone of approximately £2.5 billion per annum.

Aviation's culpability in the causation of the most significant environmental problems extends beyond global warming and includes ozone generation where this gas is harmful and ozone depletion where it is needed. Nitrogen oxide (NO_x) emissions from aircraft generate ozone where it is not wanted at low altitudes and removes it where it is wanted at high altitudes. Ozone at low altitudes (less than 15km) increases global warming. At higher levels NO_x emissions have the potential to destroy ozone. At this level ozone has the protective role of blocking harmful UV radiation.

Airports and Local Impacts

Airports are sizeable industrial enterprises with many thousands of workers who commute daily. Heathrow airport handles 54 million passengers each year and is the workplace for 50,000 people. It is probably the largest traffic generator of any kind in Europe, and the combined effect of aircraft, ground traffic, fuel storage, aircraft de-icing operations, noise, waste generation and polluted water represents a significant environmental burden for a relatively small geographical area. The Heathrow problem is repeated at a smaller scale in Manchester, Frankfurt, Paris and Amsterdam and at hundreds of smaller airports throughout the world.

The effect of noise pollution is a common and long-standing complaint from residents living in the vicinity of airports and under flight paths. Noise is damaging to human health. It interferes with communication, contributes to hearing loss, disturbs sleep, adversely effects the cardiovascular and psychophysiological systems, affects performance and disrupts social behaviour. It redefines the basis for everyday life in communities subject to aircraft noise to the detriment of local residents. WHO (1993) has estimated that about 45 per cent of the population of industrialised countries experience noise levels that exceed levels defined to protect health. The pursuit of the freedom to travel by air over longer distances subsidised by public funds is purchased at the cost of serious loss of quality of life by millions of people living around the world's airports.

The growth of aviation is enthusiastically supported by international agencies, the EU and national governments. This support contradicts other high profile policies particularly in the area of environment, sustainability and climate change. This contradiction is particularly acute in the case of the EU. The EU's position on expanding capacity to meet demand is very clear indeed:

> In the context of the trans-European networks, the key principle underlying the development of the guidelines for the airport network has been the concern to meet current and future demand for air transport, while taking due account of capacity, security and environmental protection requirements.
>
> The guidelines should thus seek to ensure that community airport capacity is able to meet current and future demand, taking into account the expected effects of the Third Civil Aviation Package adopted by the Council in June 1992.
>
> In the course of these meetings consensus has been reached on four sets of development priorities for the airport network. These include the enhancement of existing capacity, the development of new capacity, the enhancement of environmental compatibility and the development of interconnections with other networks. Consensus was also reached on the need to introduce qualitative criteria for the purpose of identifying airports of common interest as well as developed priorities.
>
> When applying the average growth rate of air transport to airports, taking account of the necessary margin of error, the passenger throughput at Community airports is expected to reach approximately 1180 million passenger movements in 2010 (arrivals + departures), which represents about twice the present passenger throughput.
>
> These figures provide some insight into the potential capacity requirements of the airport network. By the year 2000 airport capacity will need to increase by + 50 per cent in order to meet the estimated demand of 760 million passenger movements compared to 510 million movements at present (Commission of the European Communities, 1994b).

The commitment to 'predict and provide' in EU documentation could not be clearer. Equally clear is the stark contradiction with the principles of sustainable development which are explored in the next chapter. Sustainable development is the key to the EU's Fifth Environmental Action Programme, which is a formal commitment in the Maastricht Treaty supported by all 15 member states.

Airport Expansion

EU and national support for increased aviation capacity will mean a number of new runways, new airport terminals, increased car parking at airports and increased levels of motorway construction to provide the high quality access required by airport planners and operators. Airport access also involves the construction and expansion of new railways lines, tram lines and underground systems, though car access continues to dominate the travel choices of airport workers, passengers and 'meeters and greeters'.

Manchester airport in the UK predicts that passenger demand will rise from 11.7 million in 1992 to 30 million in 2005. This forecast is based on simple extrapolation of existing trends on assumptions of continuing economic growth, growth in international tourism and growth in business travel.

> Forecasts of this type, doubling or tripling passenger demand for air travel, represent a commitment to a 'business as usual' operation with no concessions whatsoever to the debate about global warming or health damage.

The forecast provides the justification for a new runway at Manchester regardless of the environmental consequences. When built, this runway will bring additional noise, air pollution and traffic congestion to the residents of south Manchester, Stockport and surrounding rural areas. It is particularly devastating for a rural environment which has already experienced extensive land take for roads and urban development. According to the Manchester International Airport 1994 Runway two appraisal:

> The runway proposal would result in the loss of 4 hectares of woodland (most of which is ancient) in Hooksbank Wood and East Woodend Wood; the grassland, scrubs and ponds in Oversleyford Brickworks, part of the adjacent grassland on the A538 road embankment, minor areas of other flower rich grassland; 4.05km of higher value edges, often with numerous mature trees; 42 ponds, 17 of which support great crested newts; and a main badger sett. The runway would also intrude into the Bollin Valley and create a barrier to the dispersal of species. A geological exposure of considerable interest would be lost. The biological character of the River Bollin and Sugar Brook would be altered.

This catalogue of environmental destruction is from the airport's own environmental statement in support of the planning application for a second runway. The statement does not consider the social and community effects of noise pollution nor the health effects of air pollution. It does not reflect on the loss of biodiversity (an important component of sustainability) and has nothing to say about global warming.

Heathrow Airport and Terminal 5

The proposal for Terminal 5 (T5) at Heathrow airport involves the addition of 30 million passengers per annum to Heathrow's existing annual throughput of 50 million. In 1994 Heathrow handled 408,000 air traffic movements (individual take off and landing operations). The proposed new terminal is larger than the existing airports of Frankfurt, Amsterdam and Paris CDG. It would amount to a new world class airport grafted on to one end of Heathrow airport in one of the already most densely populated areas of Europe.

The environmental effects of this expansion of capacity at Heathrow are acute. Tables 6.3 and 6.4 estimate the CO_2 emissions that can be expected from the construction of T5, taking into account both ground traffic (mainly cars) and aircraft activity. The calculations for aircraft only take into account the emissions of CO_2 during the take off and landing cycle.

Table 6.3: CO_2 Emissions from Passenger Car Traffic at Heathrow Airport

	1992	2016 without T5	2016 with T5
Air Passengers mppa	45[1]	60[2]	100[2]
Car journeys[3] (million) per annum	17.07	22.75	37.93
Vehicle kilometres[4] (million)	85.35	113.75	189.65
Pollution[5] tonnes CO_2	53,770	71,662	119,480

mppa = millions of passengers per annum

Notes:

1. From Transport Statistics Great Britain 1993, Table 7.1, page 147.
2. LAHT5, statement of case, 13.1.95, para 2.15, page 10.
3. Modal split is private car 42 per cent, car rental 4 per cent, taxi 20 per cent, bus and coach 13 per cent, rail and tube 20 per cent. (Source: Heathrow Environmental Performance Report, October '93 – March '94, page 24).
   The assumption made here is that 66 per cent came by car/taxi and that each vehicle contains 1.74 passengers. The occupancy figure of 1.74 is derived from Transport Statistics Great Britain, 1993.
4. For this purpose a 5km trip length is assumed. This is used to define local pollution effect. It is smaller than the distances implied in the Zurich model area (9 x 12km).
5. Assumes petrol driven car, urban conditions and takes specific emission factors from CEC (1992a) Green Paper on the Impact of Transport on the Environment COM(92) 46 final. The specific emission factor for CO_2 is 315 grams/vehicle kilometre. A 5km trip length produces a 10km journey (out & return). CO_2 = vkm x 315g x 2

Table 6.4: Heathrow Airport's CO_2 Inventory (data in tonnes)

	1992	2016 (without T5)	2016 (with T5)
CO_2 from car traffic	53,770	71,662	119,480
Aircraft emissions from LTO cycle[1]	562,600	696,000[2]	725,000[2]
Totals	616,370	767,662	844,480

Notes:

1. The data on LTO cycle CO_2 emissions are taken from Flughafen Zurich (1991). The CO_2 value per LTO cycle is 2,900 kg. The number of LTO cycles at Heathrow was calculated by taking the number of ATMs at Heathrow in 1992 (from Transport Statistics Great Britain, 1993, Table 7.1) and halving this number.
2. ATM data are taken from: LAHT5, Statement of Case, 13 January 1995 para 2.15 page 10. 2016 without T5 = 480,000 ATMs; 2016 with T5 = 500,000 ATMs.

LTO = Landing and Take-off Cycle.
ATM = Air Traffic Movement.

Terminal 5 would result in an increase in CO_2 emissions of 10 per cent when the 'with and without' T5 situation is compared in the year 2016. This increase is clearly at variance with international obligations to reduce CO_2 emissions.

Table 6.5 estimates the contribution of T5 to the level of NO_x emissions in the vicinity of Heathrow airport.

Table 6.5: NO_x Emissions at Heathrow Airport at present and in 2016

Emissions Kg per day Source/Species	NO_x (present)	NO_x 2016 (without T5)	NO_x 2016 (with T5)
Aircraft	13,826	16,903	23,493
Road traffic	2,106	2,175	2,276
Heating plant	608	752	978
Fugitive releases	0	0	0
Total	16,540	19,830	26,747

Source: Air Quality Modelling Study for Heathrow and Surrounding Area. Final Report, London Borough of Hillingdon Environment Group, April 1994, Appendix B, pages B23 and B26.

NO_x levels in 2016 with T5 are 35 per cent higher when compared with 2016 without T5. This would represent a serious deterioration in local air quality at a time when there are international agreements in place to reduce NO_x emissions.

Airport expansion is a significant environmental problem. It conflicts with sustainable development objectives, damages the atmosphere and contributes to a serious deterioration in air quality, noise and the viability of ordinary everyday activities such as use of gardens, communication at schools and conversations on the street. It also damages health – though very little detailed 'research' on the health effects of living in the vicinity of large international airports has been undertaken. Air travel is popular and represents a major new item in consumption. This is inextricably linked with tourism even though airlines often couch their advertising in terms of extolling the virtues of business travel and the advantages to the national economy of strong business connections from an important airport such as Heathrow. The reality is different – 60 per cent of British Airway's profitability derives from leisure/holiday travel.

The freedom to travel by air to exotic locations is a powerful image and is promoted through large advertising budgets. The freedom of local residents to enjoy quiet conditions while they sleep, or to breathe clean air, do not benefit from advertising and PR budgets. Airlines and airports actively promote the expansion of their industry by creating opportunities for new destinations, new experiences and new and lower fares. This active creation of a market contrasts dramatically with the official stance of British Airways, the British Airports Authority and Manchester Airport who all claim high environmental standards in their management practices whilst at the same time adding significant additional burdens to global inventories of greenhouse gases and local inventories of NO_x.

Air travel thus throws down a serious challenge to the management of environmental problems at local and global levels.

If private consumption and the pursuit of freedoms to pollute and consume resources are to be given priority over local environmental quality and local community activities, then the case for airport expansion at every world airport is overwhelming.

If continuing growth and expansion is to be challenged (as is implied by sustainable development) then some fundamental reappraisal of the concept of freedoms is overdue and some thought is needed from within the industry and government on the interplay between environment, economy and quality of life.

Air transport clearly shows that there is no chance of having one's cake and eating it. It can grow indefinitely or it can be capped. Airports can expand to double or treble their size and capacity, or they can be held to an environmental limit. The debate about sustainability provides some insight into what should be done about airports, and for what reason, but more importantly a fundamental reappraisal of lifestyle priorities is needed in order to elevate the everyday activity, the short distance trip, the local school run, interaction with neighbours and the health of children to the highest level of priority. The freedom to travel to Goa for a ten day break in January destroys the intricate web of connections that creates high quality places, healthy children and a strong sense of local identity and community interaction.

Conclusion

Air transport, long-distance tourism and their combined impact on society, culture, environment and economy present serious difficulties for policy makers. The behavioural attributes and lifestyle characteristics associated with long-distance tourism are deeply embedded in contemporary thinking about freedoms, economic growth and a globalised economy. The growth in aviation represents a fundamental threat to sustainable development which is based on clear principles of environmental capacity, demand management and reducing energy and raw material resource consumption whilst protecting biodiversity. Tourism and aviation threaten each of these principles.

The destruction of landscape and place on a global scale has its echo in the local destruction of countryside and community in towns and rural areas in Europe in the pursuit of mobility fuelled by high speeds, abundant energy and the desire to save time so as to be able to travel further in a given time budget. The logic of Britain's recent and most destructive road and motorway constructions (Twyford Down, Batheaston Bypass, Newbury Bypass) is that a time saving of a few minutes is a valuable prize well worth the destruction of woodland, nature reserves, archaeological monuments and green fields. The capacity to transport millions to holiday destinations in the Mediterranean, India and Africa is so important that damage to the atmosphere, destination areas and areas around the main European airports is a price well worth paying.

CHAPTER 7

Sustainability

Introduction

The previous chapters explored current global patterns of travel and transport use and their change over time. These patterns, it has been argued, are the result of particular socioeconomic forces. These forces act to encourage the transport of more and more people and goods over increasing distances, by modes of transport that promise – although may not actually deliver – significant time savings. Transport policies within the developed world (and increasingly in the developing world) have largely acted to reinforce this socioeconomic framework.

Policies have been predicated on the assumption that an expanding transport infrastructure is necessary to secure continued economic growth. Markets need to expand into new areas and goods need to be transported in minimum time to their far flung destinations. Transport cost, particularly in terms of time taken to access markets, is often portrayed as a significant factor in the success or failure of industry.

Policies have also attempted, and largely failed, to meet the demand for private motorised transport. This has been argued as necessary for a healthy economy to give people access to the goods and services they require, when they want them. Demand-led transport policies have also been pursued in support of the notion that the car promotes individual freedom in a way that collective forms of transport do not. Technologies associated with transport have also largely been focused on delivering these policy objectives – increasing individual mobility and increasing the speed and comfort of individual motorised travel at the expense of improving less environmentally damaging modes of transport.

It is somewhat ironic that this massive increase in personal mobility made possible by technological 'improvements', now requires technological 'solutions' to manage the demand for road space. Thus road pricing systems and advanced driver information systems are now the focus of considerable research activity and expenditure, despite their application providing only a partial approach to the problem of congested roadspace.

The environmental impacts of the global movement of people and goods are immense and will be scrutinised in greater detail later.

Needless to say there has been a growing concern, not only about the local environmental and health impacts of transport, but also about the global impacts, particularly those impacts that are the result of the massive global increase in car and air travel. This chapter will try to locate this increasing concern within the emerging concepts of sustainability and sustainable development. This will include a consideration of what is meant by the terms, how they are being used and interpreted, and what relationship exists between transport and sustainability.

Why do we Need to Develop Sustainably?

Concern about the environment is not new. Many countries have well-established legal frameworks for environmental protection and a tradition of community action that covers a wide range of environmental issues. So why do we need to adopt new phraseology to describe old problems? The answer lies in understanding sustainable development as something that goes beyond traditional notions of environmental protection.

In recent years the limitations of a partial approach to environmental protection, divorced from the economic system, have become all too apparent. In the 1960s and 1970s the development of new communications technology allowed widespread visual coverage of environmental disasters such as oil spills off Alaska in the US, and near the Shetlands in the UK, and the human and environmental catastrophe caused by the use of chemicals such as Agent Orange in the Vietnam war. New social movements began to emerge that embraced these environmental concerns and began to reconnect human society with its natural surroundings, realising that one could not exist without the other. Publication of several landmark reports such as *The Limits to Growth* (Meadows *et al.* 1972) and *Global 2000: The Report to The President* (Global 2000, 1982) served to reinforce this thinking. These reports placed human society within the global ecosystem where resources were finite and where human actions had repercussion for the future health of the planet and, hence, the viability of future human society. Most important of all, they connected environmental degradation to economic activity and questioned whether such levels and types of activity could be sustained by future generations.

As the turn of the century approaches, the speed and scale of environmental degradation has reached frightening proportions. For example, despite growing concern, the world's forests are disappearing at a rate of 15 million hectares each year. In addition, the removal of vegetation by human and animal populations is causing a serious loss of biodiversity and soil erosion to millions of hectares. It is estimated that one-third of Asia's non-desert land will become 'desertified' by the turn of the century.

Scientific discoveries such as ozone depletion and the greenhouse effect have highlighted the all too fragile relationship between the planet and its ever increasing human population. The enormity of such problems has demanded global international action and a new approach to development that seeks to embrace environmental concerns and contain human activity within environmental limits.

Defining Sustainability and Sustainable Development

In 1987, the World Commission on Environment and Development published its report, *Our Common Future*. This became known as the Brundtland Report after its chairperson, Gro Harlem Brundtland. This made explicit reference to the need for the global economy to adopt the aim of sustainable development, which it described as:

> ... development that meets the needs of the present without compromising the ability of future generations to meet their own needs.

Although this definition has been criticised for lacking a more precise meaning, it is still probably the most commonly cited definition and acts as an important reference for those wishing to explore the concept further. However, it raises more questions than it answers. For example, how is 'need' defined within our complex consumer society where needs have been socially reconstructed to mean 'wants'? Is global air transport for tourism to exotic destinations a need? How do we know what future generations will need? Their expectations and their levels of efficiency in production may be very different to ours. And at what level of economic activity are these future needs being compromised?

It is therefore hard to use this definition to construct a practical framework for precise action towards an end point of sustainability, and the sentence is more likely meant to encourage a different attitude in industry, institutions and governments, by making these forces more conscious of the long-term environmental implications of their actions, and consequently to change their approach to economic development. In as much as the report added to the momentum that led to the 1992 Earth Summit held in Rio in Brazil, these actors can be said to have had some success in achieving their task.

There is, however, a danger in that the report recommends a shift in direction of policy without giving any detail as to the size of the necessary change. Thus, policy may indeed move in the right direction, but the rate of change may not be sufficient to secure the sustainability of the planet. For example, the rate of deforestation may be slowed, but this change may not be enough to secure a level of biodiversity sufficient to meet future human needs.

In this respect the report produced by the IUCN (International Union for the Conservation of Nature), UNEP (United Nations Environment Programme) and WWF (1991) *Caring For The Earth – A Strategy For Sustainable Living*, provides a more practical and helpful definition. It defines sustainable development as:

> ... improving the quality of life while living within the carrying capacity of supporting ecosystems.

It goes on to develop a strategy defined by nine principles necessary for a sustainable society. In order to achieve this goal current generations must:

- respect and care for the community of life;
- improve the quality of human life;
- conserve the earth's vitality and diversity;
- minimise the depletion of non-renewable resources;
- keep within the earth's carrying capacity;
- change personal attitudes and practices;
- enable communities to care for their own environment;
- provide a national framework for integrating environment and development;
- create a global alliance.

Adoption of this definition requires a clearer definition of the 'carrying capacity' of the earth, and what it is to live within this. This is by no means a simple task, but it at least provides a framework for further action, rather than the vaguer definition offered by Brundtland.

Thus the concept of sustainable development represents a new agenda that, if implemented, goes beyond the traditional realms of environmental protection and nature conservation and includes:

- concern for the long-term health and integrity of the planet;
- limiting human action within 'sustainable' rates and levels;
- implying the existence of environmental features that are too important to be traded off against economic or other social benefits;
- seeing development in terms of improving the quality of human life and furthering human potential, and not simply measured by income growth.

Thus sustainable development is very much the social tool by which human societies may reach the end point of environmental, economic and social equilibrium.

Problems in Interpretation

Since the publication of the Brundtland Report the term sustainable development has become part of the common language of academics, politicians and policy-makers across the world. Some commentators have criticised the way in which it has been adopted as a guiding principle without due consideration to what it actually means. Its all too frequent use in political rhetoric has given the term a reputation for lacking substance. As a colleague noted during the 1992 Earth Summit 'anything on which John Major, George Bush and Fidel Castro all agree can't really mean anything, can it?'

One could argue that it is precisely this lack of clear meaning that allows politicians and businesspeople to feel comfortable using the term – everyone agrees that it's a good thing but no one really knows what it means.

There are certainly a range of interpretations of what needs to be done to create a sustainable society. Some interpretations commit decision makers to nothing more than business as usual with a slightly green tinge. Implementation of other, more radical interpretations, however, would involve nothing less than a revolution in the world economy and our own individual lifestyles. But this range of interpretations does not make the concept meaningless.

Action For Sustainability

The objective of achieving sustainable development has been integrated into the policy process of a wide range of governments, institutions and non-governmental organisations. The Earth Summit produced a number of important international agreements and saw the signing of the 600-page Agenda 21 – a strategy for implementing sustainable development to be adopted by all nations. The UK government is thus one of many governments now obliged to produce regular reports to the United Nations on its progress towards achieving sustainable development, as well as implementing a strategy for action on climate change and biodiversity. Action is required at all levels, from international agreements down to personal action. Local action strategies are being developed through the process of Local Agenda 21 whereby local authorities work with communities to develop strategies for protecting and enhancing the environment – both local and global.

Is a Sustainable Society also an Equitable Society?

Central to most definitions of sustainable development is the requirement that human society live within certain defined environmental limits. These limits will be based on the rate at which ecosystems can be renewed (in order to limit the depletion of natural resources) and the rate at which global ecosystems can assimilate waste from human production and consumption processes (in order to limit habitat destruction and any increase in the concentration of harmful pollutants in the environment).

These environmental limits are deemed necessary in order to ensure the survival of future generations. This notion of intergenerational equity is based on the assumption that it is wrong for one generation to consume resources at rates which deprive future generations of their ability to sustain life. Many commentators believe that if current generations accept that it is their moral duty to consider the needs of those who come after them, then the ability of the present human population to meet the needs of present generations should also be considered. It is often suggested that the global economy, in its current form, is unable to deliver an equitable distribution of resources in society, and as a result the lion's share of resources is consumed by Western developed nations at the expense of populations in the developing world.

It is theoretically possible to be concerned simply with the preservation of a healthy environment, either for its own sake or for use by future generations. Concern about how present generations meet their needs would not be relevant so long as total human activity was kept within environmental limits. This approach, however, is not supportable because it fails to recognise the link between poverty and environmental degradation: it is not possible to meet environmental targets if 90 per cent of the world's population has access to only 10 per cent of its resources, because trying to survive in a poor environment with scarce resources places enormous strain on the natural environment. This can lead to deforestation, overgrazing and soil erosion, as well as social instability which encourages mass migration and often war. Thus a more equitable distribution of resources, delivered within a framework of a socially just society, has to be an essential component of any strategy to achieve sustainable development.

Transport and Sustainability: are Current Transport Patterns Sustainable?

Sustainability is concerned with the long-term impact of human activity on the global environment. It is acknowledged, however, that these global phenomena are the result of numerous human actions that occur on a more local scale. This concern about long-term impact, the effect of which may be irreversible, largely defines priorities for a sustainable transport strategy. The following environmental concerns are therefore crucial considerations when addressing the long-term sustainability of the transport sector:

- emissions of greenhouse gases, particularly from energy consumption;
- depletion of resources, particularly non-renewable resources;
- degradation of soil fertility through erosion, salination and toxification;
- depletion of the ozone layer;
- pollution of ground water and seas;
- accumulation of toxic chemicals;
- loss of biodiversity and population numbers.

It is not always clear exactly how a large number of relatively small-scale impacts will affect the future sustainability of the planet. For example, the exact importance to future human society of the vast number of species that are becoming extinct every year as a result of human activity is simply unknown. However, it is not unrealistic to assume that this loss of species will, at the very least, deprive future societies of a significant resource in the fight against disease. It is possible, however, to be able to calculate the contribution that transport makes to habitat destruction – for example, directly, through the construction of transport infrastructure, and indirectly, through quarrying of materials necessary for the system to operate. It is also possible to calculate transport's contribution to global

The Global Car Industry

- Energy consumption by OECD countries rose by 300 per cent between 1950 and 1980, and transport is the fastest growing sector
- The US alone consumed 17 million barrels of oil per day in 1991 and this is predicted to rise to 22 million by 2010
- The transnational turnover of General Motors puts it among the GDP of the top 20 nations
- 14 per cent of US jobs are dependent on the US motor industry
- The number of private cars in the European Union, placed end-to-end, would go around the world twice
- A traffic jam comprising all lorries within the EU would stretch 4 times round the world
- If China had the same rate of car ownership as the 1980 US rate, they would circle the Earth nose-to-tail 4 times
- The number of cars in India would have to increase by 1100 per cent in order to reach British levels of car ownership (Morgan, 1994)

warming and climate change and compare this with the contribution of other economic sectors.

Transport and Climate Change

The transport sector contributes to global warming by producing CO_2 and other greenhouse gases as a result of combustion processes. A recent report (1993) by the International Energy Agency (IEA) found that energy use in the main industrial nations had increased by 300 per cent in the last 30 years. The use of energy by the transport sector has grown by similar proportions and is now responsible for over one-third of final energy use, making it the fastest growing sector. In 1992 this resulted in over 800 million tonnes of CO_2 being emitted into the atmosphere, 76 per cent of which were from road transport. Evidence suggests that, in order to avert the environmental and social disasters that may result from global warming it is necessary to cut CO_2 emissions in industrialised nations by 60 per cent by 2020 (Hughes, 1993). Some commentators believe this to be a conservative estimate and that further reductions are needed. So far 150 countries have endorsed the United Nations Framework Convention on Climate Change which commits them to the very modest reduction of returning CO_2 emissions to 1990 levels by the year 2000 – far short of the 60 per cent reduction that the Intergovernmental Panel on Climate Change (IPCC) is suggesting.

There are approximately 500 million motor vehicles on the planet, and 35 million new vehicles are produced every year. In terms of the contribution of motor vehicles to CO_2 emissions (approximately 14 per cent and growing) this pattern of consumption must be considered unsustainable. Although it may be possible to cut emissions of CO_2 from other sectors of the economy in order to allow transport's contribution to remain unchanged, this in itself will not make the sector sustainable because of the wide

The Environmental Impact of the Global Car Industry

- The car paint industry releases the equivalent of 15,652 juggernaut loads of hydrocarbons (HCs) into the atmosphere each year
- Plastics used in American cars in 1995 would fill a 878km queue of juggernauts, whilst daily new tyres laid in a line would stretch 368km
- Each car in the UK emits 45kg of nitrogen oxides per year
- Cars that are sent for scrap in the EU would create a 3km queue of juggernauts filled with shredder waste every day (Morgan, 1994)

range of other environmental impacts from this sector that also contribute to unsustainability. Principal amongst these impacts are the demands that transport makes on land and on finite material resources such as aggregates and metals. These demands are likely to increase dramatically as car ownership levels rise in developing countries and in parts of the world newly subject to market forces. The transport sector must therefore significantly reduce its impact in all parts of the world for it to be considered sustainable.

What Are the Criteria for a More Sustainable Transport System?

Based on the environmental issues outlined above, in order for transport to be more sustainable it must meet the following criteria:

- minimise its dependence on fossil fuels;
- cut its consumption of raw materials;
- reduce emissions of CO_2 and other greenhouse gases;
- cut pollution to ground water and seas;
- minimise its land use requirement;
- reduce its impact on habitats;
- reduce soil erosion caused by transport infrastructure;
- stop its use of ozone-depleting substances.

The magnitude of these reductions and the speed at which they are introduced will be dependent upon an interaction between social forces, political will and technological development. This may provide change in the right direction – but not at the rate necessary to avoid lasting environmental damage. Thus new ways must be found to ensure that transport systems and lifestyle are designed and modulated respectively in order to contain human mobility within the earth's carrying capacity.

New Approaches to Transport Decision Making

The old model of transport planning that has dominated decision making in much of the developed world has largely attempted to meet growing demand for private motoring at the expense of public transport, walking and cycling. Within this model, consideration about the environment is restricted to, at best, environmental 'improvements' for a particular project, such as landscaping or noise barriers. Opportunities for public participation by the communities affected by the scheme are minimal. Their views are often sought only after a decision to build a particular road has been taken, and their comments are restricted to the choice of route rather than whether a road needs to be built at all.

In order to design transport systems to meet sustainability objectives a new approach is necessary. The new approach would be planned by demand management concepts and clear targets and objectives linked to sustainable development principles. It would, moreover, reflect the wishes of the community and the locality rather than the long-distance traveller.

Setting Targets for Sustainable Transport

In order to change transport and planning policy to meet sustainability objectives, it is first of all necessary to know the direction that current policies are taking. The first step in adopting an environmentally led transport system is to establish reference points on which to base policy change. This requires collecting data on current transport patterns as well as predicting how this is likely to change in the future if policies and existing patterns of investment remain unchanged. Once there is a picture of where current policy is going then it is possible to determine the scope of action that is necessary to reverse those trends. In the Netherlands, where this approach was pioneered, this is known as 'trend-breaching'.

National Environmental Planning in the Netherlands

The Dutch approach to meeting the objectives of sustainability has been to develop a comprehensive package of both indicators and targets to reduce environmental impacts towards a level believed to be within the earth's carrying capacity. These have been presented within a series of reports known as the National Environmental Policy Plan. Transport is seen as a key sector on which to act if targets are to be met, and so a separate document relating solely to traffic and transport policy has also been published.

Current trends for traffic growth in the Netherlands have been analysed and various scenarios considered in order to reduce the predicted growth rate by 50 per cent. This target was chosen so that the transport sector makes its contribution to the more general targets for CO_2, NO_x, hydrocarbons and noise reduction. The scale of the changes necessary to meet the targets, if carried out, will have a significant impact on the Dutch way of living. New tools and instruments have been considered as a way of raising public awareness about the importance of environmental issues and in order to make the necessary changes without reducing overall quality of life.

Where appropriate, policy objectives may go further than merely reversing current trends. It may be possible to calculate the capacity of the local environment to absorb pollution and to set policy objectives that reduce the environmental impact of transport to this level. Alternatively, reductions may be based on a calculation of the local contribution to a global impact such as CO_2 emissions. In this case, local emissions of CO_2 from the transport sector would be calculated and a reduction in this would be based on the 60 per cent reduction recommended by the IPCC.

This process of establishing trends and agreeing objectives, based on sustainability criteria, is known as target-setting and can be applied at all levels of decision making, from local to international. However, the following general principles apply to the setting of sustainability targets, regardless of the level of decision making:

- transport must reduce its environmental impacts to within the earth's carrying capacity;
- any calculation of transport's contribution to global unsustainability must include the whole productive cycle (to include the abstraction of raw materials including fuel, vehicle production and maintenance, infrastructure construction and maintenance, and the disposal of wastes);
- the necessary changes to mobility patterns must be equitably distributed, both between societies and between individuals within those societies;
- targets should focus not only on reducing environmental impacts but also on meeting second order objectives such as improving health, reducing accidents and providing a better quality of life;
- decisions on how changes are to be made must be taken at the most appropriate level.

Choosing Environmental Indicators

By knowing how much change is necessary in order to meet sustainability objectives human societies will be in a much better position to choose the most appropriate package of policies that will meet these objectives. However, once these policies have been decided it then becomes essential to monitor both the progress towards meeting these targets and the impact that these policies are having on society as a whole.

This impact will not just extend to the local and global environment but also to the local economy and the quality of life in the community. It therefore becomes necessary to define a complementary set of indicators in order to measure progress (or lack of progress) towards the agreed objectives.

As action to achieve sustainability needs to be taken at all levels of decision making, indicators should reflect progress being made at local, regional, national and international levels appropriate to the types of decisions being made at each. As well as involving the community in target-setting, every effort should also be made to include them in choosing the indicators that monitor these targets. This type of participatory exercise has been carried out successfully in a number of communities, for example the Sustainable Seattle Initiative in the US and the Melbourne Urban Environmental Indicators Project in Australia.

The Sustainable Seattle Initiative

This initiative combines the development of environmental indicators with broader social indicators in an attempt to measure overall quality of life. The aim of the project is to 'collect, develop, translate, disseminate and publicise indicators of sustainability, in order to make them accessible to the media, the public and decision-makers' and to 'spur corrective action' (Whittaker, 1995). The indicators are chosen by a civic panel of 150 ordinary citizens after a long consultation period with the wider community.

The resulting indicators are intended to reflect global, regional and local concerns and the links between lifestyle and consumption at the local level and the solution of global problems. They range over environmental, economic and social dimensions and include:

- total CO_2 emissions;
- per capita energy use;
- number of days per year that the mountains are visible from the city centre;
- acres of protected land;
- hazardous waste production;
- unemployment rate;
- infant mortality rate;
- crime rate.

The project is still in its early stages so it is not yet possible to assess its contribution to improving sustainability, but it does offer a basis to broaden discussion about the issues of sustainability in a way that is meaningful to most people.

The set of indicators chosen by such a project will often embrace a wide range of parameters, not only measuring the impact of policies on the quality of the local, and sometimes global, environment, but also monitoring the social, economic and quality of life changes that may result from the implementation of environmental policies. For example, a policy to reduce the number of cars in the city centre may produce a range of both positive and negative impacts. It may cause a reduction in the city's global contribution to CO_2 and so improve local air quality. It may improve human health by reducing the incidence of air pollution-related illnesses such as asthma, or by reducing the number of accidents. It may also improve the quality of life for those who live in the city, and may impact positively on the local economy by boosting retail sales by producing a more pleasant urban environment. Equally, the policy could have negative effects by merely shifting traffic to another part of the city thus causing more congestion and damaging the local economy in other areas by restricting central access.

Thus each community must develop its own set of indicators that reflect local circumstances and local priorities for action based on the sustainability targets that it has identified. Community involvement is essential if many of the targets are to be met, as a number of initiatives, particularly those relating to transport, will require personal lifestyle changes. These initiatives cannot take place without the support and understanding of local residents and local organisations concerned with education, environment, transport and much more. Substantial progress in the direction of sustainable development depends on the degree to which participation and involvement of all parties is real, and a full part of the governmental process.

The points below contain some suggestions of indicators that may be relevant to monitoring the impact of transport policy in an average city. There is no prescriptive set of indicators and the list is not exhaustive. It is helpful to sub-divide indicators into three categories: primary, secondary and tertiary. Primary indicators are those that measure the key indicators of global sustainability. They reflect the principal pressures that are being exerted by human society on the planet's ecosystems. Secondary indicators measure the smaller scale, more localised impacts, and measure the actual physical state of the area being monitored. Tertiary indicators can embrace more of the social and economic trends that may be influenced by particular policies. These reflect societal response to the policy changes.

Primary Indicators

- energy use per capita;
- CO_2 emissions;
- SO_2 emissions;
- NO_x emissions;
- hydrocarbon emissions;
- levels of tropospheric ozone;
- emissions of heavy metals;
- loss of biodiversity or greenspace from transport infrastructure construction.

Secondary Indicators

- annual fuel consumption by the transport sector;
- vehicle kms per annum;
- number of cars per household;
- number of new vehicles sold per annum;
- tonnes-km of freight moved per annum by each transport mode;
- ratio of funds spent on private and public transport (including cycling and walking facilities);
- availability (and cost to user) of public/private parking bays in the central business district;
- average commuting distance and modal choice of commuters;
- percentage of total road journeys in single occupancy vehicles;
- total road capacity;
- total route kms of mass transit systems;
- total route kms of dedicated cycleway;
- percentage of inner area with access for pedestrians, cyclists and buses only;
- number and capacity of park and ride schemes;
- number and percentage of journeys of less than 5km by mode.

Tertiary Indicators

- road accident rate;
- asthma sufferers per 1000 population;
- percentage of community living with noise background rates greater than 55 dB(A);
- percentage of children driven to school;
- percentage of women who feel safe using public transport at night;
- percentage of population living within 500m of a bus/tramstop/railway station/cycleway;
- percentage of population living within 5km of essential services (shops, hospital, school etc);
- percentage of streets safe for children to play;
- GDP per capita;
- unemployment rate;
- number of business starts/failures in the central business district.

Conclusion: Policy Tools for a More Sustainable Transport System

A more sustainable transport system is one that focuses on reducing the long-term environmental impacts of transport that damage global life-support systems. Policies must therefore be chosen that:

- reduce pollution (particularly of greenhouse gases such as CO_2);
- reduce habitat destruction through the provision and use of non-motorised transport systems;
- shift reliance away from fossil fuels to low energy or renewable energy sources.

As has been argued, equity is an important component of sustainability. Transport policies should therefore be concerned with reducing the inequality in consumption of finite resources that exists between the developed and the developing world, and between individuals and groups in society.

Emphasis is increasingly being placed on developing alternative approaches to reducing the unsustainable impacts of transport. Innovative policies are being developed that challenge reliance on traditional approaches to transport planning. In particular, these policies reject demand-led transport planning as a model that has tried (and largely failed) to meet predicted demand for personal mobility, and in so doing has created its own demand. They also challenge the 'technical fix' approach to limiting environmental damage from transport. Such policies recognise that technical improvements at best offer a partial solution to the environmental and social impacts of transport. More often than not they provide only temporary relief to a particular problem, and in so doing create a different set of problems. At the same time, by relying too heavily on the emergence of technological solutions, there is a failure to tackle the underlying causes of this massive increase in personal mobility.

These alternative policies recognise that what is needed is a different approach to making transport more sustainable. Technology has a place in this, but more often than not it is low technology solutions that are found to be more appropriate and effective in meeting sustainability objectives. Such an approach recognises that the following areas of policy are a priority if a more sustainable transport policy is to be developed:

- developing land use policies that reduce the need to travel;
- improving the quality of urban life in order to limit migration to rural areas;
- limiting access by traffic to towns and cities;

- developing a strong local economy that reduces reliance on the long-distance transport of goods (particularly by encouraging local food production);
- emphasising accessibility as a priority for planning policy, rather than the more traditional emphasis on increasing personal mobility;
- moving from traditional policy tools, such as regulation and enforcement, to newer approaches, such as public awareness-raising and education;
- providing the framework of choice, comfort, convenience and affordability in non-private modes of transport to encourage the public to make lifestyle changes to their personal travel behaviour.

Sustainable transport policies transform the role of time in the urban planning process, as well as its significance as an important dimension of lifestyle. A move away from fossil fuel dependence is a move towards slower forms of transport, especially the bicycle and walking. The de-prioritising of speed re-prioritises accessibility and the importance of local facilities and neighbourhood activities. Time previously spent in traffic jams and on long commutes can be reallocated to interaction time with friends and neighbours. Paradoxically, a reduction in speed and its concomitant reduction in journey length gives people more time, reversing the historic trade-off between speed and distance. The last 40 years or so have seen the deployment of vast amounts of fossil fuel energy to generate the speed that stimulates the substitution of short distance trips by longer distance trips. Sustainability is not just about reducing per capita energy consumption or CO_2 production, but is also about enriching lifestyle and the economy. Local residents will have more time and, if they choose to dispense with the car, will have more money. The cash previously spent on cars can be reallocated to other purposes some of which will benefit local shops, local services and local activities. All this becomes possible because of the opportunity provided by a sustainability policy framework to improve environment and lifestyle opportunities.

Sustainability has the potential to deliver dramatic improvements in quality of life in ways that rising levels of demand for motorised transport and rising levels of roads and car provision never can. Sustainable development is about working towards clearly articulated goals with careful planning and allocation of budgets. It is also about consensus building rather than social engineering. The shift to a sustainable city and a sustainable society will come about as a result of the exercise of individual choice. Cities that are relatively car free will be far more popular with their residents and inward investors than those that are sacrificed to the car. Places that have low crime rates because of high levels of street activity, use of public space, and interaction with neighbours will be more attractive than the privatised and sterile worlds of car travel and streets without people. Places where children and the elderly can move around without noise assaults and breathe clean air will be more highly prized than environments that exacerbate asthma and make conversation difficult or impossible because of noise.

Public policy and spending can create these choices *and* let the market have its way. The central paradox of the free market economy that is involved in support of car ownership and use is that it is as far away from any 'free market' as it could be. The car has exterminated other choices and a choice of environments is not available. When that choice is made available we will see the attractiveness of non-car futures and reduced dependency, and will be firmly set on a path to sustainable development.

CHAPTER 8

Environment

Introduction

Environmental impacts have been integrated into the disucssion at several points in the book. In this section they are collected in a more systematic manner.

Environmental Impact of Transport

The environmental impact of transport has now become a global issue. Environmental impacts from transport in the developed world are now equalled or exceeded by those in developing countries. This is alarming given the relatively low level of car ownership and use in developing countries. Equally alarming is the advance of modes of transport that are damaging to the environment and health, while less damaging modes are retreating. Table 8.1 provides a summary of the main impacts associated with each transport mode. The impact of transport affects the global, regional and local environment. It is at each of these levels that action needs to be focused in order to reduce and mitigate the impact on the environment.

Global Impacts

Transport is mainly oil-based, and the motor vehicle is the biggest consumer of energy compared with all other transport modes. The motor vehicle is only as reliable as its fuel source, and has been influenced in the past by fluctuations in oil prices and the disruption of world oil reserves. On a global scale, motor vehicles powered solely by oil account for one-third of world oil consumption. Energy consumed by transport is closely related to air pollution, with the production of pollutants having significant effects on the pollution of the atmosphere. Fossil fuel combustion produces CO_2, CO, NO_x, and VOCs which, as previously mentioned, are precursors to tropospheric ozone and acid rain, as well as contributing directly or indirectly to global warming.

The energy efficiency of different transport modes is highly variable with more than a six-fold difference in the energy intensity between the most and least efficient modes of passenger transport. Walking and cycling are extremely efficient in energy terms and confer a number of health benefits on those who use them. However, road transport is the most common form of transport for the movement of both passengers and freight.

Global Warming

The IPCC has estimated that over the last 30 years the global mean temperature has risen by 0.3°C–0.6°C. Based on this, global warming will involve an increase in global mean temperature of 1°C above the present level by 2025 and 3°C before the end of the next century. Measures need to be taken now to reduce greenhouse gas emissions by 2030, otherwise they could reach levels equivalent to twice those of the pre-industrial period.

Global warming has a number of effects and may result in a change in climate, especially rainfall patterns which would increase the likelihood of more intense tropical storms and will have significant consequences for agriculture production. Rising sea levels due to thermal expansion of the ocean and melting of glaciers will pose a threat to wetlands, Pacific islands and atolls as well as large areas of the world's densely populated coastal regions (for example, Bangladesh). Increasing levels of risk and costs associated with accelerating coastal erosion, flooding and increases in the salinity of estuaries and aquifers can be expected.

The global average concentration of CO_2 increased from its pre-industrial levels of about 270 parts per million by volume (ppmv) to 335ppmv in 1991. This could rise to 700ppmv by 2100. Carbon dioxide is responsible for about 50 per cent of global warming. The main source of CO_2 is from fossil fuel combustion. The World Resources Institute, in its 1996/97 report on the urban environment, estimates that global emissions of CO_2 amounted to 26.4 billion tonnes in 1992. Eighty per cent of this is from fossil fuel burning and transport is responsible for 30 per cent of all CO_2 emissions in OECD countries.

The World Resources Institute presents evidence to show that CO_2 emissions are likely to rise by 30–40 per cent by 2010 under moderate growth conditions and 93 per cent by 2020 under 'robust economic growth' conditions. This compares with recommendations from the IPCC for a reduction of 60 per cent in the current level of CO_2 emissions in order simply to stabilise atmospheric concentrations of CO_2 at today's levels. It is for this reason that global warming and CO_2 emissions are such a central feature of the sustainable development debate (see Chapter 7).

Much of the future increase in CO_2 emissions will take place in the developing world, particularly India and China. Transport will play a key role in this growth as these societies motorise and adopt Western lifestyle and mobility patterns. Transport policy and traffic

Table 8.1: The Selected Environmental Impacts of Principal Transport Modes

Principal transport modes	Air	Water resources	Land resources	Solid waste	Noise	Risk of accidents	Other impacts
Marine and inland water transport		Discharge of ballast water, oil spill, etc. Modification of water systems during port construction and canal cutting and dredging.	Land taken for infrastructures; dereliction of obsolete port facilities and canals.	Vessels and craft withdrawn from service.		Bulk transport of fuels and hazardous substances.	
Rail transport			Land taken for rights of way and terminals; dereliction of obsolete facilities.	Abandoned lines, equipment and rolling stock.	Noise and vibration around terminals and along railway lines.	Derailment or collision of freight trains carrying hazardous substances.	Partition or destruction of neighbourhoods, farmlands and wildlife habitats.

Principal transport modes	Air	Water resources	Land resources	Solid waste	Noise	Risk of accidents	Other impacts
Road transport	Air pollution (CO, HC, NO_x, particulates and fuel additives such as lead). Global pollution (CO_2, CFCs).	Pollution of surface water and groundwater by surface run-off; modification of water systems by road building.	Land taken for infrastructures; extraction of road building materials.	Abandoned spoil tips and rubble from road works; road vehicles withdrawn from service; waste oil.	Noise and vibration from cars, motorcycles and lorries in cities and along main roads.	Deaths, injuries and property damage from road accidents; risk of transport of hazardous substances; risks of structural failure in old or worn road facilities.	Partition or destruction of neighbourhoods, farmlands and wildlife habitats.
Air transport	Air pollution.	Modification of water tables, river courses and field drainage in airport construction.	Land taken for infrastructure; dereliction of obsolete facilities.	Aircraft withdrawn from service.	Noise around airports.	Deaths, injuries, property damage from aircraft accidents; but slight compared with road transport.	

Source: Tolba *et al.* (1992)

demand management in developing countries is now the single most important policy area for containing the growth of CO_2 emissions and for achieving sustainable development objectives.

Carbon dioxide is only one of a number of greenhouse gases with CH_4, CFC-11, CFC-12 and HCFC-22 being the other principal sources (see Table 8.2). Other pollutants emitted from transport, such as NO_x, directly contribute to global warming or form secondary pollutants. Although CO_2 is increasing, it is not as potent as CFC-11 and CFC-12 which have a higher global warming potential.

Table 8.2: Main Sources of Greenhouse Gases

Carbon dioxide	Fossil fuel consumption, deforestation
Chlorofluorocarbons (CFCs)	Aerosol propellants, solvents, refrigerants, foam blowing agents
Nitrous oxide	a) Microbial processes in soil and water b) Biomass burning and fossil fuel combustion
Methane	Anaerobic bacteria from natural wetlands, rice paddies, rumen of cattle and other mammals, and guts of termites and other wood-consuming insects

Source: UNEP (1991)

The relative contribution of motor vehicles to global CO_2 emissions has gradually increased. In 1971, motor vehicles accounted for only 12 per cent of total global CO_2 emissions from fossil fuels. By 1985, this percentage had risen to 14 per cent. Regional differences in the emission of CO_2 can also be distinguished, with signs of stabilisation in the more developed regions such as North America and western Europe. Emissions from less developed regions of South America, South East and Central Asia, and Africa have continued to increase. In developing countries emissions of CO_2 from motor vehicles have risen by 3.5 per cent per year and account for 45 per cent of the global emissions from motor vehicles. However, the more developed regions of the US, Canada, Japan, Europe, the former Soviet Union, Australia and New Zealand, still account for a high percentage of the global total of CO_2 emissions and have per capita emissions considerably in excess of those to be found in developing countries. India and China's per capita CO_2 emissions are respectively 4.6 per cent and 11.9 per cent of the US per capita figure (19.1 tonnes per annum). The OECD average is

11.5 tonnes per annum. If the rest of the world consumed energy at this rate, total world CO_2 emissions in 2010 would be roughly triple what is otherwise projected (World Resources Institute, 1996).

Regional Impacts

Nitrogen oxides contribute indirectly to the greenhouse effect and directly to acid rain and the build up of tropospheric ozone. In 1990, about 45 per cent of total NO_x emissions in 20 European countries were attributable to road transport (Stanners and Bourdeau, 1995). This proportion rises to much higher levels in cities.

The long-range movement of air pollutants and the atmospheric deposition of SO_2 and NO_x has caused widespread acidification of terrestrial and aquatic ecosystems. Pollutants from transport have been implicated, especially in the development of regional acidification problems in North America and Europe. In Sweden, out of the 85,000 lakes greater than one hectare in area, it has been estimated that acidification affects 14,000, while about 4,000 have been classed as seriously affected. The Swedish Environmental Protection Agency (1992) estimates that if acidification continues unabated, approximately 34,000 lakes will be acidified within a few decades. Only if deposition is reduced by 75 per cent can a long-term improvement be expected.

Natural emissions of sulphur are divided equally between the North and South. However it is estimated that over 90 per cent of emissions from anthropogenic sources originate in the northern hemisphere. Sulphur deposition in Europe and North America is more than ten times higher than it would have been if it occurred naturally. Global emissions of sulphur oxides (SO_x) increased by 18 per cent in the 1970–1986 period from 57 million tonnes of sulphur to 67 million tonnes. Asia has witnessed the most rapid increase in SO_x emissions. North American levels have declined, while European values have fluctuated. During the same period global emissions of NO_x increased by one-third from 18 million tonnes to 24 million tonnes in 1986. The five largest emitters of NO_x are the US, the former Soviet Union, China, Japan and Germany.

In the EU, road transport is responsible for 2.3 per cent of total emissions of sulphur dioxide, 54 per cent of NO_x emissions and 27 per cent of VOCs. Both SO_2 and NO_x are the principal causes of acid deposition and urban smog. Improvements in vehicle technology have reduced these emissions per unit of distance travelled or fuel consumed, but any gains have been offset by the increase in motor vehicles and increase in average distances travelled. The European Commission predicts a decline in the emissions of

SO_2, VOCs and CO from motor vehicles and an increase in both CO_2 emissions and NO_x emissions.

Table 8.3: Forest Damage in Europe (%)

Country	1991
Austria	7.5
Belgium	17.9
Czechoslovakia	29.9
Denmark	29.9
Estonia	28.0
Finland	16.0
France	7.1
Germany	25.2
Hungary	19.6
Ireland	15.0
Italy	23.9
Lithuania	23.9
Liechtenstein	19.0
Luxembourg	20.8
Netherlands	17.2
Norway	19.7
Poland	45.0
Portugal	26.9
Romania	9.7
Russia	26.0
Slovenia	15.9
Spain	7.3
Sweden	12.0
Switzerland	19.0
United Kingdom	56.7
Yugoslavia	9.8

Source: WRI (1994)

The trans-boundary movement of air pollutants from transport such as oxides of sulphur and nitrogen, and VOCs (including hydrocarbons and ammonia) has resulted in the formation of acid deposition. Some of these pollutants (NO_x, HCs and VOCs) react through photo-oxidation to produce ozone (O_3) which contributes to the damage of crops and vegetation and affects human health. There is a global trend towards the increase of NO_x arising from motor vehicles, to which must be added emissions from the increasing number of aircraft. This has been estimated to be about 3 million tonnes each year, which is equivalent to about 15 per cent of NO_x emissions from automobiles. Acid deposition has caused damage to broadleaf trees and conifers in Europe. Table 8.3 shows the percentage of trees with greater than 25 per cent defoliation due to this type of pollution in Europe. In 1991, 18.5 per cent of broadleafs and 24.4 per cent of conifers were moderately or severely defoliated. 'Moderate' defoliation is defined as a 25–60 per cent loss in leaves, and 'severe' where there is over a 60 per cent loss (WRI, 1994).

Local Impacts

Increased urbanisation has resulted in a number of environmental problems unique to the city, for example, increased motorisation. This has caused greater levels of air and noise pollution. In some developing countries there has been a rural–urban exodus, with migration of the rural poor on a large scale. In 1970, 62.9 per cent of the world population lived in rural areas. By 1990 this has declined to 54.7 per cent, with a further decline of 40 per cent expected by the year 2025. Migration of the population to urban areas has been facilitated by a number of factors, including the improvement of road networks allowing easier access to major cities. Table 8.4 shows the growth of urbanisation in both developing and developed countries, and the prediction to the year 2010.

Table 8.4: Trends and Projections of Urbanisation (1950–2010)

	1950	1970	1990	2010
Proportion of the world population living in urban centres (%)				
World	30	37	45	56
Developing countries	17	25	37	52
Developed countries	54	67	73	78
Urban population (millions)				
World	730	1350	2380	4070
Developing countries	280	650	1510	3050
Developed countries	450	700	870	1020

Source: WHO (1992b)

In many major cities of the world, air pollution has resulted in WHO guidelines being exceeded on a regular basis. Worldwide, an estimated 1.1 billion urban residents are exposed to particulate or sulphur dioxide levels in excess of the guidelines set by WHO. In the US, epidemiological studies have suggested that 30,000–60,000 deaths each year can be attributed to particulate pollution (2–3 per cent of all deaths). In Jakarta, Indonesia, researchers have estimated that compliance with WHO guidelines for air pollution could prevent 600,000 asthma attacks and 125,000 cases of bronchitis each year.

Urban Air Pollution: The effects of greater industrialisation and urbanisation in the both the developed and developing world have resulted in the concentration of people in large urban agglomerations. The growth of motorised transportation has resulted in greater levels of congestion, energy consumption and air pollution. A WHO/UNEP examination of urban air pollution in 20 megacities (those cities which currently have, or are projected to have, 10 million inhabitants by the year 2000) (WHO and UNEP, 1992) showed that each of the megacities examined had one major pollutant which exceeded WHO health guidelines, 14 cities had two pollutants, and 7 had three or more which exceeded the guidelines. In nearly half of the 20 cities transport was considered the single most important cause of urban air pollution. Bangkok, Jakarta, Manila, Mexico City, Sao Paulo and Seoul had significant traffic-related air pollution and high emissions of CO, HC, NO_x and lead. In those cities where a greater proportion of the vehicle fleet was powered by diesel, such as Bangkok, Manila and Seoul, there was a higher concentration of suspended particulate matter, such as SO_2 and NO_x.

Motor vehicles in developing countries tend to be in poor condition, are badly maintained and have poor quality fuels. This, together with poor traffic management, inefficient public transport systems and high concentrations of motor vehicles, has resulted in a greater level of congestion. These factors have influenced the level of air pollution with a high proportion of the population being exposed to airborne pollutants, as well as a high incidence of road traffic accidents.

Noise: Motor vehicles are the most important source of noise pollution for the vast majority of urban residents. As previously established, noise damages health and is a serious impediment to normal everyday life, particularly in urban areas. The health implications of noise are described in Chapter 10. Forty-five per cent of the population of OECD countries is exposed to noise levels that are potentially damaging to health. Noise is socially intrusive and interferes with human activity, such as speech communication and sleep. The OECD defines noise as any acoustical phenomenon producing a sensation perceived as disagreeable or disturbing by an individual or a group. The impact of noise can be divided into three categories: interference with normal human activities, health effects and annoyance. By interfering with sleep noise can influence mood and reduce the performance of the cardiovascular system, as well as affecting intellectual and mechanical tasks. Long-term exposure to noise can cause deafness and lower auditory acuity, with noise annoyance resulting in stress and psychological and physiological side-effects.

Road traffic is a major contributor to environmental noise but in many locations aircraft and high speed trains are adding to the problem. The EU's commitment to trans-European networks, particularly new roads, new high speed trains and new airports, will seriously worsen the noise environment in Europe. Despite current regulations on noise abatement and forthcoming higher WHO standards, forecasts suggest the impact from noise will increase unless greater determination is shown by policy makers to reduce the impact of noise through reducing the amount of traffic.

Land use: Transport consumes large areas of land for the construction of roads, railways, airports and ports, excluding them from other uses. Transport has two effects on land which can be divided into primary and secondary land use. Primary land use relates directly to the construction of transport infrastructure such as roads, rail and airports. Secondary land use involves developments derived from the construction of infrastructure. For example, the construction of motorway service areas, retail development near motorway junctions, parking places and the extraction or raw materials used in the construction of transport infrastructure. In the EU roads occupy about 1.3 per cent of total land area of the region, while railway demands 40 times less land than road. Table 8.5 shows the total land area used for transport infrastructure on a global scale in the 1980s.

Table 8.5: Length of Road, Rail and Waterway per 1,000km^2 of Land Area

	Total km per 1,000km^2 of Land Area			
	Total Road	Paved Road	Rail Track	Navigable Inland Waterways
Africa	53	12	2.8	1.9
North and Central America	349	184	17.0	1.5
South America	135	15	4.9	6.6
Asia	159	76	9.9	8.2
Europe	848	705	52.7	10.0
USSR	72	54	6.6	5.5
Oceania	115	57	5.3	2.5
World average	170	88	9.5	4.7

Source: WRI (1992)

Loss of land for transport purposes is a key issue in the development of a sustainable transport policy. Land is a finite resource and has a large number of roles to play in an urban and regional system. It provides green space, habitat, ecological niches, recreational opportunity and food growing potential, and has an important role in the maintenance and enhancement of biodiversity. The quality of land in terms of its role in supporting a wide range of ecological and social objectives is as important as its quantity. An area criss-crossed by motorways or rail tracks is essentially a number of partitioned spaces each of which has to contend with physical barriers, noise and air pollution. Land allocated to roads and car parking in urban areas is land not allocated to green spaces, public spaces, cycleways, parks and attractive urban environments that define a high quality living space. Physical space is also social space, and social activities at the neighbourhood level are severely impoverished if land is allocated to roads and car parking with no provision of high quality green space and public space.

The amount of space allocated to roads and railways can be very small, typically less than 2 per cent of national land area, but the effect of this allocation on social life, quality of urban space, landscape quality, fauna and flora and peace and quiet can be very high.

Land take for transport purposes has a high correlation with the other key indicators of sustainability, energy and CO_2 production. Table 8.6 below shows how land use, energy and CO_2 parameters vary by mode of transport.

Table 8.6: Comparison of Different Modes of Passenger Travel

	Car 1	Car 2	Train	Bus	Bike	Foot
Land use	120	120	7	12	9	2
Energy	90	90	31	27	0	0
CO_2	200	200	60	59	0	0

Source: Teufel (1989)

Notes:
Land use is measured in square metres per person
Energy is measured in grams of coal equivalent units per passenger kilometre
CO_2 is measured in grams per passenger kilometre
Car 1 has no catalytic converter and car 2 has a catalytic converter

A policy designed to reduce CO_2 emissions or to reduce energy use would clearly be one intended to support modes of transport that have minimal land take requirements. In this sense the catalytic converter is irrelevant. It has no benefits whatsoever for land take, CO_2 or energy use. On the contrary, it brings with it a higher fuel consumption and increases in energy use and CO_2 production.

Road transport in Germany occupies 60 per cent more land than that for all housing purposes. Between 1981 and 1985 the amount of land allocated to transport in Germany increased by 25 per cent as a result of the construction of 8,000km of new roads, and road widening. In Germany in the late 1980s the daily rate of land take for new roads was 23 hectares, or 160m^2 per minute.

Swiss data show that land allocated to road transport purposes is five times greater than that allocated to housing purposes. On a per capita basis road transport accounts for 113m^2 per person, living purposes (house, gardens and yards) for 20–25m^2 per person.

In the UK about 2,900km^2 of land are allocated to roads. Parking occupies an additional 600km^2. Each car and lorry in the UK is responsible for over 160m^2 of concrete and tarmac, and policies that support growth in car ownership also support the transformation of both urban and rural areas into sterile landscapes where provision for the car dominates. If projections of car ownership and use in the UK come to fruition and there is no change in current policies which support car parking and road building, then an area the size of Berkshire would be required to accommodate these projections.

New road construction, engineered to very high standards in terms of vertical and horizontal alignment, is greedy for land. The Birmingham Northern Relief Road in the UK, planned to provide a new north–south motorway corridor to the east of Birmingham, is 44km in length and will require 573 hectares, the majority of which will be removed from agricultural use in an area of green land very close to Britain's second largest conurbation. This amount of land is enough to provide space for 14,500 new housing units in an area where estimates of the future demand for new homes are also large.

Land use allocations in favour of motorised transport intensify the process of dispersal and longer distance journey patterns. Walking, cycling and public transport cannot easily expand their modal share in an environment where distances between destinations are growing each year and the immediate environment of the pedestrian and the cyclist is dirty, noisy and dangerous. Land use policies have a central role in encouraging the less polluting modes of transport and increasing the attractiveness of the non-polluting modes of transport. This is the central logic of the UK government's advice to local authorities on land use and transport in its 'Planning Policy Guidance' Note No 13 (PPG13) (Dept of Environment and Dept of Transport, 1994). Minimising the demand for motorised transport is a major component of a sustainable transport strategy and can be detected in practice by monitoring the growth of land allocation to transport activities. These activities include high speed rail, motorway widening, car parking developments and airport expansion plans. If land allocations for these transport activities are rising then it is highly unlikely that we will be able to achieve much progress in the direction of sustainable development.

Land use planning has a significance that goes beyond actual land take: it has important implications for energy consumption and environmental sustainability. Travel and transport developments have interacted to allow significant land use changes. The result has been the development of more energy-intensive land use, and activity patterns which are interrelated and increase the demand for travel. The development of out-of-town retail developments such as the Metro Centre in Gateshead and Merry Hill near Dudley in the UK means greater distances are travelled for leisure and shopping activities. The absence of an efficient public transport system has also meant greater dependence on the motor car and a mutually reinforcing process of space extensive/distance intensive development that locks us into car dependency.

It is possible to break this cycle of development and dependency by focusing on land use, transport and accessibility. Integration can take place on three levels: physical; structural and operational. Physical integration requires buildings to be designed for greater accessibility to the transport system. The aim of structural integration is minimal travel for site-based activities, enabling those who wish to live within walking or cycling distance of the workplace, with facilities organised on a 'nodal' basis and along major routes. Operational integration deals with the variation in travel patterns that result from land use and infrastructural change. To influence travel activities it is necessary to integrate key aspects of public policy such as taxation on vehicles and fuel. Choice of location and mode of transport is based on travel costs which are defined by public policy, even within a free market system, and frequently exclude the external cost to the environment. Therefore, action is necessary to ensure that the real cost of transport is fully internalised, and that land use is coordinated with transport planning to reduce trip generation. The main challenge for transport planning is seen as reducing the length and number of motorised trips, whilst increasing accessibility for all everyday journey purposes.

Conclusion

The full lifecycle of motorised transport has an impact on the environment which is much bigger than policy makers or the car industry are prepared to admit. The transport sector has been implicated in either causing or contributing to a number of environmental problems, especially those related to air and noise pollution. Land take for new roads, new developments and car parks fundamentally alters urban form and structure and intensifies dependency on cars. It also damages biodiversity by partitioning land into smaller segments where the conditions for fauna and flora and their reproduction are damaged. These disparate impacts affect the global, regional and local environment, and pose a threat to quality of life. Present growth in vehicle ownership and use, both in the developed and developing countries, is unsustainable. Predictions for the next 20–30 years indicating that global car numbers will rise to 2.5 billion are evidence enough of a major impending environmental problem.

Environmental data – which now exist in abundance – reveal a serious situation that is in urgent need of attention. They do not, however, reveal the totality of effect on people. People in cities around the world now must endure noise, air pollution, traffic danger and poor health as a result of traffic. The cumulative impact of all these different assaults is more than the sum of the individual assaults (see Chapter 10). The rich can avoid the worst of the problems associated with traffic and the poor are disproportionately affected. Globally and locally, traffic is subtracting from the mass of health, welfare and quality of life.

Measures need to be taken now at every geographical scale to eradicate the environmental problems associated with motorisation and mobility. Mitigation is not enough. Sound barriers, catalytic converters, alternative fuels and tree planting around airports are not enough. The challenge to policy makers is to find ways of tackling the fundamental social and environmental inequalities flowing from traffic and high levels of mobility. A return to more sustainable modes of transport, such as walking and cycling, is necessary, together with investment in public transport. But neither will this be enough on its own. The physical amount of travel and transport is itself a problem, as is the globalisation and large-scale regionalisation that goes with it. If we are to succeed in solving environmental problems then we have to find ways of sourcing goods and services more locally, satisfying travel needs more locally and regenerating communities and economies from within.

CHAPTER 9

Transport and Equity

Introduction

In Chapter 7 we have discussed the relationship between sustainability and equity. We argued that environmental sustainability cannot be achieved unless there is also a more equitable distribution of environmental and economic resources. Equity is a theme that runs throughout Agenda 21, which recognises its importance as an essential component in any strategy that aims to achieve the dual goals of environmental protection and improved quality of life.

Despite the publication of Agenda 21, which links social conditions with environmental degradation, equity and transport are not words that are commonly linked together. The language of transport planning is more usually that of engineering, technology, economics and, nowadays, occasionally the environment. The language of social welfare is rarely heard, but it must be a fundamental consideration if a more sustainable society is to be achieved. These links between transport and equity can be summarised as follows:

i. the unequal distribution of finite natural resources, between countries and between individuals within countries;
ii. the unequal access to opportunities created by transport infrastructure and transport technologies that favour the needs of certain groups above the needs of others;
iii. the unequal distribution throughout society of the negative impacts of transport systems.

This chapter will discuss each of these three main themes and will conclude by suggesting criteria which could be used by transport decision makers to provide a more equitable allocation of transport resources.

Transport and the Inequitable Use of Natural Resources

In terms of global sustainability and the use of natural resources the arguments for greater equity within the transport sector can be summarised as follows.

Both the use of resources and their environmental effects are unevenly distributed between the developed and the developing world. Thus resource use, energy consumption, and CO_2 emissions, for example, are still largely slanted towards developed economies. It has been calculated, for example, that an average US citizen uses 100 times more fuel per annum than a Bangladeshi. Energy consumption in the major industrialised countries has increased by 30 per cent over the past 20 years. One-third of energy consumption is accounted for by the transport sector.

It is therefore argued that the developing world cannot be expected to contribute to reducing its energy use or the use of its resources at the same rate as the developed world when the latter has both contributed more to global unsustainability and, as a result, has greater economic power and greater technological resources to reduce its impacts. As discussed in Chapter 8, an equitable and sustainable response to the threat of global warming would require industrialised nations to reduce their emissions of CO_2 by 60 per cent by 2020. In March 1997 the EU agreed to a 15 per cent reduction in greenhouse gases on 1990 levels by the year 2010 (European Information Service, 1997).

The UK in 1995 claimed that it would easily achieve its CO_2 reduction/stabilisation targets and the secretary of state for the environment, John Gummer, offered a further 5–10 per cent reduction on 1990 levels to be achieved in the 2005–2010 period. This is still considerably short of the reductions required for the achievement of climate change objectives and in the case of the UK will be achieved with an increase of CO_2 emissions from the transport sector. The key political question of how to provide for increases in developing countries so as to permit some economic 'catching up' has not been addressed. Providing for increases in southern Europe or in developing countries whilst cutting CO_2 emissions in the developed North is central to the achievement of equity objectives but is distinctly unpopular with the governments of northern Europe and the US.

Much of the global poverty caused by economic inequality is in itself an important causal factor in encouraging unsustainable living practices which lead to further environmental degradation. For example, those living on or below the poverty line will overgraze soil for food production or deforest for fuelwood in order just to survive. And because of their lack of economic power these people are often denied the technologies that would not only improve their life quality but also lessen their environmental impact.

The unsustainability associated with living below minimal income levels is associated with local environmental degradation. This can be seen in those parts of the world where the search for fuelwood leads to complete deforestation. The environmental impact of highly mobile consumers in the US or Germany is, however, considerably greater as large parts of the globe have to be allocated to food production, materials production and energy extraction in order to support the high levels of consumption in these developed societies. The 'ecological footprint' of these high consuming groups is much bigger than of the low consuming groups.

Quantifying the size of an ecological footprint is very difficult. In the case of London an estimate has been made by the Sustainable London Trust. London's footprint is defined as the land area required to feed the city, to produce its timber and to re-absorb its CO_2 output from fossil fuels through photosynthesis. London's ecological footprint extends to 20 million hectares, 125 times its actual surface area of 160,000 hectares, and almost equivalent to the productive land area of Great Britain. Much of this land is located outside of the UK and in the developing world. The land area required for carbon absorption is 1.5 hectares per person, or 10.5 million hectares for London's population as a whole. Clearly reducing the size of the ecological footprint of developed countries and regions is a high priority and transport must play a major role.

Per capita CO_2 emissions give another clear indication of non-sustainability and the size of an ecological footprint. The US in 1992 produced 19.13 tonnes of CO_2 per capita which compares with 9.78 tonnes per capita for the UK and 0.88 for China. It is not difficult to see why exhortation from developed countries to reduce CO_2 emissions is met with some scepticism in Beijing or New Delhi.

The consumption levels of the wealthy drive a global economic system that ensures that lifestyle requirements in New York or London have an impact on the environment in Bangkok and Goa, on the upper atmosphere, and on what is grown in Kenya or Chad. The maintenance of the lifestyles of the opulent is accompanied by the destruction of remote environments and intervening spaces. This has a close parallel in the impact of the affluent closer to their home communities. Most cities in Britain experience large daily tidal flows of traffic, part of which consist of affluent commuters who live in rural idylls and drive to work or their park and ride destination. Their journey into Manchester, Birmingham or Liverpool, for example, takes them past residential areas where poorer people live, and they impose noise, air pollution and traffic danger on those poorer groups. The poorer groups have to pay the price for the convenience, lifestyle and consumption patterns of the richer groups.

Finding Globally Equitable Solutions

If the premise that sustainability must be concerned with a more equitable distribution of resources is accepted, then concern with achieving merely global reductions of energy use or CO_2 emissions does not provide an adequate solution. Instead it should be asked: how equitable is the current distribution of resources used by global transport systems? And how can these be redistributed in such a way that combines environmental objectives with the need to maintain human well-being?

When searching for appropriate solutions, it is important to remember that the inequitable distribution of resources not only occurs between countries of the North and South, but within them. Thus, for example, new highway infrastructure in a developing country may in fact benefit economically only a small, already wealthy, business elite. A more sustainable and equitable use of economic resources may instead have resulted in investment in better public transport or in improving accessibility to essential services such as schools or health centres.

It must also be remembered that policy decisions that aim to redistribute resources from developed to developing countries may also have significant social impacts in the developed world, in part because of the economic inequalities that exist within those wealthier nations. For example, raising fuel prices in the West, in an attempt to reduce overall consumption, may succeed in its aim, but in so doing may seriously disadvantage poorer sectors of the community. This is not to say that such redistribution should not occur, but that it should be done within a policy framework that considers social impacts and aims to minimise hardship caused to groups already disadvantaged. In this instance, for example, the raising of fuel prices in the medium to long term could be coupled with a programme to improve energy efficiency and a programme of investment in public transport. In this way fuel savings may be made and social costs minimised.

Those that acknowledge equity as key to achieving a more environmentally sustainable society would argue that the following should be an intrinsic part of any strategy for achieving sustainability:

i. Any reduction in the global use of resources or the volume of pollutants produced by the transport sector should be distributed according to the amount of environmental damage that each country is responsible for, and any reduction should be distributed proportionally throughout the population so that wealthier groups absorb a larger share than poorer groups, and low income/no-income groups are protected.
ii. There should be a transfer of clean transport technologies to developing countries, or the resources necessary for them to produce their own cleaner technologies where appropriate should be supplied in order to ensure that the environmental impacts of those countries are minimised.

iii. That transport infrastructure development adopts new models of consultation and participation that:

- reflects local transport needs, particularly those of women and disadvantaged groups;
- gives the highest priority to journeys of less than 5km in length and to the improvement of noise and air quality;
- is appropriate for the economic circumstances of the population;
- acknowledges the importance of local knowledge and understanding about the environment;
- seeks to educate and empower the local population to participate fully in the decision-making process.

Inequality of Opportunity and the Role of Transport

Environmental concerns are not the only reason for being concerned with equity and transport. Transport systems exist for a purpose: as a means to obtain ends. An unequal distribution of, or the inaccessibility of those 'means' to certain sectors of the population, will result in those groups being denied the opportunities that transport can bring.

Mobility is rarely an end in itself (except in some varieties of tourism); more often than not it is a means to a variety of different ends. These 'ends' can be social, leisure, economic or essential for maintaining life itself – as in the case of the emergency services. The justification for adopting particular transport policies or investment decisions are that they provide certain quantifiable economic and social benefits to society. These are often expressed in terms of the economic benefits they bring – in terms of cost savings for industry, job creation opportunities or the chance to expand markets. Often these so-called benefits are expressed as time savings, for example reducing the time taken by employees to get to work or the time taken for goods to reach their destination. However, a time-saving for one group in society may produce time penalties for another – in particular those with lower economic and political power.

A Transport System For Whom?

Transport policy, in recent years, has been largely concerned with increasing the mobility of the economically important sectors of the economy, that is to ensure that workers, goods and consumers should be able to get to more places, more quickly and at any time in order to boost the consumption of goods and services. In the

UK this has been interpreted as encouraging private mobility at the expense of public transport, walking and cycling, and mobility has been equated with accessibility – as long as personal mobility increased so people's access to goods and services increased. It was also assumed by planners that everyone was equally mobile, when in fact one-third of the population does not have access to a car. As a result cities are now congested, there can be up to 20km queues on to motorways, and non-car users are unable to use out-of-town shopping facilities. The fundamental assumption used by transport planners and politicians to promote their vision of the 'great car economy' must therefore be questioned.

Valuing Time in Transport Policy Making

This book has highlighted that time saving is a fundamental objective of transport planning and investment. Time saving is frequently used to justify substantial investment in transport infrastructure, particularly road building. Vast resources are channelled into the development and application of new time-saving technologies designed to improve economic efficiency and provide more leisure time for the working population. Often, however, those who have access to these new technologies tend to use the potential savings not for more leisure time, but in order to travel greater distances. These potential time savings (in many instances congestion means that the time saving potential of these technologies is never fully realised) stimulate responses on the part of individual and collective behaviour that increase distances between functional centres such as work, home, schools and shops on the often false premise that it will take less time to reach them. Of course for those who do not have access to a car, or the resources necessary to use public transport (if it exists), these places simply become inaccessible or only accessible at a severe time penalty.

Whose Time is More Valuable?

A particularly pointed graphic from a German transport text has the unusual caption 'How fast must Grandma run?'. This is reproduced as Figure 9.1. It shows that traffic engineers have intervened to give priority to drivers at the expense of elderly pedestrians. A deliberate decision has been taken to steal time from the grandma (in this example) and give it to the motorist. All traffic engineering and infrastructure planning embodies the theft of time in some shape or form and its redistribution to wealthier groups.

Figure 9.1: How Fast Must Grandma Run?

This is the speed pedestrians must cross the road when the light is green

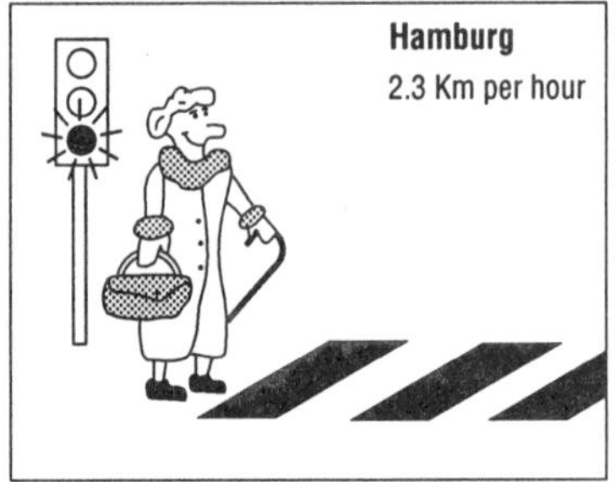

Source: Seifried (1990)

Infrastructure planning also involves decisions about what kind of travel is important and which journey purposes and destinations are to be favoured. The range of the population whose time is considered worth saving is limited. Both public transport and road infrastructure tend to concentrate on connecting workers or consumers to the main regional economic centres, often the central business district. Public transport, if it is provided, will frequently be concentrated along these main routes and the services concentrated at peak commuting times. This approach to transport planning rests on a number of assumptions: that those who wish to use the system are employed, that their need is for a single daily journey to and from home to work or shops within standard working hours, that their time is valued more highly as economic actors than other non-working sectors of the population, and that as workers they can afford to pay relatively high travelling costs.

Of course the reality is somewhat different. At any one time a substantial group of the population will not be in paid employment, either through unemployment, sickness, retirement or because of childcare responsibilities, and increasingly those in work are in part-time employment. Women in particular are often in the position of having to juggle a multiplicity of daily tasks. Time geography studies on women in London with children under five years old have helped to identify the complexities of many women's daily lives when confronted with limited mobility, limited financial resources and a public transport system that is poorly designed to meet their needs. A typical day, for example, may involve taking children to different schools in different locations, going to a part-time job, returning to pick up a child from nursery, doing the shopping (increasingly facilities are located at out-of-town locations) picking up another child from school, taking them to evening activities and meeting them afterwards, and, for an increasing number of women, finishing the day with a late shift and returning home late at night. Add to this the regular trips to doctors, the hospital and the welfare services and the total inadequacy of current transport planning to meet their needs soon becomes apparent.

Transport planners and those who plan land use and influence the pattern of local development often fail to consider these complex patterns or the time it takes to travel across town or out to isolated industrial estates or factory sites using public transport. Not only are these daily patterns far more complex than most planners assume, but in general women also have very limited time and money in which to achieve their multiple daily tasks. These everyday routines are often viewed as unimportant or trivial compared with the more important need to deliver workers to their place of work on time, or the objective of some politicians to increase personal motorised mobility in order to support the automobile industry or to maintain the car as status symbol for the economically successful and the symbol of individual freedom. Studies of complex travel patterns, particularly by women, have highlighted the disadvantages many women face in trying to pursue employment or leisure opportunities caused not only by a lack of childcare facilities but also by restricted mobility. This often results in a sense of isolation and depression.

Another common assumption made by planners and service providers is to assume that the users of public transport are both able-bodied and unburdened. Those wishing to make use of public transport facilities are often the elderly, people with a disability or those with shopping or young children to look after (again, mostly women). Too long a walk to bus stops or stations or steps up into vehicles or trains may make the use of these facilities almost impossible. This can lead to the exclusion of the very groups in society who are reliant on public transport for their mobility.

Public Transport for All?

An experiment recently undertaken in London monitored the experience of two women pushing children in double buggies and carrying shopping bags as they tried to cross London using only public transport. A journey that should only have taken one-and-a-half to two hours took nearly five and was possible only because other people stopped to assist the women at a number of stages in the journey. Detailed features of transport systems and urban design such as steps, escalators, the boarding height of buses and trains, the layout of stations and the availability of toilets all become very important for a journey made with children, shopping or any kind of mobility disadvantage.

These problems of everyday use are a serious deterrent to walking and the use of public transport. Difficulties are compounded by the presence of traffic. Trying to cross roads, even with pelican crossings, is extremely hard and stressful. The urban system has moved so far in the direction of satisfying the needs of the person in the car that it acts as an efficient deterrent to those who struggle on as pedestrians or cyclists. In combination with the fear of attack and molestation, these disincentives to walk and cycle create a powerful inducement to own and use a car, thus exacerbating the problem for others and adding to the pressure for yet more car ownership and use. This represents a serious equity and environmental problem.

Transport systems and technologies in the developed world have largely failed to meet the basic needs of their users. They share this characteristic with transport systems in developing countries where the bulk of new investment is allocated to highway projects when less than 5 per cent of the population have access to a car. In many developed countries it is still normal to find buses with steps, railway stations with many changes of level and underground systems that are unfriendly particularly to the elderly and disabled. A sustainable transport system has to be equitable and accessible to all groups if it is to play a full role in minimising demand for motorised transport.

Of course it is not only the poor design of public transport facilities that makes shops and services inaccessible to certain groups. The situation is made worse by policies that assume an almost universal access to a car for meeting essential daily needs. Thus, prioritising time savings of car users can have a very negative impact on the time budgets of non-car users. First, because zoning based on car access has both separated traditional functional centres and placed distances between essential services that make them accessible only by car. And second, because the infrastructure provided for vehicular traffic can divide communities and provide physical barriers preventing, or making it difficult for non-car users to reach their destination and taking up more of their time by having to find a safe place to cross or by walking further in order to avoid busy roads.

Yago (1984) argues in his account of the decline in the US that zoning and land use controls in that country effectively created a car-oriented and car-dominated society. Transit (public transport) could not possibly compete over large distances and from suburb to suburb and so it declined in importance.

Safe Routes to School in Denmark

The problem of school transport and the loss of freedoms for school children has already been described. The extra traffic demands that result from the decline of walking and cycling to school pose a serious problem for urban transport management, particularly in morning rush hours. School transport needs can be met by a combination of land use planning, traffic management and public transport measures that will increase accessibility for all, reduce inequalities and save the time of escorters. In Denmark, and now in the UK, a number of local authorities have worked with school authorities, pupils and parents to 'audit' children's most common routes to school, identifying potential traffic hazards. Routes have been altered to provide better facilities, roads traffic-calmed, and priority changed in favour of cyclists and pedestrians where hazards were seen to exist. In many instances this has helped to encourage parents to let their children travel to school independently rather than be driven.

Schools transport solutions show the way for a range of other specific travel purpose situations where careful consideration of the detail of journey patterns and the objectives of transport and urban planning can improve quality of life, reduce costs, reduce inequalities and improve the environment. Journeys to hospitals, places of work, local government offices and universities offer a number of solutions to the traditional problem of the car commute but require coordination and cooperative planning on the part of a number of agencies.

Who can Afford to Travel?

Affordability is a vital consideration in encouraging a modal split towards more equitable and more sustainable forms of transport. It is a major factor in achieving the desired goal of encouraging people out of their cars. This is unlikely to happen in any meaningful numbers in situations where car travel, after initial purchase, remains significantly cheaper than public transport alternatives.

Equally important is the need to consider whether all sectors of the population can afford to use the system. A public transport system which is efficient and attractive may as well not exist if the sectors of the population who are most reliant on it cannot afford to use it. For those on low income, for example, the unemployed, the elderly, many women and many members of the non-white population, any increase in transport costs, particularly public transport, will affect them much more severely than those on average earnings. For low-wage earners or those seeking work, travel costs may be the deciding factor in a calculation about whether or not to take up an offer of employment. Again, flexibility, both in terms of service times and ticketing, is an important consideration if more complex daily travel patterns are to be catered for. Any policy changes away from through ticketing or travelcards for multiple journeys are most likely to affect those whose travel patterns are the most complex and who can least afford the additional costs of buying a number of single journey tickets.

A Safe System for All

Safety is another important social welfare consideration that must be fully integrated into any strategy for promoting more sustainable forms of transport. Whether or not people feel safe in public spaces is an important factor affecting many people's travel patterns and their quality of life. Unfortunately, safety and security considerations are frequently sacrificed in pursuit of cost saving and staff reductions. Safety in public spaces is an issue that affects the whole population, but is often more acutely felt by those groups who feel more vulnerable to attack – for example, women, the elderly, and the black community.

Safety, transport, equity and the environment are issues that are very closely linked. People tend to feel safe using public transport when they are confident that other people will also use it. However, as staffing of public transport is reduced people will feel safer using their cars, or if they don't have that option they simply won't go out. The more that people use their cars, the less revenue is available for investment and improvement of public transport facilities and the less people want to use them. And as more people use their cars, the emptier the streets and other public spaces become, adding to the feeling that public transport is unsafe.

In this way, the pursuit of time savings on the part of those in cars adds a significant time penalty to those without. As local facilities and local public transport declines so the penalties for non-motorised transport increase. For those groups who are most directly affected by increasing levels of inaccessibility and increasing levels of physical isolation and insecurity, the time penalty is expressed as varying degrees of imprisonment at home. The slang expression 'doing time' is an apt description of the loss of freedom associated with the social impact of the car on society as a whole.

Women's Safe Transport

Clearly the best long-term approach to ensuring a safer environment for groups who feel more vulnerable in public spaces is through better urban design and by providing mixed-use urban centres that do not empty of people as soon as the shops close. Restaurants, cafes, theatres and cinemas, mixed in with residential accommodation, can all help to create a vibrant urban space that feels less threatening to its users. Clearly this cannot always be achieved, and once outside this area streets may again become quiet. A number of initiatives have tried to overcome this problem and to stop women feeling that safe mobility at night is only possible through the use of a private car. A number of women only night-time minibus schemes have been tried in the UK where, for a small extra charge, the user will be taken home to her front door. These schemes have had a mixed response as they can be expensive to operate and have been criticised for appearing to take women off the streets, thus making public spaces at night even emptier and even more given over to men.

A scheme in the Netherlands called the train–taxi scheme aims to integrate more closely train services with local taxi services. Instead of hoping that a taxi will be there on arrival at a station, or having to phone late at night and wait for it to arrive, often when no one else is about, a train–taxi ticket can be bought and paid for when buying the train ticket. Taxis are then there to meet the train and take the ticket holder anywhere within the town for a pre-paid set charge. One city in Germany has developed a similar arrangement with its local bus company. After buses stop running at night shared taxis leave from the bus station at regular intervals. They charge a flat rate fare marginally higher than the bus fare and drop the passengers off at their door.

Transport and the Unequal Distribution of its Negative Impacts

We have already seen how many groups in society are being denied access to services, and have a reduced life opportunity simply because of their lack of personal mobility. Unfortunately, reduced life opportunity is but one of a number of serious negative impacts – both environmental and social – that result from the increase in mobility throughout Western society. It is often argued that 'society', through the democratic process, has collectively decided that the benefits of increasing mobility outweigh the disbenefits. These disbenefits, therefore, must simply be tolerated by society as a price worth paying.

As we shall see, however, these disbenefits are not evenly distributed throughout society, and it is often the most disadvantaged groups and those least able to be heard who bear the brunt of the disbenefits and who pay directly through their health and their quality of life for other people's mobility.

The Destruction of Community

Many countries throughout the Western world are facing a crisis in many of their cities. A crisis the symptoms of which include migration, ghettoisation, deindustrialisation, under-investment in public services and infrastructure, rising crime, drug taking and social deprivation. It is not suggested that the growth of road traffic is responsible for these urban problems. Nor is it suggested that the adoption of more environmentally sustainable transport policies will act as a panacea to all of society's environmental and social ills. But there is mounting evidence to suggest that increasing traffic growth, much of it from more pleasant suburbs or commuter towns and villages, can have a detrimental effect on the ability of residents to build community links and develop a sense of place for which they feel some sense of responsibility. This decline in social interaction may in turn damage both community links and important social support networks.

Appleyard (1981) in his classic study of street life in US cities, *Livable Streets*, provides considerable evidence regarding the impact of various levels of traffic on street life and home life using case study material. In those streets where traffic was heavy, traffic-related problems such as noise, pollution and road danger were cited as the most bothersome by the residents. In these streets people took the least care of the outside of their houses, taking little interest in the street itself and wanting to withdraw from it. Very few residents knew any one else in the street and adapted to the heavy traffic flows by keeping windows closed and restraining children from going outside. In comparison in the streets with little traffic children played together in the road, neighbours talked to one another, the outside areas were well maintained by the residents and the street was generally thought to be friendly, quiet and safe.

Property on streets with high traffic flows and poorly maintained public spaces is likely to be considerably cheaper to rent or buy than on quiet, well-maintained streets. Thus those streets with much poorer social and environmental quality are likely to attract residents from poorer backgrounds. Often, such households will be less able to afford childcare and will be responsible for looking after young children themselves. This supervisory role becomes a major time constraint when there is no safe outside space for children to play in. The fact that many poorer households, for reasons of unemployment, ill heath or lack of resources, are unable to go elsewhere means that they will be affected by the negative aspects of heavy traffic on the street much more than those who are able to go elsewhere for work or leisure. Their sense of isolation, through the destruction of wider support networks and their lack of a sense of place (which Appleyard showed diminished with increased traffic flows), is likely to be more acute, making it more likely that they will experience mental illness. Of course, such households are the least likely to own, or have access to, a car of their own.

Car-free Living in Bremen

Bremen developed the first car-free living area in Germany in 1992. There are now (at the time of writing in mid-1996) 26 schemes either built or at an advanced stage of planning in Germany, as well as significant schemes in Amsterdam, Rotterdam and Vienna. Car-free living is increasingly seen as an attractive and feasible alternative to supplying the expensive infrastructure required by car dependency and substituting green space, play space and public space for the concrete and tarmac of car dependency. The original Bremen scheme (Hollerland) has been discontinued though a smaller version (Grünenstrasse) has gone ahead. Residents living on the estate undertake not to own a car, and only a few parking spaces are provided on the perimeter (and even these are mostly for visitors to the area). A car sharing scheme is available for the residents to use if they so wish, but it is assumed that most journeys will be undertaken by public transport, walking or by bicycle. Buses depart regularly for town and a new tram system will be developed that will begin operation soon after residents move in. So far demand to live on the estate has been very high, as the space that on a normal estate would have been taken up with roads, garages and parking spaces has been used to provide green space, a kindergarten and play space for children. It is expected that pollution levels and accident rates will be considerably lower than in other comparable areas.

There has been some interest in car-free living in Britain, but as yet no development. Cambridge and Nottingham county councils have discussed the idea and Lothian regional council has produced some guidelines which include a detailed plan for Edinburgh which would involve developing a 1.4 hectare area for 120 car-free residential units in the area currently occupied by Gorgie Goods Yard (a former railway yard).

The benefits of car-free zones are listed as:

- improved quality of life: more space to live in, more pleasant surroundings with no traffic congestion;
- safety: no car traffic, no road accidents;
- a good place to bring children up with more contact with other residents and a strong sense of community;
- clean air and a clean environment, with no intrusive noise from vehicle engines and the slamming of car doors;
- being part of an exciting new development;

- financial savings: the average cost of running a 1000cc petrol driven car, including depreciation, fuel and insurance, is around £3,117 per year (AA information hotline). The cost of renting a small car can be around £1.50 per hour.

Car-free zones are thought to be attractive to developers because of:

- fewer roads and infrastructure requirements with an exemption from present requirements on providing parking areas;
- the potential to develop more houses on a given site and a chance to make innovative use of the freed space;
- the possibility of developing 'problem sites';
- continuing high-profile media interest.

Children and Traffic

A significant component of social injustice and inequity is the impact of traffic on the everyday life of children, particularly in the developed world. Children are deprived of their freedoms to move around independently in an urban or rural area. The spatial dispersion of activities and longer journey distances make them highly dependent on adults and their cars, and deprive them of independent learning and socialisation experiences. Their exposure to air pollution, both in the car and on the roadside, makes them susceptible to asthma and a number of other respiratory diseases (see Chapter 10), and a road traffic accident is the single most common cause of death among school-age children. Noise pollution affects their learning abilities and speech acquisition, and these depredations impinge more on poorer groups and lower social classes than they do on the wealthier sections of society.

Child pedestrian accidents exhibit a steep social class gradient. In England and Wales children from social class V households are over seven times more likely to die as pedestrians than children from social class I (see glossary). Similar gradients exist for comparison between white population groups and black population groups in British cities. Black children are far more likely to be killed or injured in a road traffic accident than are white children. This is rarely measured in the UK but in Germany a comparison of 5,000 child road traffic accidents in 15 cities has quantified the likelihood of injury by the categories 'German' and 'foreigner'. The results show a clear disparity with a higher level of risk associated with the category 'foreigner'. The results are summarised in Table 9.1.

Any road traffic accident statistics must be interpreted with great caution. There are enormous problems with reporting and registering accidents and injuries which are likely to lead to an underestimation of accidents and injuries to, for instance, Turkish children in Berlin or Asian children in Blackburn and Preston. There is abundant evidence that under very dangerous circumstances parents withdraw their children from risky environments producing the counter-intuitive result that very busy streets and streets with lots of speeding traffic can often have low accident rates.

Table 9.1: Number of Injured Child Pedestrians and Child Cyclists by Age Group and Ethnic Definition

	German		Foreigner	
	0–5	6–14	0–5	6–14
Number of accidents	467	3,192	392	959
Number of children	253,465	501,908	85,713	123,271
Percentage of injured children	0.18	0.64	0.46	0.78

Source: Bundesminister fur Verkehr (1985) Germany

Whatever the reasons for this large variability in the social and ethnic impact of road traffic accidents it remains a serious public health and social/environmental concern that transport systems discriminate strongly against the poorer and more vulnerable groups in society.

In Manchester in the late 1980s, 82 per cent of all children killed in road traffic accidents were pedestrians and 12 per cent were cyclists. The deployment of resources into road safety is the exact opposite of what is suggested by these figures. Most effort and expenditure goes into activities to protect the occupants of vehicles (who are largely protected already by mass and metal). Vehicles with air bags, reinforced passenger compartments, sophisticated braking systems, anti-roll bars, side impact protection and so on are designed into the vehicles that are designed to drive at speeds of well over 150kph and are driven by drivers who often exceed speed limits as a matter of course. Under these circumstances equity considerations are blatantly disregarded in favour of policies that support the larger vehicle, the adult driver, the wealthier traveller, the speeding male, and those with more control and influence in so-called democratic societies. A child has no vote and a poor child has very little choice about daily activity patterns, types of journey and opportunities that can be exploited. This child will spend a lot of time on the street and the street is a very dangerous place.

Child injuries and fatalities in road traffic accidents are higher in many parts of the developing world. In China the child death rate in this category is five times higher than in Britain. This high fatality rate is a consequence of the juxtaposition of high performance vehicles, particularly on rural roads, with high levels of usage of public space (including roads) by children. The implications of this juxtaposition are enormous. China currently has approximately five cars per 1,000 people and still manages to kill 50,000 people each year in road traffic accidents. This total is approximately the same as that of the US where car ownership is approximately 600 per 1,000 population. China's road trauma epidemic is only just beginning and will represent one of the most significant global public health problems of the twenty-first century. India, Bangladesh and large parts of Africa and South America will also come to have the dubious distinction of sharing this most recent manifestation of freedom and economic progress from the world's car manufacturers.

The impact of traffic on children has a major role to play in redefining their space–time perceptions and the nature of their experiences. At a very fundamental level this was identified by C. S. Lewis in his 1955 autobiographical book *Surprised by Joy*:

> I number it among my blessings that my father had no car, while yet most of my friends had, and sometimes took me for a drive. This meant that all these distant objects could be visited just enough to clothe them with memories and not impossible desires, while yet they remained ordinarily as inaccessible as the Moon. The deadly power of rushing about wherever I pleased had not been given me. I measured distances by the standard of man, man walking on his two feet, not by the standard of the internal combustion engine. I had not been allowed to deflower the very idea of distance; in return I possessed 'infinite riches' in what would have been to motorists 'a little room'. The truest and most horrible claim made for modern transport is that it 'annihilates space'. It does. It annihilates one of the most glorious gifts we have been given. It is a vile inflation which lowers the value of distance, so that a modern boy travels a hundred miles with less sense of liberation and pilgrimage and adventure than his grandfather got from travelling ten. Of course, if a man hates space and wants it to be annihilated, that is another matter. Why not creep into his coffin at once? There is little enough space there.

The deprivation of detailed local knowledge and social interaction at a small geographical scale as a training exercise and developmental experience for the future practice of social skills, environmental awareness and problem solving abilities is a consequence of the annihilation of space through the conquest of time. The view put by C. S. Lewis may be more metaphysical than practical and more spiritual than scientific but it very clearly identifies a major cultural and psychological shift that is of the greatest importance to our understanding of what has happened over the past 40 years, and what we must do to design and create healthy cities and sustainable futures.

Conclusion: a New Approach to Decision Making

Who is making these decisions on our behalf? Those most affected by many transport planning decisions are often the most poorly represented in the decision-making process. Women, for example, are still severely under represented at both the political level of decision making and the more advisory professional role which, in the UK, is still dominated by male engineers. Below is an example of a female politician in Sweden describing the problems she encountered on the planning and transport committee when trying to get ideas across about how women were experiencing traffic problems in their city:

> It is extremely difficult to sell one's ideas ... because the engineers and architects and the male politicians tell us to formulate our experiences in their terms first. It is difficult for us female politicians to make ourselves understood and to be taken seriously.

Thus the agenda is set and the scope of possible solutions is largely determined by a social group which is largely unrepresentative of the population as a whole. The language used by the professionals is often technical, scientific and rational. It is not easily understood by the lay person and is not amenable to the language of how people feel about, or experience, their surroundings unless backed up by statistical data. Policy solutions are either approved or rejected in terms of their technical merit rather than a consideration of their social good.

It is also important to consider how decisions are made. The traditional approach to transport planning within the UK has been for professionals to propose route options and for this to be followed by a period of consultation. For major projects this is also followed by a public inquiry. This is an extremely limited approach and does not allow the need for the project itself to be questioned.

In order to achieve the goal of equitable sustainable development a radical re-examination of existing models of transport decision making is required. New methods should seek to empower communities and build on local knowledge systems. In developing countries it is this local knowledge which has often preserved the environment for generations. This is often ignored and instead

Western models of development, largely based on infrastructure projects, are imposed from above.

Delft, in the Netherlands, has been attempting over a number of years to remove traffic from the old medieval centre of the city. As part of this initiative it has been renovating some of the main city squares, which were once used merely as car parks, and transforming them into pleasant mixed-use areas full of vibrant cafes and friendly open spaces. The redesign, however, has not been carried out by the council but by the residents themselves. After setting out that their overall objective was to remove the parking spaces, the council then set up a number of half-day workshops with the necessary facilities, and gave the task of the design of the squares over to the residents. The results speak for themselves, as these areas now provide an important social space in the city, which the residents rightly feel is their own.

New models of decision making must consider those issues largely ignored by the planning process: safety, daily time budgets and travel patterns; accessibility rather than simply mobility. There is a danger that the new environmental agenda of sustainability will simply apply new constraints on mobility regardless of social consequences, where, for example, mobility is rationed by ability to pay, as in the case of road tolls and fuel price rises. This approach can only be acceptable if it provides an alternative that is efficient, attractive, affordable and safe, and is designed to reflect and meet the needs of its users, not just the more powerful groups in society.

CHAPTER 10

Traffic and Health

Introduction

Traffic represents a major global public health problem. In most parts of the world there is a very low level of awareness of the impact of traffic on health and even less awareness of the combined effects of air pollution, noise, traffic danger, social isolation and stress on human health. The rise in traffic volumes and the degree of exposure of large numbers of the population to this increased volume continues with little serious effort made to reduce the scale of the problem. In most countries there is an overwhelming pressure to build roads and airports and add infrastructure to existing transport networks.

In the US, where epidemiologists have estimated that 30,000–60,000 deaths can be attributed to particulate pollution per annum (WRI, 1996), the majority of which is vehicular in origin, there is also strong governmental support to build 2,900km of new road – the 'NAFTA Superhighway'. This highway would connect Indianapolis, Bloomington and Evansville (Indiana) to Memphis (Tennessee), Shreveport (Louisiana) and Houston (Texas). It would then link to Mexico via Loredo (Texas).

A similar situation exists in Europe where the EU's trans-European networks include the construction of an additional 12,000km of motorway standard road, in eastern Europe and the former Soviet Union where there are grandiose plans to construct major new highways, and in much of the developing world where transport infrastructure is still linked to economic development in the minds of policy makers and international funders such as the World Bank. The 1995 list of projects from the World Bank includes the Nairobi–Mombassa road in Kenya, new highways in Ghana and Thailand, an Argentinean national airport and a trans-Kalahari highway from South Africa to Namibia. Additional infrastructure is intended to stimulate additional traffic which equates with economic development. In poorer parts of the world this additional traffic will increase road traffic accidents and in all countries the upward cycle of car ownership and use will add additional pollution and noise, each of which is associated with damage to human health.

Road traffic accidents are already a serious problem. In 1990, globally there were 420,000 deaths and 9 million injuries as a result of road traffic accidents. The death and injury rate is higher in low car ownership countries than in high car ownership countries. Road traffic danger is particularly acute where cars are powerful and street activity is still dominated by pedestrians and cyclists. The Heidelberg Environment and Forecasting Institute (see glossary) estimates that by 2030 the annual total of road traffic accident deaths globally will be over 2 million with over 50 million injured. The number of deaths worldwide from road traffic accidents in the 1995–2030 period is predicted to be over 50 million. This scale of mortality puts road traffic at the forefront of public health concerns and in numerical terms ahead of many cancers and respiratory diseases (Teufel *et al.*, 1995).

Road traffic accidents each year on a worldwide basis create about 800,000 permanently handicapped people. The Heidelberg Institute estimates that this annual total will rise to 5.7 million by the year 2030. Cumulatively, road traffic accidents will have created approximately 100 million handicapped individuals over the 1995–2030 period. This presents enormous problems for poor countries and poor families, and underfunded healthcare systems.

In Germany one person is killed on the roads every 50 minutes and one injured every minute. However, there are no reliable estimates for the numbers killed, injured or handicapped as a result of exposure to air pollution, heightened blood pressure and cardiovascular problems as a result of noise, nor any estimates of deaths and injuries arising from wars fought over oil resources, or climatic change and severe weather problems arising from global warming. In other words, there are no estimates of the amount of psychological damage done to millions as a result of grief and distress arising from the death of children, parents or friends in road traffic accidents, and no estimates of the psychological distress caused everyday through the need to avoid dangerous roads, restrict the activities of children, remain indoors and use urine-soaked underpasses whilst traffic has the priority at ground level. All of these factors damage health and in combination they damage health more severely than any of them in isolation.

WHO defines health as a 'complete state of physical, mental and psychological well being'. The daily experiences of a large proportion of the world's population exposed to traffic noise, traffic-related air pollution, danger and social isolation is a long way from this definition. The significance of traffic from a health point of view lies in its vigorous growth rates (particularly air transport), the willingness of governments to sacrifice health concerns when faced with traffic growth estimates and the sophistication of the industry to organise itself globally to motorise areas such as China, India, Africa and Latin America. On current trajectories, and on the evidence of current institutional responses, traffic related mortality and morbidity will rise dramatically in the twenty-first century.

Evidence of the Links between Exposure to Traffic and Damage to Human Health

The UK Transport and Health Study Group (see glossary) has produced a useful summary of the ways in which transport influences health. These are divided into health-promoting and health-damaging groups.

i. **Health-promoting**
   Enables access to: employment, education, shops, recreation, social support networks, health services, countryside; provides recreation and exercise.
ii. **Health-damaging**
   Accidents; pollution: carbon monoxide, nitrogen oxides, hydrocarbons, ozone, carbon dioxide, lead, benzene; noise and vibration; stress and anxiety; danger; loss of land and planning blight; severance of communities by roads.

Community health studies have shown the links between well-developed social networks and the maintenance of a healthy population. Good social networks appear to reduce non-cancer mortality.

Transport alone cannot deliver rich social networks but it can go a long way to providing the right preconditions. The decline of walking deprives many of the possibility of social interaction and reasons for wanting to be in a car often include feelings of insecurity on the street and the need for private defensible space. Jane Jacobs, writing in the United States in 1961, describes the preconditions for social interaction very clearly. At the centre of her account of what makes cities vital and attractive places is the street as an arena for social interaction, sustained by a large variety of uses and mixed residential, service, retail, shops and so on. On this street there is a continuous movement of people, all supervised informally by other people, and there is a shared responsibility for supervising the children. The street depends on the volume of pedestrians and the attractiveness of its varied uses for its success. The result is a neighbourhood that works, a reduction in crime and an increase in feelings of security and well-being.

Donald Appleyard (1981) also based his work in the US, and in a highly original piece of research in San Francisco showed the extent to which heavy traffic deprived local residents of social opportunities and a sense of belonging. Residents were physically deprived of public space and of the use of outdoor space for community purposes. Those living on heavily trafficked streets (16,000 vehicles per day) reported an average of 0.9 friends per person and 3.1 acquaintances per person compared with 3.0 and 6.3 respectively on lightly trafficked streets (2,000 vehicles per day).

The Transport and Health Study Group in the UK has identified exercise from walking and cycling as a factor in reducing the risk of ischaemic heart disease (see glossary). Quoting a number of health studies, it shows that men who walk or cycle to work have a lower rate of death from ischaemic heart disease than do those who travel by car. Public transport users fall in between these two groups.

Cycling and walking provide easy and cheap access to physical activity which sustains physical fitness. The reduced rate of coronary disease among those who exercise has been noted by several authors, and higher levels of physical fitness appear to delay all-cause mortality, primarily due to lowered rates of cardiovascular disease and cancer. Physical fitness is an essential condition for good health. Modern lifestyles, particularly those involving the journey to work by car, the office job and sedentary activities are not conducive to health and are accurate predictors of a number of cardiac and hypertension problems.

The British Medical Association produced a report in 1992 which demonstrated the beneficial health effects of cycling. Cycling reduces the risk of cardiovascular disease and contributes to lowering blood pressure. It encourages psychological well-being and keeps weight down. There is very specific evidence that regular exercise, such as cycling, can counter depression and improve mental health.

Air Pollution

Air pollution causes a number of basic adverse health conditions. It:

- aggravates cardiovascular and respiratory illness;
- adds stress to the cardiovascular system forcing the heart and lungs to work harder;
- reduces the lung's ability to exhale air and speeds up the loss of lung capacity;
- damages both the cells of the airways respiratory system and the lungs even after symptoms of minor irritation disappear;
- may contribute to the development of diseases including bronchitis, emphysema and cancer.

These health effects are not felt evenly amongst the population and there are a number of groups at a greater risk for a given level of pollution. These are:

- pre-adolescent children;
- individuals with asthma;
- individuals with pre-existing cardiovascular disease;
- individuals with pre-existing respiratory disease;
- people over 65;
- pregnant women.

Approximately 18 million people, or 38 per cent of the population of England, were in at-risk groups from air pollution in the early 1990s. This includes 2 million people with asthma, 1.1 million of whom are children.

The global threats posed by air pollution (including vehicle sources) have been addressed by the Worldwatch Institute in Washington. Ozone pollution in the US, as a result of the interaction of sunlight with automobile NO_x emissions, is a major health problem. In 1988, the air in New York City violated federal health standards on 34 days, two or three times each week throughout the summer. In Washington DC, the same standard was exceeded every third day on average throughout the summer. In Los Angeles in the same year federal standards for ozone were exceeded on 172 days. In the US 382 counties are out of compliance with US Environmental Protection Agency standards for ozone.

Vehicle emissions may be responsible for a number of serious diseases including cancers. The late Simon Wolff of University College London examined the hypothesis that leukaemia 'clustering' as well as national leukaemia incidence in the UK is related to non-occupational exposure to benzene formed by petrol consumption and from petrol evaporation. He found a statistically significant association between car ownership and acute myeloid leukaemia, the cancer specifically associated with benzene exposure, as well as between all lymphoproliferative diseases and car ownership (Wolff, 1992). The research methodology based on geographical variation in car ownership and leukaemia data for the same spatial units cannot demonstrate causation. It does, however, indicate a need for further research.

There are important contributions to the cancer debate in community based health studies. Savitz and Feingold (1989) observed that rates of leukaemia were higher in areas of higher traffic density in a study of childhood leukaemia incidence in Denver, Colorado, in the US. Whilst the authors of this study make a plea for cautious interpretation they conclude that their results indicate an association between traffic density near the home occupied at the time of diagnosis and childhood cancer – even when confounding variables are taken into account. Evidence of increasing risk with increasing traffic densities was found for the total number of cancers and leukaemias.

Blumer, Blumer and Scherrer (1989) carried out a statistical comparison of two groups of subjects in Netstal, Switzerland. One group lived in the vicinity of a heavily trafficked road and the other 400m away from the main road with no through traffic. At the end of 1958 in the houses located within 25m of the main road 25 persons of the 232 adults in the group had died of malignant tumours (11 per cent). In the control area three persons of the 259 residents had died of cancer (1.2 per cent). The study linked the higher mortality on the heavily trafficked street to higher concentrations of particulates, mainly heavy polycyclic aromatic hydrocarbons.

An epidemiological study carried out in Hamburg in 1989 (Ippen, Fehr and Krasemann), observed a 12 per cent increase in cancer incidence for men on 'heavily trafficked' streets when compared with lightly trafficked streets. Heavy traffic was defined as more than 30,000 vehicles per day. Taking data from the Hamburg cancer registry this study calculated rates for heavily trafficked areas and compared them with Hamburg-wide rates. Lung cancer rates in the heavily trafficked areas were 34 per cent higher than expected, and colon cancer stood at 68 per cent higher. There was no attempt to control for cigarette smoking or dietary factors.

A wide ranging study undertaken by Siemiatycki *et al.* (1988) identified associations between several types of cancer and ten types of exhaust and combustion products. This study carried out interviews with 3,726 men aged between 35 and 70 in Montreal, Canada who had been diagnosed as suffering from cancer. The most important results were the associations between squamous-cell lung cancer and both gasoline and diesel exhaust. Gasoline exhaust was also associated with rectal cancer and diesel exhaust with colon cancer.

The South Coast Air Quality Management plan in the US which covers the urban area of Los Angeles, and Orange, Riverside and San Bernardino counties in California, is based on a highly sophisticated model which determines the total population exposed to air pollution both before and after pollution controls. The Regional Human Exposure Model (REHEX) calculates the daily exposure to air pollution by each member of nine demographic groups living in 32 pollution 'exposure districts'. The demographic groups were distinguished by age, working status and whether or not they worked indoors, outdoors or predominantly in an automobile. The model translates concentrations of ozone and particulate air pollution recorded at monitoring stations into actual amounts of pollution inhaled by each of the demographic groups using 1,000 time–activity patterns and six exercise states.

The conclusion reached through the application of the REHEX model was that nearly everyone living in the south coast area is exposed to concentrations of ozone or particulate pollution that exceed federal or California public health standards. School–age children, college students and adults working outdoors were judged to experience the highest ozone exposure per capita.

The south coast study identified nearly 1,000 studies to identify pollutants of interest and their health effects. The report focused on morbidity effects from ozone and on mortality and morbidity effects from particulate matter. Five morbidity effects were analysed for exposure to ozone pollution: mild cough, eye irritation, sore throat, headaches and chest discomfort. Using dose-response coefficients from the scientific literature and the results of the REHEX analysis the study predicted that reducing ozone pollution to meet the federal public health standard would eliminate annually 121.7 million occurrences of mild cough, 191.6 million eye irritations, 179.0 million sore throats, 107.4 million headaches and 64.5 million cases of chest discomfort.

The south coast plan translates these health benefits into monetary values as part of the argument for paying the very large bill associated with cleaning up California's air. It is aimed at all sources of air pollution, though in the Californian context pollution from California's 16 million vehicles is a top priority and the main reason why zero emission (electric) vehicles are the favoured option for reducing pollution from mobile sources.

The American Lung Association estimated that in 1990 in the United States as a whole an 'upper bound of about 120,000 excess deaths attributable to air pollution in 1985 is reasonable and that a lower bound of approximately equal likelihood is about 50,000'. Vehicles produced 40.5 per cent of the total discharge of pollutants examined but the authors concluded, conservatively, that vehicles were responsible for 15–25 per cent of the total health costs from air pollution. In effect they were concluding that vehicle emissions prematurely killed between 10,000 and 24,000 people each year. This assumes a 20 per cent apportionment of air pollution to vehicles which is extremely conservative when in the US automobile exhausts contribute 66 per cent of the nation's total CO pollution, 43 per cent of the NO_x pollution and 34 per cent of the reactive HC pollution.

EU figures show a higher proportionate responsibility for the contribution made by cars and vans: (CEC, 1992a)

- 56 per cent of NO_x pollution;
- 67 per cent of VOC pollution;

- 50 per cent of SO_2 pollution;
- 80 per cent of CO pollution;
- 30 per cent of particulate pollution.

This would signal the presence of a larger health problem in Europe.

A study of 7,445 children aged between nine and eleven years in Munich in 1993 and involving direct measurement of lung function showed that high rates of road traffic diminish forced expiratory flow and increase respiratory ailments in children. These results were statistically significant, and controlled for smoking, indoor air pollution and social class.

The question of 'control' is crucial in health studies and has been addressed in, for example, the Lancaster Study in the UK.

The Lancaster Study

The Lancaster University Environmental Epidemiology Research Unit carried out an investigation into the links between traffic and health in 1992. This study used traffic data from local authorities and a questionnaire on the health experience of residents on the same streets supplied with traffic data to establish whether or not there was a relationship between traffic levels and health experience. The result of the investigation was that there was a clear, statistically significant relationship between the amount of traffic and the number of symptoms of poor health reported by residents. As the traffic level went up so did the amount of illness.

The symptoms in the study were: blocked/runny nose; sore/red eyes; cough; breathing difficulties; headache; lack of energy; and sore throat. The results were statistically significant for five of these seven symptoms.

The Lancaster study is important because it established a statistically significant relationship between traffic and poor health. More importantly, it did this through having controls for factors like smoking, other sources of pollution and income. The confirmation of a link between traffic and health has not arisen from the effect of 'confounding' variables. An example of an important confounding variable is poverty. If poor people live on heavily trafficked streets and we know poor people are more likely to be ill then the finding of a link merely confirms that poverty makes people ill. The Lancaster study used a statistical method that allowed the link to be investigated independently of such confounding variables.

In its 1992 review of motor vehicle air pollution WHO concluded: 'Motor vehicle traffic and its emissions seriously damage the health of urban populations.' Of relevance to the public policy debate and the protection of human health is the conclusion about air quality monitoring:

> It has been incontrovertibly established that ambient (outdoor) air quality measured at fixed monitoring stations designed to represent community exposures in general, significantly underestimates the exposure to primary motor vehicle air pollutants (lead, carbon monoxide, particulates and hydrocarbons) of many population subgroups. People in vehicles in heavy traffic, people walking/working along busy streets and people whose homes front onto busy streets are all exposed to both noise and air pollutants at much higher concentrations than reported by the community monitoring networks.

Traffic related air pollution is a particularly serious problem for children. They breathe in a larger quantity of air per unit of body weight and are, therefore, more vulnerable than adults to problems associated with air pollution. They are nearer to the ground than adults and smaller children in particular breathe in air from a level that approximates to the level of a vehicle exhaust pipe. Children are also more active than adults and this increases the volume of air they breathe in and the exposure of the deeper recesses of lung tissue to air pollutants. Children are the societal equivalent of the 'canary in the cage' used by miners until very recently. In most contemporary urban environments they show many signs of 'falling off the perch' and there is still very little effort in the direction of fundamental redesign of urban environments to make them child friendly. One study reported in 'The Environment for Children' suggests that over two million children suffer from chronic cough as a result of urban air pollution in Latin America.

The report of the Royal Commission on Environmental Pollution, published in 1994, has added to the information available on health impacts. This report refers to a five-fold increase since 1983 in the number of families in the UK applying for disability grants because their children have severe asthma. There has been a marked increase in the incidence of respiratory problems in recent years. Between 1976 and 1987 acute attacks of asthma more than doubled in England and Wales (from 10.7 per 100,000 patients a week to 27.1 per 100,000 patients a week). The greatest increase was in children (from 13.5 to 74.4 per 100,000 in the 0–4 age group, and from 17.4 to 58.9 in the 5–14 age group).

The Royal Commission points out that a number of factors in addition to traffic are implicated in the increase in respiratory disease. It also points out that transport emissions account for 90 per cent of emissions from all sources in the case of CO and 57 per cent in the case of nitrogen oxides (NO_x). It also identifies the very clear association between increases in nitrogen dioxide (NO_2) emissions and human health. In the case of the December 1991 smog episode in London the poor air quality was directly associated with 160 excess deaths (additional to the expected rate) during a four-day period. The cause of this poor air quality is described by the Royal Commission thus:

> The correlation of concentrations of nitrogen oxides with concentrations of carbon monoxide and the absence of correlation with sulphur dioxide strongly suggests that vehicle emissions were the dominant source of pollution.

Benzene

The Royal Commission has identified benzene as one of the more serious pollutants arising from exposure to traffic. Benzene is carcinogenic and vehicles are 'the most important source of exposure to benzene for people in urban areas who do not smoke, are not heavily exposed to other people smoking, and do not encounter high concentrations of benzene in the workplace'.

Ninety-eight per cent of UK emissions of benzene are from car exhausts. Measurements of air quality show that half the sites tested near busy roads or petrol stations exceed the standard recommended by the Government's Expert Panel on Air Quality Standards (EPAQS) of 5 parts per billion (ppb) as a running annual average. EPAQS has urged the government to set a deadline for reducing the air quality standard to 1 ppb. Measurements made by TBV Science, a consultancy firm, reported by the Environmental Data Service (ENDS) show that 25 per cent of those taken at 40m from a busy road were above the 5 ppb level.

WHO does not recommend a guideline for benzene because no safe level of exposure is known.

Particulates

There is currently a great deal of concern about the health damaging effects of fine particulate matter emitted from vehicle exhausts. Two studies in the US reported by WHO in 1995 suggest that life expectancy may be shortened by more than a year in high versus low particulate communities. Fine particulate matter, referred to as PM_{10} because each particle is less than 10 microns in diameter, has been implicated in fatalities in the US in up to 60,000 deaths per annum. A similar calculation for Britain reported in *New Scientist* (Brown) in 1994 produced an estimate of up to 10,000 deaths per annum.

PM_{10} is largely traffic-based and has been implicated in increases in mortality in the work of Dockery and his colleagues (Dockery, D.W. *et al.*, 1993). Particularly strong associations have been found for cardiovascular mortality and respiratory mortality in six cities where patients were tracked over 16 years.

Table 10.1 summarises the results of a large body of empirical work which identifies the relationship between increases in particulate pollution and increases in mortality and a number of other indicators of health.

Table 10.1: Summary of Short-term Exposure–response Relationships of Sulphates, $PM_{2.5}$ and PM_{10} with Different Health Effect Indicators

	Estimated Change in Daily Average Concentration Needed for Given Effect (in μg/m³)		
Health Effect Indicator	Sulphates	$PM_{2.5}$	PM_{10}
Daily mortality:			
5 % change	8	29	50
10 % change	16	55	100
20 % change	30	110	200
Hospital admissions for respiratory conditions:			
5 % change	8	10	25
10 % change	16	20	50
20 % change	32	40	100
Bronchodilator use among asthmatics:			
5 % change	–	–	7
10 % change	–	–	14
20 % change	–	–	29
Symptom exacerbations among asthmatics:			
5 % change	–	–	10
10 % change	–	–	20
20 % change	–	–	40
Peak expiratory flow (mean pop. change):			
5 % change	–	–	200
10 % change	–	–	400
20 % change	–	–	–

Source: WHO (1995a)

A wide range of UK and international reseach material on vehicle pollution and human health was brought together at a conference in London in May 1994 (Read, 1994) and some of the more relevant conclusions are summarised below:

> Recent evidence has convincingly shown that death rates from heart and lung disease are up to 37 per cent higher in cities with high levels of fine particulates.
>
> More research is needed in the UK to estimate the public health effects of air pollution; the need to do this for particulates is urgent.
>
> People exposed to high traffic levels experience more respiratory symptoms and worse lung function than people who live in areas with less traffic.
>
> Three traffic-related pollutants: particulates, nitrogen dioxide and ozone, are all associated with a fall in lung function and an increase in respiratory symptoms in healthy people as well as those with asthma (Walters, 1994).

Phillips (1994) wrote:

> It is a highly plausible hypothesis that environmental exposure to the traffic pollutants discussed above poses a carcinogenic risk to the public.
>
> As vehicle pollution is a major source of Polycyclic Aromatic Hydrocarbons in urban areas, an increase in emissions of particulates which can carry PAHs into the lungs, particularly from diesel vehicles, is likely to increase lung cancer risk. However, the magnitude of the increase in risk is difficult to estimate at present.

According to Goodwin (1994):

> Vehicle pollutants in Britain frequently exceed international guidelines. There is a growing body of evidence to suggest that, at levels experienced in the UK, these pollutants have significant adverse effects on health.
>
> These adverse effects include: respiratory problems including an increase in the severity of asthma, reduced lung function, cough, breathlessness, wheeze and respiratory infections. Mechanisms have been discovered which explain how air pollutants may cause wheeze, enhance allergic airway disease including asthma and hayfever, and predispose to infection.

Research from the US suggests that people who live in areas with high concentrations of particulates are at increased risk of premature death from heart and lung disease including lung cancer; people with pre-existing heart and lung conditions and the elderly are most at risk. The risk of exposure to particulates for people living in urban Britain is still not known.

People with coronary heart disease are at risk from levels of carbon monoxide experienced in urban areas; an increased likelihood of chest pain with exercise may limit their activity and adversely affect quality of life.

Over the next decade emissions of most types of vehicle pollution are predicted to fall. However, particulate emissions, which are of considerable concern for health, are predicted to rise significantly. In the longer term, by 2010, the overall outlook is unfavourable.

In the absence of further technical improvements, or a different approach to transport provision, emissions will begin to rise once more by around the year 2010.

Direct research into vehicle pollution and health has only recently begun in the UK and more research is needed. The effect of particulate exposures on people living in urban areas is possibly the most urgent.

Recent concern about the health effects of vehicle pollution has coincided with a remarkable shift in thinking on transport policy. The evidence from research into health effects reviewed here gives further weight to the economic and environmental reasons for adopting new transport strategies.

Ozone (O_3)

An increasingly common problem in developed countries is photochemical or summer smog, largely derived from the action of sunshine on NO_x pollution in combination with VOCs. The largest source of both these compounds is the motor vehicle. In the UK in 1992 road transport was responsible for 53 per cent of NO_x and 46 per cent of VOCs (Dept of Transport, 1996).

In the summer of 1995 large parts of Europe experienced hot, dry and sunny anti-cyclonic weather conditions which are associated with O_3 pollution episodes and warnings of poor air quality. Ozone, a strong oxidant, is naturally formed through the influence of ultraviolet radiation from the sun. It is the predominant constituent of photochemical smog, and damages plants, materials and human tissue. Proteins such as enzymes, on the surface and in the interior of cells, as well as unsaturated fats, are attacked in living tissues by ozone. It also damages respiratory tissue, causing disturbance that can lead to inflammation. Symptoms associated with O_3 pollution include coughing, dryness in the mouth and pains in the chest.

Laboratory experiments have shown that O_3 can invade the body and cause damage in various parts: in the white and red blood corpuscles, in the circulatory system, the liver, the endocrine glands and the central nervous system. The effects of O_3 on health depend on the length of exposure, concentration in the air and intensity of inhalation. The most important factor seems to be concentration, and extremely high peak levels are more harmful than lower average excesses.

Children and young people are more sensitive to high levels of ozone than older people. Mild effects (irritation of the eyes, nose, mouth, and headache) have been related to concentrations as low as 120μg/m^3. Healthy individuals can experience a slight difficulty in breathing after exposure for six hours to concentrations of 160μg/m^3 and more serious symptoms such as pain in the whole respiratory tract and severe irritation of the trachea at 320–360μg/m^3.

Table 10.2 summarises the relationship between ozone (O_3) concentrations and a number of health outcomes.

Table 10.2: Health Outcomes Associated with Changes in Peak Daily Ambient Ozone Concentrations in Epidemiological Studies

Health Outcome	Change in 1–h O_3 (μg/m^3)	Change in 8–h O_3 (μg/m^3)
Symptom exacerbations among healthy children and adults or asthmatics – normal activity:		
25 % increase	200	100
50 % increase	400	200
100 % increase	800	300
Hospital admissions for respiratory conditions [a]:		
5 %	30	25
10 %	60	50
20 %	120	100

1–h = one hour
8–h = eight hour

Source: WHO (1995a)

Note:
[a] Given the high degree of correlation between the 1–h and 8–h O_3 concentrations in field studies, an improvement in health risk associated with decreasing 1– or 8–h O_3 levels should be almost identical.

When O_3 exposure occurs in combination with other air pollutants (NO_2, SO_2, sulphuric acid, nitric acid and CO) the various substances accentuate each other's harmful effects. Ozone also contributes to the formation of aerosols, small airborne particles which themselves have adverse effects on health.

There is a clear connection between heightened O_3 levels and increased mortality from respiratory diseases, slight difficulty in breathing and asthma symptoms. Hospital admissions are also correlated with episodes of O_3 pollution.

Ozone pollution episodes are more common in rural and suburban areas than in city centres where large amounts of NO_x break down the O_3 molecules. In southern Europe or in hotter temperatures there may not be such an urban–rural gradient. According to WHO calculations concentrations above the lower WHO one-hour guide exposure value of 150μg/m^3 occur over practically the whole of Europe.

Ozone levels vary from year to year depending on weather conditions. During the hot summer of 1989, when a lot of O_3 was formed, some 367 million people were exposed to levels higher than the upper WHO guide value of 200μg/m^3. Excluding city centres in northern and western Europe, 38 per cent of the population were in areas where the 200μg/m^3 level was at some time exceeded. The greatest excesses occurred in southern England, the Benelux countries, northern France, Germany and Switzerland. The highest local values were recorded in the south of England and around Lisbon in Portugal. Ozone levels were much less in 1985, when the summer was cool. Nevertheless, 16–22 per cent of the whole European population was estimated to have been exposed to 1-hour values of more than 200μg/m^3.

In 1989 the population of Europe was exposed to an average level of 139μg/m^3. In 1985 it was 130μg/m^3. Taking the figure of 90μg/m^3 – the level at which long-term exposure will cause reduction of the lung function – 431 million persons, or 65 per cent of Europe's population, were living in places where that level was exceeded, even in the cold year of 1985. In northern Europe 63 per cent of the population outside the big towns were estimated to have been so exposed in 1985, and 93 per cent in 1989.

Depending on the weather, an increase of 220,000 to 1.9 million cases of cough and eye irritation amongst children can be expected in a single year as a result of short episodes with high concentrations of ozone. Children living in the southern parts of the Benelux countries and adjoining parts of Germany and France are likely to be the most affected.

Ozone pollution episodes are likely to increase in the future. The growth in car numbers and distances driven by vehicles will ensure that the benefits of catalytic converters are cancelled out after the year 2010 in most of Europe. Catalytic converters reduce the amounts of NO_x and VOCs emitted by vehicle exhausts but they cannot provide enough relief to compensate for growth in the vehicle fleet and the growth in distances travelled each year. Ozone pollution is unusual in that it can move over large distances. Traditionally, road builders in the UK argue that emissions from road vehicles will reduce to background levels and will be undetectable at distances of more than 200m from a road. This overlooks the fact that 'previous' emissions still exist and add to those background levels, if only marginally. In the case of O_3, the pollutant can move continentally and can arrive at ground level from the stratospheric layer (10–50km above the earth's surface). Ozone pollution episodes are intensified by periods of clear, hot, sunny weather which maximises the availability of ultraviolet radiation at the earth's surface. This was the case in O_3 pollution episodes in May 1995 in the UK and throughout Europe in the summer of 1995.

The seriousness of O_3 pollution has been recognised in Germany which introduced a new law to combat summer smog in August 1995. The new law provides powers to ban vehicles from the road and impose speed limits should the concentration of O_3 exceed $240\mu g/m^3$ at three separate measuring stations in one region over a one-hour period. The one-hour period recognises the importance of short-lived high concentrations for human health. Longer periods for averaging purposes would not identify these peaks.

The Extent of Health Damage

The World Health Organisation (1995b) has estimated the number of Europeans living in places where WHO guidelines were exceeded in the early 1990s. This information is reproduced in Table 10.3.

The WHO estimates reveal a bleak picture:

- 6,000–13,000 premature deaths among people over 65 due to SO_2;
- 89,000–203,000 people suffering intensified chronic respiratory problems due to SO_2;
- 58,000–99,000 extra cases of disease in lower respiratory organs of children due to NO_2;
- a 2–3 per cent lowering of lung function in 60 million people due to NO_2;
- 220,000–1.9 million children suffering coughs and eye irritation from O_3.

The WHO estimates reveal a great deal about the extent of health damage from pollution. They cannot, however, begin to quantify the damage that goes beyond the physiological – including psychological damage from noise, the disruption of everyday life and damage to communities and the elderly from fear and stress.

Table 10.3: Number of Europeans Living in Places where WHO Guidelines were being Overstepped in the early 1990s

Pollutant	Time period	Guide-line (μg/m³)	Numbers exposed according to statistics (millions)	(%)	Total number exposed (calculated) (%)
Sulphur	24 h	125[a]	144[d]	46	34
dioxide	1 year	50[a]	22	20	9
Nitrogen dioxide[e]	24 h	150[a]	21	23	8
Ozone	1 h	150[b]	105–367[d]	63–93	63–93
	1 h	200[c]	105–367[d]	16–56	16–56
	1 year	90	431[d]	65	
TSP[f]	24 h	120[a]	29	95	
	1 year	60	18	61	
Black	24 h	125[a]	14	23	
smoke[f]	1 year	50[a]	14	23	

Notes:

a WHO guidelines
b Lower guideline
c Upper guideline
d According to model calculations
e Exceeded only in urban areas
f Data insufficient for calculating total exposure.

TSP = Total suspended particulates

Source: WHO (1995b)

Noise

Exposure to levels of traffic noise that make speech difficult, disturb sleep and damage human health is now the norm in urban areas throughout the world. The vast literature on vehicles and air pollution has tended to dominate the technological agenda set for the motor vehicle and the environment. There is no noise equivalent for the catalytic converter and if there were we would have to deal with an even more intractable problem in the form of a silent vehicle capable of speeds of up to 100kph infesting urban areas. This is not likely to prove attractive to urban residents already retreating from public spaces and terrified of road traffic accidents.

Noise is a problem which affects everybody. Noise is unwanted sound. It is most commonly expressed as the A-weighted sound pressure level in decibels – dB(A). Typical sound pressure levels range from 20 dB(A) in a very quiet rural area to between 50 and 70 dB(A) in towns during the day time, to 90 dB(A) or more in noisy factories and discotheques to well over 120 dB(A) near to a jet aircraft at take off.

The extent of the noise problem is large. Every third dwelling in Denmark is exposed to non-acceptable traffic noise. Between 1973 and 1978 the population of the US exposed to non-acceptable road traffic noise almost doubled. Non-acceptable traffic noise is defined by the OECD as noise levels exceeding 65 dB(A). In large cities more than 50 per cent of the population are exposed to levels in excess of 65 dB(A). The OECD predict a deterioration in noise environments. They identify road traffic noise as the biggest single source of noise nuisance followed by aircraft noise and identify the spread of noise over time as a major source of concern. As mobility levels rise and as spatial dispersion accelerates, noise levels diffuse through space and time to spread the misery through previously quiet space–time slots.

The percentage of city residents living with unacceptable noise levels varies with the type of city (see Table 10.4).

Table 10.4: Percentage of Population Living with Noise Levels Greater than 65 dB(A)

Amsterdam	19
Detroit	60
Paris	50
Sydney	10

Source: WHO (1993)

Noise levels are related to speeding behaviour and since speeds of cars and lorries have increased on uncongested roads over the last 20 years so have noise levels. The majority of motorists and lorry drivers break speed limits and contribute through aggressive acceleration and braking to excessive noise. This contributes to the serious noise problem particularly for those urban and rural residents who live within 1km of a motorway. The interaction of tyre and road surface on these roads produces a continuous background hum that lasts throughout a 24-hour period and is more noticeable at night when other local sources of noise have shut down. If congestion problems are resolved on local roads and motorways, then speed levels will rise and lead to a further deterioration of the noise environment. Noisier conditions for urban residents can be expected to follow from the introduction of road pricing measures where these measures reduce traffic volumes, and, in uncongested conditions, encourage higher speeds.

Health Effects of Noise

Noise interferes with communication, particularly speech, and causes severe problems amongst those groups where there is an existing hearing problem or for whom high quality communication is particularly important. This group includes school pupils, those undertaking language training and those immigrant groups who are learning a new language. The speech level in relaxed conversation at home is approximately 55 dB(A). For 100 per cent sentence intelligibility the speech level should exceed the background noise level by 10 dB(A). Efficient communication is impaired on most heavily trafficked streets or in areas near such streets where there are other sources of noise. Communication difficulties are unacceptable disturbances to normal social interaction and are a contributory factor in the abandonment of public space, abandonment of walking and loss of contact with friends, neighbours, colleagues and children in the outdoor environment. For the elderly or those with some hearing loss, a noisy environment is a serious handicap to basic social interaction and well-being.

Indoor noise levels of less than 45 dB(A) are recommended by the WHO 1993 review of noise standards if 100 per cent speech intelligibility is to be guaranteed. Whilst it is possible to produce indoor noise levels lower than this level through double and triple glazing and acoustic engineering, it is important to recognise that health and well-being require the facility of living indoors with open doors and windows, using balconies, terraces and gardens. The street is also a key element in the urban fabric and is the location for the vast majority of unplanned contact with friends and neighbours. Communication and interaction will take place in all these situations and even more so in southern Europe or other parts of the world where long periods of sunny, dry weather make outdoor activities more common. This has important implications for motorised transport and its predicted growth. If noise levels that are deemed acceptable on health grounds by the WHO are to be achieved then there will have to be a substantial shift away from motorised transport towards quieter modes and/or a substantial shift of motorised transport into tunnels where noise levels can be contained. The tunnel option is usually too expensive and it is unrealistic to expect tunnels to get rid of all the traffic that currently makes life in Brussels, London or Bangkok so unpleasant.

Noise is responsible for sleep disturbance. The constant background noise of a motorway and the peak noise events associated with motorbikes and lorries are disruptive of normal sleep patterns. Noise exposure causes difficulty in going to sleep, disrupts sleep itself, wakes the sleeper and contributes to tiredness in the morning.

Noise during sleep is responsible for a number of primary physiological effects. These include increased blood pressure, increased heart rate, vasoconstriction, change in respiration and cardiac arrhythmia. The day after noise exposure can reveal a number of secondary effects including increased fatigue, decreased mood or well-being and decreased performance. Long-term effects on psycho-social well-being have been related to noise exposure during the night. These reactions have been shown both in laboratory and field conditions to be induced by road traffic noise with maximum levels exceeding 40 dB(A).

Habituation to noise does not seem to take place and exposure to increasingly severe noise levels exacerbates the negative health effects. To avoid the negative effects on sleep patterns the sound level should not exceed 30–35 dB(A) in the bedroom. When sound levels rise to 45 dB(A), which is very common in all urban areas at night-time, particularly where lorries are present, sleep disturbance takes place.

Noise affects the cardiovascular system. Traffic noise is correlated with increases in blood pressure, as is aircraft noise. Since air transport is predicted to double in numbers of passengers carried by 2005 this represents a significant and increasing source of health damaging noise. Studies of health around airports have shown that in those environments with heavy noise (67–75 dB(A)) cardiac disease, doctor's calls and the purchase of medicines are more frequent than in quieter environments (46–55 dB(A)).

Noise has been shown to produce a number of impacts on physical health including nausea, headache, irritability, insomnia, abnormal somnolence, argumentativeness, reduction in sex drive, nervousness and loss of appetite. Aircraft noise studies have also found associations between noise and gastrointestinal ailments.

Noise is associated with a number of mental health conditions and increased rates of treatment and admissions in psychiatric care. There are closely related effects on social behaviour that reduce helpfulness, stimulate aggressiveness and give rise to extreme judgements of others. Noise is not sufficient to produce aggression but in combination with provocation or pre-existing anger/hostility it makes aggression more likely.

In 1993 the World Health Organisation updated its noise standards and replaced those that were published in 1980. The new standards take into account the importance of outdoor activities and the need to reduce noise levels in those locations. They also take into account the importance of susceptible groups, and of high quality sleep and communication, particularly for schoolchildren. The recommended standards are:

- Inside bedrooms, 30 dB(A)
- For steady state-continuous noise and for a noise event, 45 dB(A)
- For balconies, terraces and outdoor living areas, 55 dB(A)
- Night-time outdoors the noise should not exceed, 45 dB(A)
- In schools and pre-schools noise levels should not exceed, 34 dB(A)
- For outdoor playgrounds the level should not exceed, 55 dB(A)
- In hospitals the sound level should not exceed, 35 dB(A)

Noise Standards in EU Member States

Noise standards and approaches to noise regulation vary throughout Europe. This has led to different levels of protection being provided for residents affected by noisy developments. In the case of high speed trains this results in a situation where the same route, for example, London–Brussels–Paris–Cologne, has to meet four very different sets of requirements imposing different standards on the construction of the line.

In France, under the Municipal Code, mayors have the power to limit or prohibit noise that 'disturbs the public tranquillity'. In addition, mayors have the power, under Article 90 of the Decentralisation Law of 7 January 1983, to prevent or stop 'pollution of all kinds', which includes noise. Articles 101–104 of the health department regulations also allow mayors to stop noise pollution.

In Germany, noise is regulated by the Air Quality Control Act. There are strict controls for noise from road construction, trams and trains. These controls have led to much of the high speed train (HST) network being put in underground tunnels or in surface tunnels (box-like constructions that sit on the surface and completely enclose the track and associated equipment). Thirty-one per cent of the Stuttgart to Mannheim HST (total length 100km) is in a tunnel, and much of the route is through rural areas. German noise regulations specify a daytime limit for housing areas of 59 dB(A) and a night time limit of 49 dB(A). The limits are more stringent for schools, old people's homes and hospitals and more lenient for industrial areas. These limits were set in the Verkehrslarmschutzverordnung of 1990 (Traffic Noise Protection Law).

In the Netherlands, noise zones are defined around railways, airports and residential areas. The Noise Abatement Act 1979 sets preferred and maximum limits for noise loads (that is, aggregate noise levels) within zones. The noise limits for residential areas are as follows:

	dB(A)
Level to which insulation must reduce noise in residential rooms	35
Day	50
Night	40

Noise levels are set for classrooms in schools when external noise rises above 55 dB(A). Classroom noise should not exceed 30 dB(A). This also applies to bedrooms in old people's homes and wards in hospitals and nursing homes.

Maximum permissible noise loads, in dB(A), for railway noise have been set:

	From 1 July 1987	*From 1 January 2000*
Preferred load	60	57
Maximum permissible load	73	70

Source: Commission of the European Communities (1991b)

The Dutch approach sets noise standards that respect the nature of the protection required, for example, for schools and residential areas. This results in substantial remediation measures to protect the population from noise. Noise protection in Germany and the Netherlands gives protection levels to local residents and schools considerably in excess of those available in Britain.

Conclusion

Noise and air quality standards have been set to protect human health. They point very clearly in the direction of reductions at source rather than reduction via mitigation measures. This is in line with the thrust of the EU's Fifth Environmental Action Programme which puts the emphasis in environmental policy on reductions at source rather than attempts to reduce the problem once it is established.

Noise and air pollution from road and air traffic can be reduced by reductions in the demand for transport and by transfers to other modes of transport where appropriate, and by substitute activities where appropriate. In this sense a noise reduction strategy, for example, is identical to a greenhouse gas reduction strategy and a strategy to improve the quality of life and environment of urban residents. In all three cases, the principles of sustainable development and sustainable transport can provide a solution and can protect human health to a degree that is impossible with the transport policies and growth potential for motorised transport of the late twentieth century. The future for human health, like the future for planetary health, is distinctly bleak in a hyper-mobile, car-dependent, and infrastructure-hungry future.

The WHO definition of health quoted earlier in this chapter challenges the acceptance of the current levels of the impact of motorised transport on health globally. Traffic damages health and does not engender a complete state of physical and psychological well-being. Our dependence on motorised transport, moreover, deprives large numbers of people access to basic facilities, such as adequate shopping facilities, which in its turn damages health. Finally, motorised transport deprives large numbers of people of basic, inexpensive and socially satisfying exercise such as walking and cycling. A number of diseases are made more likely in the case of overweight individuals and exercise has a number of benefits for the maintenance of physical and psychological well-being. A fundamental and wide ranging audit of the health benefits and disbenefits of our transport systems would reveal a major deficit.

CHAPTER 11

Resolutions

Introduction

The present environmental crisis caused by the growth in motorised transport and its associated environmental impacts has been a consequence of the interrelationship of social, historical, economic, environmental and political factors. Transport growth has been fuelled by increasing population, development and urbanisation. In its turn the growth of motorised transport influences the land use system to increase the scale of urbanisation, the distances to be traversed and the intensity of car dependence.

These factors have fostered the growth in motorisation which now threatens the social fabric of society and quality of life. In attempting to resolve the problem of transport it is necessary to examine transport policy in a holistic and comprehensive manner. Action needs to be taken with regard to each aspect of the problem and on a multiple level, and which covers the global, regional and local environments. By taking measures to deal with transport problems at each level some progress can be made towards achieving a more sustainable transport system.

The management of transport has traditionally involved the maximisation of capacity and efficiency of networks, the improvement of safety and the improvement of accessibility for the car and lorry. The different types of measures used to manage transport have varied by mode and by country. The present impact of transport can be addressed in a number of ways in order to ensure that the environmental impact is reduced. These could include better utilisation of existing modes, implementation of best practice technology, reducing the impact of modes through technological means, shifting to less damaging modes of transport, and reducing the total amount of travel undertaken. In this chapter a number of the approaches and tools which are available to policy makers to assist them in working towards a solution to transport problems will be reviewed.

In the main, these approaches and tools are to be found wanting. They emphasise technical measures that are available to reduce emissions, a belief in new forms of technology, materials and fuels that will make cars environmentally friendly and put forward only a limited number of regulatory interventions designed to reduce air pollution and noise pollution.

Regulatory Measures and Agreements

Measures to regulate the transport sector have mainly dealt with the micro or local impacts of transport. These include vehicle emission limits, speed limits, traffic lights, restriction of the use of transport spatially, temporally and car and lorry bans.

With the introduction of new technological and scientific developments there has been an increasing concern over national and global impacts of transport. The regulatory measures applied within the transport sector have become more diverse and have covered a wide range of areas on a national and global level. A number of international agreements exist which directly or indirectly relate to transportation. The transport sector's contribution to global air pollution is an important consideration in the determination of international agreements to limit air pollution. Protection of the atmosphere has been dominated by concern over transboundary air pollution, climatic change and the depletion of the ozone layer for which a number of international conventions have been agreed.

The 1979 United Nations Economic Commission for Europe (UNECE) Convention on Long-range Transboundary Air Pollution (LRTAP) was a response to the increasing concern over acidification which had been experienced in western Europe and North America. The convention was signed by 34 industrialised nations in North America and Europe. Article 1(b) of the convention defined long-range transboundary air pollution as:

> ... air pollution whose physical origin is situated wholly or in part within the area under the national jurisdiction of one state and which has adverse effects in the area under the national jurisdiction of another state at such a distance that it is not generally possible to distinguish the contribution of individual emission sources or groups of sources.

As well as taking measures to prevent long-range transboundary air pollution, signatories within the framework of the convention are encouraged to share information and results of monitoring, and eventually develop strategies to combat such pollution. The convention provides a framework of cooperation for monitoring and evaluation, and has led to a number of agreements (known as protocols) concerning sulphur emissions, NO_x and VOCs. The Sulphur Protocol and the Nitrogen Oxides Protocol provided quantitative requirements to control and reduce emissions and fluxes of harmful substances. For emissions of sulphur, parties were required under the convention to reduce them by 30 per cent by 1993 using 1980 levels as a basis.

Under the Nitrogen Oxides Protocol, parties were required to reduce national emissions by December 1994 so they did not exceed 1987 levels. As well as being required to exchange information on monitoring and technology, parties under the convention were required within two years after the protocol came into force to introduce unleaded petrol – especially along main international transport corridors – to facilitate the circulation of vehicles equipped with catalytic converters.

A further protocol under the LRTAP convention, signed in Geneva in 1991, covers the control of emissions of VOCs. This protocol was a response to the threat to human health and natural resources caused by tropospheric ozone or smog. VOCs form ozone which reacts with NO_x in sunlight resulting in photochemical oxidants. Parties to the VOCs protocol are required to reduce emissions of VOCs by 30 per cent by 1999 using 1988 levels as a basis.

The UNECE Convention and its protocols have also developed the notion of 'critical loads' and 'critical levels' for air pollutants. Critical loads are defined as a quantitative estimate of the exposure to one or more harmful pollutants below which significant harmful effects on specified sensitive elements of the environment do not occur, according to present knowledge. Above the particular level of critical loads damage to the environment will occur. Critical levels refer to the concentration of pollutants which are in the atmosphere for a specific time of exposure below which direct adverse effects on human beings, plants, ecosystems or material assets do not occur, according to present knowledge. The extent of the impact varies with each pollutant and concentration of exposure. It is still not known exactly what relationship there is between the concentration of pollutants and the actual impact.

Concern over transboundary environmental impacts from development projects led to the Espoo Convention on 25 February 1991. From this came the Convention on Environmental Impact Assessment which requires parties to take effective action to prevent, reduce and control significant transboundary environmental impact from proposed activities. Transboundary impacts should be considered at the project level and, where possible, be applied to the environmental impact assessment of policies, plans and programmes. Within Appendix I of this convention transport projects are included in the list of activities which, if they are likely to cause a significant adverse transboundary impact, parties are required to notify an affected party. Transport projects include the construction of motorways, express roads, lines for long distance railway traffic, and of airports with a basic runway length of 2,100m or more.

Climate Change

One of the more recent conventions relating to the protection of the atmosphere is the Framework Convention on Climate Change which, together with Agenda 21, resulted from the 1992 United Nations Conference on Environment and Development (UNCED) in Rio in Brazil. This Framework Convention, together with Agenda 21, has a number of consequences for the transport sector. The objective of the Framework Convention on Climate Change is to stabilise operational gas concentrations at a level which would prevent dangerous anthropogenic interference with the climate system. Stabilisation should be achieved within a timeframe sufficient to allow the ecosystem to adapt naturally, so ensuring that food production is not threatened and economic development can proceed in a sustainable manner. The Framework Convention came into force on 21 March 1994. Although it lacks binding agreements it states that industrialised countries should aim to reduce greenhouse gas emissions to 1990 levels by the year 2000. Agenda 21 provides a programme for sustainability to be achieved at various levels in a number of different sectors. Chapter 7 of Agenda 21 concerns the promotion of sustainable human settlement and development. Within this chapter, Section 6 covers the promotion of sustainable energy and transport systems in human settlements with the objective:

> ... to extend the provision of more energy-efficient technical and alternative/renewable energy for human settlements and to reduce the negative impacts of energy production and use on human health and environment.

Activities which need to be undertaken to provide a comprehensive approach to human settlement should include the promotion of sustainable energy development in all countries. This includes the promotion of an efficient and environmentally sound urban transport system. Thus all countries should adopt an urban transport strategy which encourages a high occupancy of public transport. Non-motorised forms of transport should be encouraged with the provision of safe cycleways and footways in urban and suburban centres. Land use and transportation planning should also be encouraged to reduce the demand to travel. In addition, attention should be given to effective transport management and the efficient operation of public transport and maintenance of transport infrastructure.

Chapter 2(b) of Agenda 21 concerns conservation and management of resources for development. It has a section dealing with transport. The basis for action is outlined below:

> The transportation sector has an essential and positive role to play in economic and social development, and transportation needs will undoubtedly increase. However, since the transport sector is also a source of atmosphere emissions, there is a need for a review of existing transportation systems and the most effective design and management of traffic and transportation systems.

The objective of the programme on transportation is to develop and promote cost-effective policies which limit, reduce and control harmful emissions and other adverse environmental effects of the transport sector. Six activities were outlined which governments, in cooperation with intergovernmental and non-governmental agencies, should undertake. These are outlined as follows:

1. Development and promotion of cost-effective, less polluting and safer transport systems and partially integrated urban–rural mass transit networks, as well as an environmentally sound road network taking into consideration the needs of sustainable economic social development.
2. Facilitate access to and transfer of safe, efficient, resource efficient, less polluting transport techniques at the international, subregional and national levels. This is of particular importance for developing countries with appropriate training programmes.
3. Action should be taken to strengthen efforts at collecting, analysing and exchanging relevant information on the relationship between transport and the environment, with emphasis on the systematic observations of emissions and the development of a transport data base.
4. Cost-effective policies and programmes should be promoted including administrative, social and economic measures, in order to encourage the use of transportation modes that minimise adverse impacts on the atmosphere in accordance with national socio-economic development and environmental priorities.
5. Mechanisms to integrate transport planning strategies and urban and regional settlement planning strategies should be developed and enhanced with a view to reducing the environmental impact of transport.

6. Within the framework of the United Nations and its regional economic commissions, the feasibility of convening regional conferences on transport and the environment should be studied.

(Agenda 21: Chapter 2(b): Conservation and Management of Resources for Development UNCED, 1992).

Other issues such as population growth and development of human settlements are also relevant to the transport and environment debate. Increasing population growth will have consequences for the environment and the quality of life. Rapid population growth increases the pressure on resources and communities which eventually leads to environmental degradation. If current population and energy consumption trends continue, then by 2025 developing countries could be emitting more than four times as much CO_2 as developed countries do today. The world's motor vehicle fleets will increase by 2.5 per cent a year, outstripping the 1.7 per cent annual increase in human population. In addition, population growth was addressed at the United Nations Conference on Population and Development held in Cairo in September 1994. This attempted to address issues within this area such as gender equality and empowerment of women, reproductive rights, and access to and availability of family planning.

The condition and quality of human settlements will also have a significant role in the future, for 56 per cent of the world's population are expected to be living in urban areas by 2025. The development of more sustainable and people-friendly cities is important, and changing the role of urban transport will play an important part in achieving this. The UN addressed the issue of human settlements in its 1976 'Habitat Conference' which was held in Vancouver, Canada. This conference addressed local environmental problems such as housing, shelter, infrastructure, water, sewage and transport.

Chapter 7 of Agenda 21 deals with promoting sustainable human settlements, and after UNCED it was agreed to hold a second conference on human settlements – Habitat II. This was hosted in Istanbul, Turkey in June 1996. The conference addressed the progress made since the 1976 conference, and adopted a general statement of principles and commitments to formulate a global plan of action to halt the deterioration of global human settlements. Better management of human settlements will be necessary if sustainable development is to be achieved with increasing urbanisation and associated car use.

A number of measures, therefore, have been undertaken on a global and regional scale to reduce the impact of transport and its associated environmental effects. These have provided a framework for action. Action will also be required at the local level where a large component of transport impacts are located. These actions include the setting of emission limits.

Emission Limits

WHO has set guidelines and standards for air quality for 28 substances based on their effect on human health. As previously stated, these include guidelines for SO_2, NO_2 and O_3 pollutants. International limits and European limits for emissions have been set, as well as national limits which tend to vary from country to country.

In 1960, the problem of smog in Los Angeles was linked with motor vehicle emissions. This led to the State of California setting emission standards which were then followed by emission standards for tailpipe exhausts. The 1970 US Clean Air Act required motor vehicle manufactures to reduce by 90 per cent the pollution of HCs and CO within a five-year period and NO_x within a six-year period. This forced the motor industry to develop the necessary technology, which resulted in the catalytic converter (ERL, 1992). The development of tailpipe emission limits within California have resulted in similar limits being adopted by the US government, the European Commission and UNECE. The development of such standards have tended to become much stricter over the years.

The EU has been active in a number of areas related to transport and the environment. The European Community Fifth Environmental Action Programme Towards Sustainability requires that overall quality of life should be maintained and irreparable damage to the environment be avoided. Transport is one of the target areas of the plan with the objective to achieve 'sustainable mobility', and contain the environmental impacts caused by transport. A host of EC directives relating to emissions from motor vehicles (70/220/EEC) have been adopted. These include emissions from diesel engines (72/306/EEC), (88/77/EEC), the sulphur content of fuel oils (75/716/EEC), sulphur dioxide and particulates (EEC/80/372), lead in air (82/884/EEC), nitrogen dioxide (85/203/EEC), and lead in petrol (85/210/EEC). The proposed 1996 EC standards (EEC/89/433) for emissions from passenger cars are 0.5g/km for HC and NO_x, 2.2 g/km for CO and 0.08g/km for particulate matter. These standards are similar to the 1994 US government standards, but they are less strict than the 1994 California standards.

Technological Fix

While policy instruments may be more effective in dealing with the problems arising from transport, a number of pollution control technologies have been developed which have reduced to a certain extent the local impact of transport. Exhaust emissions from motor vehicles have become an increasing problem with the rise in traffic. Several industrialised countries are now making efforts to reduce the level of vehicle emissions. In 1990, the state of California developed a plan for light vehicles which took effect in 1994. Over the 1994–2003 period, an increasingly large proportion of the car fleet will be made up of vehicles with low emissions. By 2003, 75 per cent of the fleet is expected to consist of cars emitting up to 0.045g/km of non-methane HCs. From 1994, heavy vehicles have not been allowed to emit more than 5.0g of NO_x, 1.3g of HC, 15.5g of CO and 0.10g of particulates per brake horsepower-hour (Swedish EPA, 1992).

Technological advances have concentrated on a number of areas which have examined the modifications of engines, anti-pollution devices such as the three-way catalytic converter, the use of alternative fuels and potential for electric or hybrid motor vehicles (ERL, 1992). Technology can reduce specific emissions per vehicle kilometre but cannot work indefinitely to compensate for an increase in kilometres driven. In the UK, the effect of catalytic converters will have largely disappeared by 2015 as increased vehicle use more than compensates for improved engine efficiency and catalytic converter technology.

A focus on exhaust emissions misses the importance of the whole lifecycle of the vehicle and the environmental impact of all the stages involved in raw material extract, processing, manufacturing, and use and disposal. Improvements in exhaust emission performance are only a small part of the much larger picture of environmental pollution.

Engine Technology

The efficiency of the internal combustion engine is influenced by a number of factors such as the type of fuel used, the compression ratio (the way fuel and air are introduced), as well as the ignition and engine cooling systems (ECMT, 1993). Manufacturers are improving the operation of engines such as basic performance, drivability, safety and reliability, and reducing the amount of emissions without affecting the fuel economy. The air-to-fuel ratio influences the varying amounts of pollutant emitted with different types of engines and the use of catalytic converters.

Lean burn engines operate at a fuel–air ratio of 18:1–21:1 compared with 14.7:1 for normal engines. This makes it more fuel efficient and reduces the emissions of NO_x and CO, but increases the content of HCs.

Engine technology in combination with a number of other environmental design features has produced a new generation of vehicles with much reduced environmental impacts when measured on a 'per vehicle' basis. The Volvo 'Environmental Concept Car' (ECC) uses aluminium to reduce the mass of the vehicle by 12 per cent compared with similar steel body cars. It reduces rolling resistance by 50 per cent through the use of special tyres and its drag coefficient is 30 per cent lower than a corresponding model. Its power is provided by a diesel-powered gas turbine engine that generates electricity and recharges its own batteries. The gas turbine engine is not connected to the wheels. The energy generated can be stored in batteries or used directly to drive the electric motor that in turn drives the wheels. The car can be driven on the batteries alone which meets the Californian zero-emission requirements, that is no exhaust emission at all. The gas turbine operation will meet the ultra low emission standards (ULEV) of future Californian legislation. Hydrocarbon emissions are one-tenth of California's 1992 Model Year Standards, and NO_x emissions are approximately half. The ECC is a significant improvement on the internal combustion engine and virtually eliminates waste heat. The engine or power plant in the ECC can operate at a constant speed which significantly improves fuel economy and reduces air pollution.

Amory Lovins at the Rocky Mountain Research Centre in the US has taken the design several steps further in a 'concept ultra-light hybrid' that he designed and tested on a computer.The Lovins Supercar would weigh less than half that of a conventional car with a fuel economy of at least 1.5 litres/100km. This vehicle could travel more than 300km (for example, London to Manchester) on 4.54 litres of petrol and can switch between fuels for its electricity generation plant. Carbon dioxide emission would be 85 per cent lower than current models can achieve and NO_x emissions even lower.

Clearly new technology has a great deal to offer in improving the design of vehicles to reduce air pollution. The same technology does not, however, address the problems of energy use in manufacture, land take, road traffic accidents and community disruption. The Volvo ECC or the Lovins hybrid will still require the conversion of large parts of the world's cities into parking lots and freeways and will still demand new highway capacity that will crisscross the landscape, consume vast amounts of materials and divide communities. A full audit of the environmental impact of vehicles of any kind has to take into account social, neighbourhood and community impacts which are conspicuously absent in the Lovins and Volvo technological fixes.

Catalytic Converters

The three-way catalytic converter is the principal technology for reducing emissions from motor vehicles and has been used worldwide. The EC required that all new vehicles sold after 1993 were to be fitted with a catalytic converter. The catalytic converter enables the reduction of HCs, CO and NO_x. It works by removing oxygen from NO_x and converts HC and CO to CO_2 and water. Cars fitted with converters are required to use unleaded petrol, because leaded petrol damages the catalysts used.

Although catalytic converters reduce some emissions at the local level, they do not reduce CO_2 emissions. In practice, a car with a catalytic converter uses more fuel than one without, and so causes a CO_2 penalty. For the cleaning process of a catalytic converter to work effectively it must reach a temperature of 300°C, which it gets to after it has travelled for 1km. On a cold morning a car must travel for one to two kilometres to reach the 300°C threshold. In this cold state the engine emits as much CO and HCs as it would in warm conditions over a distance of 375km and 160km respectively (Swedish Environmental Protection Agency, 1992).

Catalytic converters add to the pollution levels of rare metals used in the manufacture and add to disposal problems at the end of their life. There is clear evidence that their effectiveness declines as they age, thus reducing the size of the pollution reduction claimed for a given number of cars or vehicle-kilometres.

Alternative Fuels

To deal with the pollution and energy costs from the private car, attempts have been made to replace conventional gasoline and diesel fuel with cleaner burning fuels. These have included alcohol-based fuels such as ethanol and methanol, compressed natural gas, liquefied petroleum gas, and electricity. Although alternative fuels may be preferable to existing fuels, all of them will have some impact on the environment, especially if the full lifecycle of fuel is considered from production to consumption.

Those alternative fuels which are carbon-based are considered the best because they have smaller molecules and are similar to gasoline. These molecules tend to burn more cleanly than gasoline because they have few, or no, carbon–carbon bonds, and the hydrocarbons which are emitted are less likely to generate ozone. Those fuels which involve the combustion of larger carbon–carbon bonds require a more complex series of reactions which increases the probability of incomplete combustion.

Alcohol

Biofuels such as ethanol and methanol are less polluting than fossil-based fuels, have a low carbon and sulphur content, and can be produced from biomass resources which are considered renewable. They tend to have a higher energy content per volume than other alternative fuels and require minimal changes in the existing distribution network of motor fuel. Ethanol can be produced from biomass, while methanol can be obtained from natural gas, coal, wood or organic waste.

Methanol has a number of advantages as an alternative fuel. It can reduce by 90 per cent the emissions from motor vehicles that form ground level ozone, which is considered a major urban pollutant. Due to the properties of methanol it is possible to design vehicles which are much more energy efficient. However, vehicles which run on methanol have been criticised for emitting twice as much of the carcinogen formaldehyde as gasoline currently emits. In the US, an estimated 75 cancer cases each year are due to the formaldehyde in vehicle emissions.

The only attempt to develop a substitute for oil products on a large scale with biomass occurred in Brazil in response to the 1973–74 oil crisis. Ethanol produced from alcohol-distilled sugar cane has been used widely. The first ethanol-fuelled cars appeared in 1980 in response to the National Alcohol Programme which was established to reduce oil imports in 1975 a year after the crisis. In 1986 alcohol production stood at 11.8 million m^3, or almost 27 per cent of the total fuel consumption in the transportation sector. In 1988, 90 per cent of Brazilian cars that were produced were equipped with alcohol-burning engines and one in four of the 14 million Brazilian cars were running on alcohol. Whilst there is a substitute for petrol there is none for diesel and demand for diesel has continued to grow. Diesel now represents a large share of demand for oil products. Table 11.1 shows the transport fuel consumption in Brazil between 1975 and 1987.

Table 11.1: Transport Fuel Consumption in Brazil

Year	Diesel (%)	Petrol (%)	Alcohol (%)	Total (million toe[1])
1975	40.3	59.2	0.5	18.6
1979	47.8	44.6	7.6	22.4
1983	52.8	30.7	16.5	21.8
1987	52.3	20.8	26.9	27.9

Source: de Oliveira (1991)

Note:
[1] Tonnes of oil equivalent

Ethanol use leads to a reduction in polluting emissions to the order of 57 per cent CO_2, 74 per cent HC and 13 per cent NO_x. In 1990, 3 million vehicles were registered in the city of Sao Paulo, of which 30 per cent were alcohol-fuelled, 60 per cent gasoline-fuelled, and about 10 per cent used diesel. Approximately half of the gasoline-fuelled vehicles regularly used 'gasohol' (a mixture of gasoline and anhydrous ethanol). The use of these fuels in Sao Paulo has actually affected ambient air concentrations of pollutants. Lead pollution fell from between 1.0 and 1.1 micrograms/m^3 of air in 1976 to between 0.1 and 0.6 in 1983, before a limit was set for 0.4 millilitre (ml) of tetraethyl lead/litre (l). These levels have tended to remain low despite a significant growth in vehicle numbers. However, the combustion of alcohol increases ambient concentrations of aldehydes, which are volatile organic compounds and precursors to O_3 smog.

The practicality of converting to biomass fuels is difficult to assess. A US study has shown that it would be possible for the US agriculture sector to accommodate a large biomass industry of more than a thousand million tonnes of biomass crop per year which could produce 8.4 million gigajoules (Gj) methanol or 9.9 million Gj ethanol. This would of course require large amounts of land to be converted to fuel production. For instance, if corn was used as a raw material it would result in almost 40 per cent of the harvest being utilised to supply only 10 per cent of automotive fuel demand. An average Brazilian distillery producing 180,000 litres/day requires 11,000 hectares of land for sugarcane production. In Brazil some distilleries are cultivating over 55,000 hectares, removing land from food cultivation and concentrating land ownership (de Oliveira, 1991). Waste from alcohol production produces 13 litres of stillage for each litre of alcohol, which creates another category of waste that requires new policies and solutions to eliminate environmental problems.

Natural Gas

Liquid petroleum gas (LPG) and compressed natural gas (CNG) have been considered as alternative fuels. It is possible to reduce emissions of ozone-forming pollutants by as much as 50 per cent if vehicles are converted to run on CNG. Light vehicles powered by natural gas have been estimated in America to emit about 0.03 to 0.06g/km of CO and about 0.25g/km of NO_x. LPG consists of butane and propane and is a by-product of petroleum and natural gas production. It is one of the most widely used alternative fuels with about 3.9 million LPG-powered vehicles worldwide. LPG production requires high capital expenditure to prepare gas for liquefaction. It therefore tends to be unavailable in such large quantities as to be a suitable alternative for gasoline and diesel oils.

By compressing natural gas to a pressure of 160–180 atmospheres, a fuel can be obtained which is easily transported and stored. CNG has been used for many years in Europe, the US and New Zealand. The use of CNG requires modifications to fuel systems and changes in maintenance and equipment. CNG is considered a safe option and is less polluting than conventional (petrol and diesel) fuels. However, it still has a number of difficulties in terms of vehicle technology and distribution systems. More importantly, natural gas is a non-renewable fuel and therefore, in the long term, will not be able to sustain demand.

Hydrogen

Hydrogen has been considered as another possible solution to the transport fuel problem in the long term. Hydrogen is less polluting than fossil fuels, and waste products consist only of water vapour and small quantities of NO_x. But it has a number of problems regarding its source, storage and use.

Hydrogen may be derived from natural gas although, as with other fossil fuels, the supply is limited and non-renewable. The alternative solution has been the production of hydrogen via the simple, though expensive, process of electrolysis, where an electric current is passed through water to produce hydrogen ions (H^+). The source of electricity would need to be obtained from renewable energy technology such as photovoltaic cells to ensure production is sustainable in the long term. Hydrogen is also difficult to store in vehicles. This is because H^+ ions only liquefy at temperatures below -253°C. This also poses problems for the distribution of the fuel.

Electric Vehicles

Electric vehicles have also been proposed as a possible means to reducing urban air pollution because they produce zero emissions at the point where the vehicle is in use. In California, stringent clean air regulations have encouraged the use of zero-emission vehicles. In September 1990, California adopted new regulations which required 40,000 zero-emission vehicles to be introduced and in use by 1998, 100,000 vehicles by 2001 and 200,000 vehicles by 2003. A number of other countries (Canada, France, Germany, Italy, Japan, the Netherlands, Sweden, Switzerland and the UK) are also undertaking research within the area of electric vehicle technology. In addition, the European Commission, the European Electric Road Vehicle Association and the World Electric Vehicle Association are conducting research.

The electric vehicles which are presently available commercially are able to travel between 50 and 80km in urban areas, and reach speeds of between 70 and 90 km per hour. The benefits of electric vehicles include low emissions of CO, NO_x and HCs, particularly in urban areas where the problem is particularly severe. Emissions will be shifted from street level to the stack of the power station. Emissions of SO_x may increase, except in those countries which have stringent emission standards or efficient power plants. Although electric vehicles provide a partial solution to the poor air quality in urban centres, they transfer the problem from one area to another. The only way to make them more environmentally favourable is to ensure that the electricity is from a renewable source.

Zero-emission vehicles have nothing to offer urban areas in terms of noise pollution, traffic danger or the conversion of car-friendly space into people-friendly space. They may also encourage nuclear power generation which has its own dangers.

The benefits of alternative fuels compared with gasoline are presented in Table 11.2.

Table 11.2: The Benefits of Alternative Fuels Compared with Gasoline

	Methanol	Ethanol	Compressed Natural Gas	Liquid Gas Petroleum	Electricity
Feedstock size/diversity	++	–	++	–	++
Environmental impacts	++	++	++	++	++
Vehicle cost	0	0	–	–	—
Vehicle utility (range, luggage space)	0	0	—	0	—
Vehicle performance	0/+	0/+	—	–	—
Current fuel operating cost (high demand)	–	—	0	0	0/+
Future fuel operating cost (high demand)	++	–	+	0	0/+
Refuelling convenience (time, complexity)	0	0	—	—	—

Source: Gray and Alson (1989)

++ Much better than gasoline
+ Somewhat better than gasoline
0 Similar to gasoline
– Somewhat worse than gasoline
— Much worse than gasoline

The use of methanol appears to offer the most advantages on a number of criteria as established by Gray and Alson (1989). However, as discussed above, methanol production requires land to be taken away from food cultivation which would have very serious implications for health and equity in certain countries in particular, for example, India and China.

Although technological measures may go some way towards reducing the impact of motorised transportation on the environment, either by changing the fuel to a renewable one or improving engine efficiency, any potential gain from technological fixes will ultimately be cancelled out by the increase in growth in traffic and consumption of fuels.

Life-Cycle Approaches

The discussion of alternative fuels in isolation carries with it a risk of distortion and unreliable estimates of environmental impact. A life-cycle approach overcomes these disadvantages and examines in detail all the stages of a vehicle's life, the life of its components, the use of fuels and its final disposal. At each stage energy is used: for example, in the extraction of raw material resources, in their transport, in processing and all the intermediate transport and distribution involved in the sophisticated motor vehicle manufacturing industry. Such energy use is closely associated with CO_2 emissions and with a number of other pollutants. When alternative fuelled vehicles are analysed in terms of their whole lifecycle, their environmental performance is poorer than if one fuel was compared with another fuel in isolation. Figures 11.1 and 11.2 summarise the results of a life-cycle analysis.

Figures 11.1 and 11.2 show life-cycle greenhouse gas emissions for OECD Europe for both electric vehicles and alternative fuel cars. The advantages of electric vehicles in terms of greenhouse gas reduction are only available when the fuel source is nuclear or renewable. Ethanol and methanol from wood give very little improvement over conventional fuels. Each of these alternative fuels also creates new problems. Nuclear power (feeding electric vehicles) poses a number of unresolved issues relating to pollution and waste disposal and the growing of 'fuel crops' removes land from food production.

The search for zero-emission vehicles and alternative fuels is a search for a technical fix that will permit rising levels of resource consumption and land take whilst adopting some of the concerns of sustainable development. The underlying assumption behind technological arguments for motorisation is that there is no need to reduce the demand for travel, no need to pay attention to the negative social and equity consequences of motorisation, no need to pay attention to global warming and no need to pay attention to global issues of resource availability and energy supply as a result of, for example, China and India moving towards European levels of car ownership and use.

Figure 11.1: Electric Vehicle Life-cycle Greenhouse Gas Emissions (g/km of CO_2 equivalent in urban driving)

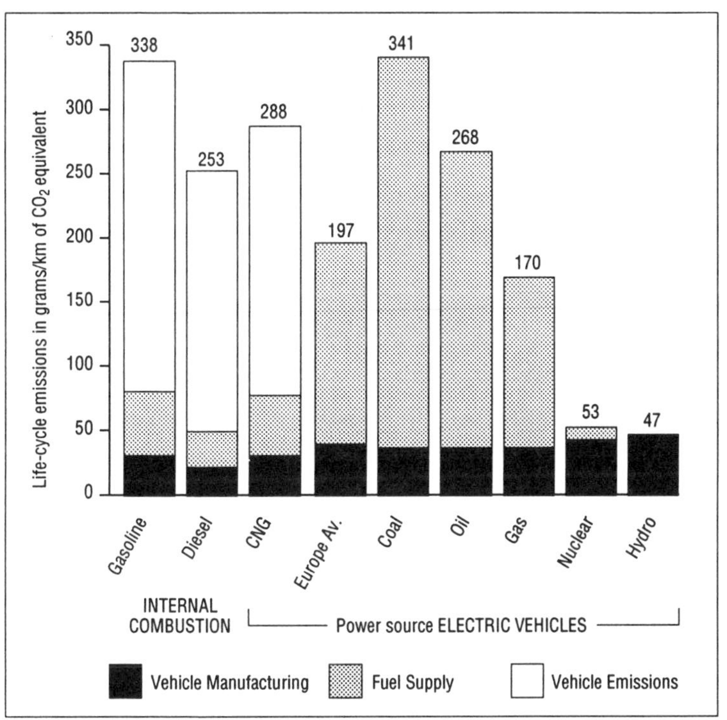

Source: OECD (1993a)

Action to reduce the demand for transport, implement the full content of sustainable development proposals and address issues of local and global equity will require more fundamental change than one of engine and vehicle technology. These include fiscal measures and land use planning measures.

Figure 11.2: Life-cycle Greenhouse Gas Emissions for Alternative-Fuel Cars (g/km of CO_2 equivalent)

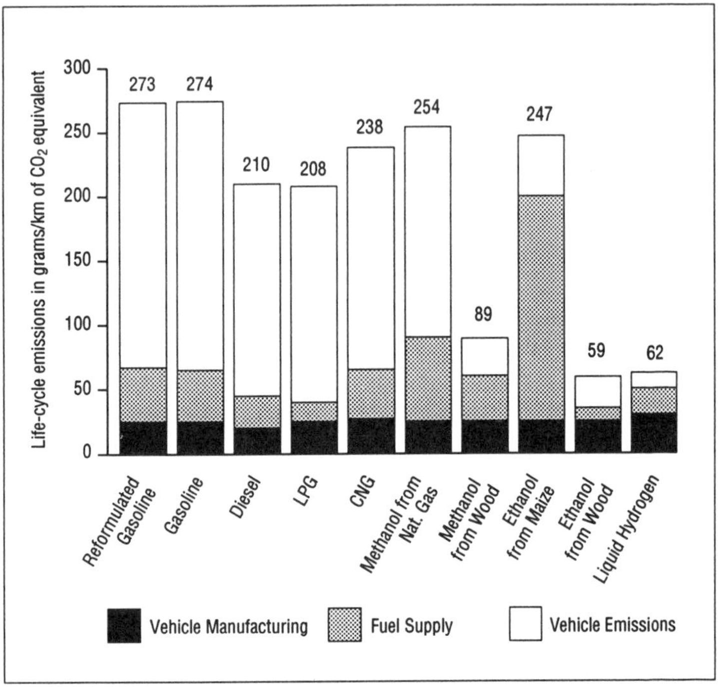

Source: OECD (1993a)

Fiscal Measures

The European Fifth Environmental Action Programme, together with a number of national environmental strategies, gives prominence to the need for fiscal and economic incentives as strong signals to everyone involved in production and consumption of the 'true' costs of energy consumption, transport, waste generation, water use and raw material consumption. This approach is often referred to as environmental taxation or green taxation but has deeper roots in the 'polluter pays' principle and in von Weizsäcker's phrase 'prices should tell the ecological truth' (von Weizsäcker and Jesinghaus, 1992).

The experience of derelict land reclamation, the management of landfill sites and the spiralling cost of transport infrastructure have shown the extent to which the costs of supporting the full lifecycle of any human activity are considerably in excess of the price the user pays. In the case of transport, the external costs are very large indeed and have been estimated to be three to five times greater than the total income in all forms of taxation.

In the case of car trips, the Umwelt- und Prognose Institut in Heidelberg (an environment forecasting institute) estimates that all forms of taxation from car purchase and use in Germany cover 25 per cent of the costs they impose in terms of air pollution, noise pollution, accidents, road construction and maintenance. In the case of lorries this falls to approximately 18 per cent. This is effectively a large subsidy to motorised transport which then influences the level of demand. The polluter pays principle clearly implies that these costs should be recouped from those who benefit from the car or lorry journey. In European discussions this attempt to recoup the full costs of any particular activity is known as internalising the external costs and applies equally to waste disposal, raw material extraction (for example, oil), energy production and transport.

Ecological Taxation Reform

Weizsäcker and his colleagues at the Wuppertal Institute have taken these ideas much further with a proposal for wide ranging and fundamental change in the whole taxation system. Ecological taxation reform (ETR) is designed to shift the burden of taxation from labour to raw materials, energy and pollution. The objective is to maximise economic gains arising from high environmental standards whilst reducing the materials and energy intensity of society. The total tax take would not increase, the reform would be constrained so that it was not regressive (that is, the poor would not be disproportionately penalised) and the objective would be to steer the whole economy in the direction of sustainable development.

In the case of transport, ETR would lead to a steep increase in the costs of motorised transport and a reduction in the costs of public transport and collective transport. The prospects for walking and cycling would improve dramatically as their benefits, from a cost point of view, became apparent, and there would be new market opportunities for retail leisure and employment opportunities based on local supply of goods and services as the costs of longer distance transport increased. This restructuring would not take place overnight but would happen over a 30 to 40 year period so as to minimise the potentially disruptive impact on firms and organisations and ease the transition to land use patterns of residential, work, school, shop and health activities based on the assumption of reduced travel.

External costs in transport can be internalised in a variety of ways. Existing systems of fuel taxation transfer resources from the car and lorry owner to the state. It would be very simple to calculate the full external costs of road transport and recoup these through increased levels of fuel taxation. The Netherlands has an environmental component in its fuel taxation of 6 pence/ litre, as do Norway and Sweden. The EU is also planning to harmonise all fuel taxes throughout Europe. It remains to be seen whether or not the EU will give priority to its own self-declared objectives in the Fifth Environmental Action Programme to reduce environmental damage at source. Increased fuel taxation presents a policy instrument that can achieve this objective but has met powerful opposition from those groups who see reduced transport costs as the primary lubricant of economic growth and full employment.

There are a number of other methods that can reduce the subsidy to motorisation and increase the degree of internalisation of external costs. They include car parking fees, road pricing, distance–weight taxes for lorries and the abolition of complex systems of supporting car use, for instance through company car schemes and employer provided car parking arrangements. The provision of cars, car parking places, and contributions to car maintenance costs by employers to their staff or by self-employed individuals to themselves, remains a substantial block to any move towards internalisation of external costs. It is also a major source of inequality since these same benefits are rarely extended to those individuals who walk or cycle to work.

Some caution on internalising the external costs of transport is necessary however. A strategy aimed at reducing the demand for transport by implementing the full force of the polluter pays principle is a logical use of market forces. But this still misses some important policy objectives that can be identified for transport. A policy change in the direction of increased fuel taxation would need to pay attention to the degree of financial 'insulation' from the policy that subsidised motoring represents in the shape of the company car and free car parking. It would also need to provide a framework for alternative travel arrangements in the short, medium and long term.

A framework for alternative travel arrangements would involve improvements to public transport systems (short term) and improvements to the urban environment that would favour walking and cycling (medium term). In the long term changes in the land use system would bring locational patterns into line with the advantages of walking and cycling, thus bringing about a fundamental reduction in the demand for transport.

Road Pricing

Economic measures have also been used to regulate the demand for road space which is considered a limited resource, especially during peak hours of the day and at particular congestion 'hot spots'. Tolls have been charged on some roads and bridges in Europe and North America since the eighteenth century. In 1964, the Smeed Report gave prominence to the concept of road pricing in Britain. The report argued that individuals should be charged for the congestion which they cause. Although the economic arguments were accepted at the time, the possibility was rejected for technical reasons given the unreliability of metering systems and cost of implementation. Today, with advances in technology, electronic road pricing has been developed. This is where either the number plate of a car or 'smart cards' are used to register the presence of a vehicle and implement the charge. The aim of road pricing has been to reduce congestion by charging users for a good which has normally been considered free. Secondary benefits have been a reduction in noise and air pollution and in the number of accidents. Road pricing aims to deter people from using their vehicle at a particular time and in a particular place. This aims to reduce the amount of non-essential traffic, such as that for leisure activities, and provide greater accessibility for important 'essential' business trips. Those important business vehicles such as goods delivery vehicles and emergency vehicles are normally exempt from any charge. A number of cities, Singapore, Hong Kong, Stockholm, Oslo and Trondheim included, have already installed some form of road pricing.

Road pricing has given rise to a number of concerns which have included equity, particularly where disadvantaged members of society, such as the disabled and low income families, could not afford to pay the cost. Road pricing may also encourage traffic to be diverted to minor roads which pass through towns and villages which are unsuitable for large amounts of traffic. Concern for civil liberties has been associated with electronic pricing due to the possibility of monitoring individual movements via an electronic register of car plates and billing systems.

Road pricing is an imperfect device for achieving its own declared objectives. There is already a large element of traffic suppression in congested urban areas and it is unlikely that road pricing will make much of an impact on roads that are already congested. Equally, it is very likely that road pricing will displace traffic to non-priced roads or lower-priced roads.

In the medium to long term, road pricing could act as a tax on central area activities and deflect development to suburbia or out-of-town locations. These are precisely the locations where traffic growth is high and where activities are more car dependent. The consequences of this process could be the 'doughnut' city characteristic of some American urban centres – empty in the centre surrounded by a ring of development.

Cycling, Walking and Public Transport

Walking and cycling are of the greatest importance in any assessment of transport, urban design, environmental impact and application of sustainable development principles to urban areas. They are far more important than public transport, which in its turn is far more important than the car.

Both cycling and walking can be considered the only truly environmentally friendly modes of transport which can be sustained in the future, especially when one considers that distances travelled within urban areas are of mainly short distances which are capable of being undertaken on foot or by bike, given the right conditions. A number of measures can be introduced which encourage more cycling and walking. For cycling, safety is an important aspect and measures include actions such as segregated cycleways, special arrangements at junctions, limiting the speed of motor vehicles, and provision of direct and continuous, safe-cycle paths. In addition, safe, secure and covered bicycle parking facilities near main transport nodes is essential.

Walking can only be encouraged if it is taken seriously as a mode of transport. Walking, like cycling, needs high levels of safety and security, clear pavements, clearly defined networks of routes and clear linkages into other policies, such as 'safe routes to schools'. Walking can be encouraged by the provision of new and more direct routes, the removal of traffic, the reduction of speeds and the physical redesign of cities and neighbourhoods to give priority to pedestrians. For both walking and cycling, the most effective stimulus is likely to be vehicular traffic reduction and a reduction in air pollution, noise and danger. Land use changes which increase the densities of facilities in a location will also stimulate these modes.

In the Netherlands, cycling accounts for 29 per cent of all journeys and 8 per cent of passenger kilometres travelled. This is quite high when compared with an average of 4 per cent of journeys within the UK. In 1992, the Dutch ministry of transport published a bicycle master plan which set out specific targets to be achieved. These included an increase in the number of kilometres travelled by bicycle by 30 per cent by the year 2010, compared with 1986.

The Dutch city of Delft developed a bicycle network in 1982 based on three levels: the city level, the district level and the sub-district level. The network consisted of two large tunnels; three bridges; 3.3km of new bicycle track; 2.6km of streets which are bi-directional for cycles but one-way for cars; 8.5km of bicycle lanes and tracks; and 10km of new asphalt pavement. These improvements to the Delft bicycle network resulted in changes in the modal split and saw the use of the bicycle increase from 40 per cent to 43 per cent. This increase was due to a shift from other modes.

In the UK, the city of York has achieved a high level of cycle use through careful planning and prioritisation of walking and cycling above motorised modes. Approximately 20 per cent of journeys to work in York are by bicycle, which should be compared with the national average in the UK of 3 to 4 per cent. York has been awarded the title of Britain's No. 1 Cycling City by *New Cyclist* magazine and is now developing a 120km pedestrian network. In addition, York has traffic-calmed about 20 per cent of its street network and brought about a 40 per cent reduction in accidents since the 1981–85 base period. York's experience shows very clearly what can be done even within the poorly funded and deregulated world of UK transport policy.

Land Use and Planning

The contribution land use planning could make in reducing the number of trips undertaken by an individual (trip generation), was recognised as early as 1963 when Colin Buchanan produced his report 'Traffic in Towns'. The report focused on land use and transport and examined the long-term effects of road development on the urban environment in Britain. Whilst acknowledging the benefits of motor vehicles, it also identified the negative impact of noise, visual intrusion and accidents. The report suggested the design of compact cities based on the principle of circulation to serve environmental areas. Environmental areas were defined as relatively free of traffic, and designed in a manner whereby traffic was related in character and volume to the environmental conditions being sought. Applying this concept produces a cellular structure consisting of environmental areas set within a network of distributor highways.

With increased suburbanisation and people moving from the city to the outskirts, there has been an increase in the home-to-work journey and to everyday facilities. Travel and transport developments have interacted to allow significant land use changes. The result has been the development of more energy-intensive land use and activity patterns. Land use planning has been shaped by the increasing dominance of the motor vehicle as the main mode of transport. Dependence on motor vehicles has increased with both decentralisation of activities and the siting of large shopping complexes out-of-town, further intensifying dependence on the motor vehicle. This process has been to the detriment of inner city centres which have tended to become less attractive locations.

A number of measures have been taken to deal with transport and land use in congested cities. By developing more compact cities, where there are shorter distances to the workplace and recreational activities, the need to travel can be reduced. A study by the departments of environment and transport (DoE) in Britain examined the extent to which land use planning could contribute to reducing the demand for travel, and hence CO_2 emissions. The study concluded that planning policies in combination with transport measures could reduce the projected transport emissions by 16 per cent over a 20 year period. A 10–15 per cent saving in the use of fuel and hence emissions from passenger transport might be achieved through land use change at the city/region scale over a 25-year period (DoE, 1993). In March 1994, the UK government published planning policy guidance (PPG13) on transport to meet the commitments made towards implementing sustainable development. The guidance aims to ensure that local authorities coordinate land use policies and transport programmes so as to reduce the growth in the number and length of motorised journeys and to encourage alternative modes of transport which have a lower impact on the environment. The guidance encourages the implementation of a form of location policy in Britain which sites development projects near adequate transport facilities and reduces dependency on the car. Measures to reduce car use include limiting car parking space, traffic management, provision of facilities for cyclists and pedestrians and improved location decision-making to ensure that developments are accessible to public transport.

In the Netherlands the concept of 'location policy' has been adopted in national physical planning policy. One of the main aims of current Dutch policy is to reduce the level of mobility and the use of motorised transport while stimulating the use of bicycles. In the past, the long-term implications of choosing a particular site were given little attention, resulting in poor accessibility due to large volumes of traffic. Location policy involves the siting of new business and services at appropriate locations accessible by both car and public transport. Each company will tend to have its own transport needs. The role of location policy is to ensure that the company is sited in the most effective location. For example, companies with high numbers of employees will be sited near public transport facilities, while a company with a low number of employees or which requires greatest use of motorised transport will be sited near a main road or at a motorway junction. The location policy divides sites into 'A' , 'B' and 'C' locations. These are described in Table 11.3:

Table 11.3: Location Policy Categorisation

A-Locations: Very accessible by public transport, such as sites near main public transport facilities, central stations in large urban areas. Accessibility by motor vehicles is of secondary importance, car commuting is restricted.
B-Locations: Sites which are reasonably accessible by both car and public transport. Situated on main urban trunk roads or near motorway exits. Parking geared towards business and services with a moderate dependence on motorised transport.
C-Locations: Mainly car-oriented locations which are sited near motorway exits on the fringe of urban areas and poorly accessible by public transport. Limited number of employers. Directed towards supply and distribution of goods by road

(Source: based on Hilbers and Verroen, 1992).

The city of Groningen in the north of the Netherlands has taken action to integrate traffic and transport planning. The main aim of transport policy has been to enable the city to be more accessible while restricting car traffic and promoting alternative, less polluting modes. Public transport and bicycles are given priority while car traffic is restricted selectively. Traffic which is economically necessary, for example city centre deliveries, is unaffected, while non-essential commuter traffic is curbed. The approach of Groningen to deal with traffic growth within the city has improved the quality of the urban environment. The city has encouraged cycling and walking by restricting the use of cars and more pedestrianised areas have been created. Transport and physical planning have been integrated to deal with the actual need to travel from home to work or to public facilities. The measures have influenced the modal split of the residents of Groningen, and now about 48 per cent of the residents go by bicycle to work, 31 per cent by car, 5 per cent by public transport and 17 per cent by foot. The city council estimates that bicycle use is 10–15 per cent higher than other cities of comparable size, whilst the use of the car is 15 per cent lower.

In Europe a number of cities have begun to take an interest in becoming car free, with the city of Amsterdam leading the way. On 25 March 1992 a referendum was held in Amsterdam on whether or not action should be taken to make the city car free. Just over 52 per cent of those who voted in the referendum voted for a car-free city, and, although not conclusive, this was endorsed by the city council. Measures contained in Amsterdam's plan include reducing the number of parking places, improving public transport and giving priority to trams and buses.

European cities demonstrate a wide variation in the degree of dependence on different modes of transport. The importance of public transport in Stockholm or Zurich is the result of policies to develop that mode of transport as part of an overall strategy aimed at turning the tide of congestion and stemming the harmful consequences of pollution. In comparison, non-motorised modes of transport are dominant in Groningen and Munster (see Table 11.4) reflecting the prominence given to these modes in those cities.

Table 11.4: Percentage of Journeys by Different Modes of Transport in Selected European Cities (various years 1984–1989)

	Foot/bike	Public transport	Car
Groningen	60	8	32
Munster	55	7	38
Bologna	40	30	30
Munich	36	24	40
Amsterdam	35	25	40
Zurich	29	42	29
Hanover	27	24	49
Stockholm	12	55	34
UK	6	14	71

Sources: Mainland European data from 'Handbuch der Kommunalen Verkehrsplanung, Economica Verlag', 1993. UK data from 'National Travel Survey', 1985/86

Table 11.4 very clearly shows Britain's poor performance in providing genuine choice or alternatives to the domination of the car.

In practice, sustainable transport solutions at the local level, particularly in urban areas, will involve elements from all major policy areas including support of the alternatives to the car, land use planning, fiscal measures to internalise externalities and car-free concepts to reassert the primary importance of people and places as opposed to cars and roads. It will be for each city to decide what it wants to deliver by way of quality of life for its residents in the twenty-first century, and where its priorities lie amongst this rich diet of policy options.

Project and Policy Appraisal

In the planning system, project appraisal has been used to ensure full consideration is given to the environmental impacts which result from transport projects such as the construction of road and rail infrastructure, airports and runways. Environmental impact assessment (EIA) is becoming an increasingly important environmental management tool used to assess the impact of such development projects on the environment.

EIA stems from the US 1969 National Environmental Protection Act (NEPA) which was introduced during a period when environmental protection was being recognised as a legitimate political objective, when people were demanding greater accountability from politicians generally, and when 'experts' were challenged to provide technical justification for projects and development proposals. Since the passage of NEPA over two decades ago, some form of EIA has been adopted by the majority of Western industrialised countries. In addition, a number of developing and eastern European countries and a substantial number of agencies have incorporated EIA into their activities. The European Commission adopted directive 85/337/EEC in 1985: The Assessment of the Effects of Certain Public and Private Projects on the Environment. Principle 17 of the Rio Declaration states that EIA should be used as a national instrument to assess the likely significant adverse impact of proposed activities on the environment.

EIA can be described as a process for identifying the likely consequences for the biogeophysical environment and for man's health and welfare of implementing particular activities and for conveying this information, at a stage when it can materially affect their decision, to those responsible for sanctioning the proposals (Wathern, 1988).

The EIA process consists of a number of steps of which the production of an environmental impact statement (EIS) is just one. The approaches to EIA have tended to be diverse in practice, for example in the type of projects subject to EIA and the different ways EIA has been integrated into the planning process. The application of EIA to transport has been mainly project based, with one mode of transport being considered in isolation. Due to the nature of EIA, it has been mainly constrained to individual projects and has received increasing criticism for coming at a late stage in the decision making process.

EIA tends to be reactive rather than proactive and therefore only allows proposals to be either accepted or rejected. By the time the EIA stage has been reached, it is too late to consider alternatives. In the case of road transport, once a decision has been made to build a road the alternatives considered are concerned with the different alignments of the road or other changes to the infrastructure design. Consideration of cumulative impacts, such as transboundary impacts, are very rare. EIA only addresses the direct impacts of a development and does not consider the cumulative impacts of a development project. A localised, project-based EIA fails to go far enough in identifying the project's contribution to higher level environmental problems, for example, the contribution of a road scheme to tonnes of air pollutants which result in the formation of acid rain.

The mid-1990s has witnessed a large number of damaging road projects proceed where an EIA has been seen as part of the evidence in support of the scheme. Twyford Down near Winchester in the UK represents a watershed in the development and reputation of the EIA as a process that can help to protect landscape and the environment.

The Twyford Down cutting and the destruction of archaeological and historical landscape, and sites of importance for plant life, was supported by an EIA. This is not an isolated example and reveals the EIA as a seriously flawed process of dilution and manipulation designed to support the political process that has already decided that road expansion is preferable to rail or increases in demand for transport are preferable to reduction.

With increasing concern over the nature of global and regional environmental problems there have been attempts to apply EIA at the strategic level to policies programmes and plans. Increasingly, international agreements and conventions are setting objectives and targets to achieve environmental sustainability in a wide range of areas. Some form of strategic environmental assessment would provide a means of ensuring these objectives are met. A number of international organisations have now recognised the need for strategic environmental assessment (SEA), including the EU, the OECD and UNECE. The European Commission prepared a draft directive on SEA in 1992, while a number of national and state governments have begun to advocate some form of policy appraisal, including Australia, Finland, Germany, Hong Kong, Japan, the Netherlands, New Zealand and California.

The transport sector has been identified as a suitable area for the application of SEA. This would enable consideration to be given to the total impact of road construction programmes such as those presently being pursued by the British government and by the European Commission in its trans-European road network. The value of SEA in the transport sector is that it would enable informed choices to be made at an early stage in the decision-making process where they are most important. This would enable more general and strategic issues to be resolved, including the role of different transport modes, land use policies and transport policies. A more multi-modal approach to dealing with transport problems could then be developed, rather than an over-dependence on road-based transport which is a feature of the present planning approach.

An SEA was undertaken on the European high speed train network, which was proposed by the EU. One study developed alternative scenarios for the outline plan that has been developed by the Commission. It concluded that a high speed train network could make a 'positive' contribution to the natural environment and could change the modal split of intercity traffic. Other studies have included the Betuwelijn Cargo Rail Line proposed by Dutch Railways in 1992, and the road programme proposed in Nordrhein-Westfalen in 1993.

An SEA requires that explicit objectives are set for the development under consideration. This is of considerable value in the transport policy sector where large expenditures can be associated with very large objectives. Objectives can either be quantitative in the form of specific targets or qualitative in the form of statements of intent. For example, to reduce the transport sector's contributions to national CO_2 emissions by x per cent by the year 'z'. Such targets may be based on international agreement such as the UNECE agreements discussed earlier. Once objectives have been set a number of options can be pursued to ensure that the objectives are met. These include technological measures, fiscal measures and land use planning measures.

In 1989 the Dutch government produced its second transport structure plan which it is possible to view as a transport policy which has resulted from strategic planning. The plan is based on sustainable development and developing a transport system which finds a balance between individual freedom, accessibility and environmental amenity. The plan has been coordinated with physical planning and environmental policies and the full impacts of the transport sector are covered. It has set specific policy objectives and targets which have provided guidance to project-based EIA. Although the Dutch transport plan is not considered an SEA in itself, it has a strong link with an environmental impact study at a strategic level and its effect is comparable to that of an SEA. By having explicit objectives and targets the Dutch have been able to monitor the progress made towards achieving the targets they have set. For example, the Dutch set a target to reduce NO_x and HCs by 20 per cent from road transport by 1995, and by 75 per cent by 2010. For CO_2 emissions from road traffic, the Dutch set a target to stabilise emissions at 1989/90 levels by 1995, and to reduce them by 10 per cent by 2010. In September 1993 the Dutch ministry of transport published the first annual evaluation report of its transport plan. This showed that emissions of both NO_x and HCs had been reduced and the 1995 target was within reach. This has been due to the introduction of catalytic converters, the use of which was encouraged by fiscal incentives. Emissions of CO_2 from the road sector have continued to rise, however, and the target for 1995 has not achieved. Emissions of NO_x and CO_2 from freight transport have also increased whilst those from personal car transport have decreased.

Although SEA may pose methodological problems in its implementation, it will enable greater attention to be given to the environmental impact of transport at an early stage, and will enable a wide range of options to be available to deal with transport problems. It requires objectives and targets to be explicitly stated, and this in turn requires national governments to articulate clearly a transport policy which in many countries (for example, Britain) can be vague. The impact on the regional, national and global level will also be taken into consideration, which is a contrast to the present project-based EIA which only considers a single action or project on a local or regional basis.

One of the main benefits of SEA is that it provides a mechanism to implement sustainability.

With the rise in the number of international agreements and treaties, and the setting of specific targets, SEA will provide a systematic mechanism through which progress towards achieving these targets can be maintained and adjusted.

Conclusion

A large number of measures can be used to resolve the impact of transport on the environment and to steer cities and regions towards a sustainable future. These range from the local to the international level, and from the short to the long term. Each individual measure discussed in this chapter has advantages and disadvantages. None of these measures used in isolation can provide a solution to the transport problem. Although technical fixes and fiscal policy may make some progress towards mitigating the impact of using roads, and discouraging people from using their motor vehicles, they do not go far enough.

To achieve a more sustainable transport system a package of measures need to be taken to reduce the need to travel and to reduce the environmental impact of transport. Emphasis should be placed on more strategic planning and the integration of environmental and physical planning and transport policies, which are objective-led and which set specific targets. Good, reliable, comfortable alternative solutions to motorised transportation need to be developed. Further action will need to curb the unsustainable growth in motorised transport, which threatens quality of life and alienates people from their surroundings and local environment.

The extent to which governments and international agencies will enforce and implement such measures will depend on a number of varying political and economic factors. Their interpretation of the concept of sustainable development will play an important role in the measures adopted. As discussed in Chapter 7, sustainability can be divided into weak and strong sustainability. In the context of transport, technological fixes alone such as engine efficiency and the development of electric vehicles will not solve the problems of transport, and are therefore considered weak measures. They may even contribute to non-sustainability through the continuation of 'business as usual' strategies beyond critical thresholds.

Strong sustainability measures are those which grasp the nettle of restricting individual mobility whilst improving accessibility and reducing the actual need to travel and thus the demand to travel. Fiscal measures may play a prominent role within this area, although there is always the issue of inequity associated with such measures. It is almost inevitable that the wealthy in society will continue to travel relentlessly by any mode regardless of changes in the price of transport. Nevertheless, land use planning can reduce the need to travel for everyday activities and so benefit lower income groups by reducing the total cost of their journeys.

Sustainable development in transport means far more than restricting the demand for travel. It means increasing accessibility by non-motorised modes of transport, improving health and quality of life and benefiting households and individuals financially by removing the 'necessary' element in much of car ownership and use. Sustainable transport means more choice and more freedom to do without a car if that is thought appropriate. This itself can benefit the average UK car owner by at least £3,000 per annum.

Before such objectives can be achieved they must be clearly articulated at local and national level, and clearly incorporated into a democratic process of choice and accountability of the kind available in the Local Agenda 21 process. SEA stimulates the formal process of objective-setting and brings sustainable development that much nearer. However, a thorough overhaul of the democratic process, accountability and the rights of individuals over their local environment is needed before transport and land use decisions will contribute to the achievement of sustainable development objectives and WHO objectives for human health and welfare. In the next chapter the steps that will move transport and land use in this direction are identified.

CHAPTER 12

Solutions

There is no shortage of possible solutions to transport problems. Most parts of the world have an example of a strategy or policy that has been implemented to reduce the volume of traffic in urban areas, provide high quality alternatives to the car, improve air quality and make different arrangements for the movement of freight. The number and diversity of excellent alternatives is testament to widespread ingenuity and creativity. However, a lot of mindless transport planning and road building still occurs, almost blind to the developments of the last ten years. Transport planning, or, more correctly, political decision making reinforced by transport planning, can still show absolute obedience to the discredited 'predict and provide' philosophy which continues to underlie much of the expansion of road building and aviation planning.

As previously stated there is, of course, an economic logic which underlies such planning. But this logic fails to explain its past failures and fails to address the problem of centralisation and longer distances in contemporary Europe. The economic logic also fails to address the extent to which the vast majority of congestion in and near urban areas is associated with short distance car journeys and local travel. Roads built to speed urgent export orders to long distance destinations frequently provide very expensive travel opportunities for the trips to supermarkets and local schools.

Examples of good and bad planning abound in both developed and developing countries. The developing countries, with their large informal sectors and reliance on pedestrians, rickshaws and cyclists, have a great deal to pass on to urban administrations in the so-called developed world. The fact that these countries frequently view their most common modes of transport as a problem rather than as a solution requires a clear response from within these countries, as well as from the developed world, that these characteristics are desirable. And they are desirable because they are inexpensive, socially equitable, have a low energy consumption, are highly flexible, use very durable vehicles which perform very well indeed on a life-cycle analysis, are largely non-polluting and are well suited to the detailed design of the built form of the cities in which they operate. They may not be perfect but they are an excellent base for further development.

The rush to high levels of motorisation in eastern Europe and in the developing world requires a considered response from the developed world. Funding the building of roads and setting up vehicle manufacturing plants is not a considered response.

Clearly there are difficulties with the translation of problem specification and analysis into policies capable of delivering solutions. This book is intended to be a part of that process designed to facilitate and accelerate this translation. The existence of alternatives and the existence of analyses is not enough. A deeper and broader debate involving all sections of the community and involving all aspects of education and participation in decision making is just as important as (and more than) any scientific analysis.

In the developed world there are several important preconditions for change on a larger scale already in place. These include:

1. The hard evidence that traditional policies are not working – more vehicles lead to more traffic congestion, and new roads do not relieve traffic congestion, nor do they create jobs.

2. The health evidence and the prevalence of poor air quality demonstrates the need for a new direction. Respiratory disease and raised susceptibility to heart problems affect all social classes. Health damage is one of the very few democratic consequences of motorisation. Poor air quality warnings are now the norm in Britain during any period of still, warm and sunny weather, and air quality inside a vehicle is worse than at the roadside.

3. There is now abundant evidence that noisy environments damage health and well-being and that traffic is the dominant source of noise for most urban residents around the world. The search for peace and quiet in the developed world is one of the causes of urban decline and longer distance journeys as people abandon city living for rural idylls.

4. Road traffic accidents blight the lives of millions and even though accidents preferentially affect the poor and the disadvantaged, they kill a large number of young middle class people and draw attention to the need for alternatives to the private car.

5. It is possible and desirable for many people to live very happily and successfully without a car. They already do so (regardless of income group) in many parts of London, Paris and Berlin, and social mores can change to emphasise the advantages of not owning a car. In many smaller towns and cities it has proved possible for the proportion of non-motorised trips to reach as

high as 50 per cent. Delft in the Netherlands is an example of cycling success.

6. The advantages of owning a car will only be maintained if ownership (or in some cases use) is restricted. If every individual in the 17–80+ age group able to drive chose to drive for every journey greater than 500m, and expected to be able to park their car at every shop, GP surgery, school, college, workplace, bank or hospital, then the circulation system of any urban area with a population of more than 50,000 would collapse. If leisure and tourism trips continue to be largely car borne and increased free time leads to more leisure trips, then rural as well as urban areas are in difficulty. The collapse of circulation systems could be so severe it could only be rescued by the physical redesign (that is destruction) of the urban area to create a blend of freeway parking lots that leave very little of the city recognisable.

7. The loss of countryside and woodland to new roads in Britain has generated an unprecedented wave of social protest and non-violent direct action. This has exposed the failure of the political system to handle choices and conflicts, and revealed deep flaws in the democratic system itself. Attention will have to be paid to repairing this system.

   The flaws are multi-dimensional and include the inability to sustain a genuinely participatory decision-making process where local residents are key players in making choices. They also include the manifestly unfair and unbalanced public inquiry system where substantial financial resources, legal representation and expert witnesses are deployed against local residents and parish councils which have no access to funds. The public inquiry into the Birmingham Northern Relief Road was a very clear example of this fundamentally undemocratic process. The flaws go deeper, however, and reveal an inability to reconcile local versus national interests; and in the case of the European Union and the North America Free Trade Area (NAFTA), national versus international interest. At what point does a local concern for a high quality environment become tradable against a national policy goal (for example, an additional terminal at Heathrow airport) or against an international policy goal (for example, the NAFTA superhighway or the new bridge between Malmo in Sweden and Copenhagen in Denmark)? Both T5 at Heathrow airport and the new bridge between Denmark and Sweden bring with them substantial environmental impacts. Local concerns for clean air and low noise environments do not weigh heavily in the larger scale politics of transport infrastructure.

The bigger the organisation taking the decisions the more likely that local communities will be ignored. Just as big takes precedence over small, so short-term thinking takes precedence over long-term thinking, completing the space–time distortion of decision making and the destruction of the environment. It is this complex and manifest failure of the public policy process that has stimulated large-scale social protest against roads and bridges in the UK, Denmark and Sweden and the Pyrenees.

8. The environmental debate, particularly with respect to the activities of the private sector, multinational firms and national enterprises, has matured into an ethical debate. Is it ethically acceptable for a large company to be instrumental in destroying the landscape through road construction, or the atmosphere through flying aircraft? The ethical company in the twenty-first century will need to be alive to these issues and to the human rights violations that are associated with transport projects in developing countries.

9. The private sector itself sees road freight as increasingly unreliable due to congestion. Congestion disrupts the core principles of distribution and manufacturing which extol the virtues of accurate timing and perfect coordination of many different flows. Time organisation created the world of logistics at the same time as seeding its own destruction.

10. The whole transport system is increasingly in disrepute as a result of the large amounts of money that it absorbs for the very poor returns that are obtained. As climate change becomes more obvious, crop damage from ozone pollution and acidification more prevalent, and the economic consequences of spiralling mobility more severe, attitudes will shift towards more accountability and better value for money.

11. Perceptions are changing about the 'benefits' of car ownership and use. Car ownership is a substantial financial burden (at least £3,000 per annum in the UK at 1995 prices) and car use imposes substantial time penalties. The car has usurped the language of freedom and time saving whilst reducing freedoms and ensuring that people spend more time in vehicles travelling to destinations that are further away.

12. There is a growing awareness that children in the developed world are suffering as a consequence of higher levels of motorisation and car use. Their independent freedom and mobility has been eroded, their lungs are in poor condition and their sense of geography, place and community is degraded.

> This has serious and little understood consequences for their adult life and for society as a whole.

However, preconditions for change do not necessarily bring change. This still depends on an unpredictable mixture of cultural change, institutional change and political vision. Ultimately it depends on the psychological and political processes described in the prisoners dilemma later in this chapter. Whatever the probability of change it is increasingly clear that the present trajectory of spatial dispersion, vehicle use, pollution and transport investment cannot be continued into the indefinite future.

The question of change is even more problematic in developing countries. From their perspective, developed countries have gone through a number of stages that have produced high levels of per capita income as well as a number of other advantages that stem from purchasing power. This has been achieved through resource exploitation, indeed through direct exploitation of the resources of developing countries. The current proposition that we are all in this together and should all reduce, for instance, energy consumption, pollution and resource exploitation thus is likely, and understandably, to meet with robust rejection from developing countries. They will have to find their own path and the behaviour of the developed countries vis-à-vis their consumption and materials exploitation will be a large factor in what developing countries are likely to do.

Wolfgang Zuckermann (1991) who works at the Paris-based transport consultancy EcoPlan has advanced 33 solutions designed to achieve a 'new and less car-dependent existence'. He is very clear these solutions do not form an exhaustive catalogue and that the list must evolve over time and from place to place; solutions that work tend not to come out of 'cook books' but from detailed observation of local circumstances and local consensus on what should be done. The experience of the city of Amsterdam in introducing a car-free city concept has shown that the most important ingredient in change is political will and the skills needed to work within local democratic institutions. Nevertheless, some intellectual and practical pump-priming is always a good idea. Zuckermann's 33 solutions are as follows:

1. radically redesign the conventional car;
2. help car owners become aware of the true costs of using their vehicles;
3. place restrictions, or a total interdiction, on car advertising;
4. carefully design total, partial or temporary car bans in city centres;
5. traffic-calm and modify streets to give non-car users a greater share of street space;

6. use cells and mazes to protect local areas from through traffic;
7. create mixed-use pedestrian zones;
8. use parking policy as an instrument to restrict car use in cities;
9. formulate policies to prevent or punish infractions effectively;
10. strictly regulate, and place higher taxation on, trucks;
11. make cities, suburbs and the countryside more walker-friendly;
12. make bicycle use more appealing by creating a bike-friendly infrastructure;
13. close damaged roads to motor vehicles and turn them over to non-motorised transport;
14. integrate taxis into overall transport planning;
15. introduce semi-public paratransit services to provide a real alternative to private car use;
16. use pools and high occupancy vehicles for commutes to work where walking, cycling or public transport is not practical;
17. allow hitch-hiking to take its rightful place in an overall transport strategy;
18. restore local rail for efficient freight and passenger movement and as a car restraint measure;
19. use trams and light rail systems to replace private cars in cities;
20. separate busways in cities to stimulate public transport;
21. use city-wide fare cards to boost public transport;
22. use easily administered road pricing to control the number of cars on the road;
23. increase fuel taxes to discourage car use;
24. inform the public about government subsidies of automobiles to create political pressure for their removal;
25. rethink the concept of suburbs to make sterile dormitory communities into living towns;
26. plan new towns as integrated and car-independent communities;
27. bring back corner, village and general stores as well as open-air markets to stimulate suburban walking and prevent car trips to distant superstores;
28. use telecommuting to cut down the number of vehicles on the road;
29. arrange lives to be less car dependent;
30. stop giving bad advice and dirty cars to developing countries;
31. introduce consciousness-raising, role-modelling and education about the worldwide effects of the car;
32. introduce stricter attention to energy efficiency on the part of drivers;
33. carefully consider the necessity for each car trip.

Zuckermann's 33 solutions are very helpful as a template that can be applied to local situations. It is very important, however, to be clear about some basic principles.

Spatial Mobility, Lifestyle and the Demand for Transport

The growth in car traffic and the growth in lorry traffic has not come about because of a shift from rail to road, or from any mode, to private motorised transport. The car and the lorry have completely changed the spatial patterning of activities and created the demand that supply side policies try to satisfy in a hopeless and ultimately doomed attempt to satisfy what cannot be satisfied.

In wealthy and highly motorised countries (for example, Germany and the Netherlands) more than 50 per cent of car kilometres are spent on trips for leisure and holidays. Additionally, shopping has become a leisure activity – a trend more advanced in the UK than in any other European country. Car ownership creates new mobility patterns. Unlike most other examples of consumption the product (the car) is not only consumed but plays an active role in redefining the rules of consumption so that over time higher and higher levels of car use become necessary to carry out the same basic task.

The car creates a lifestyle that only the car can satisfy. Spatial structures specifically based on cars can't be served by public transport, foot and bike.

Markus Hesse (1995) at the Ecological Research Institute in Berlin and Wuppertal describes this very succinctly:

> Society as a whole is trapped by the automobile. Since lifestyle is the root problem solutions have to be very creative indeed in unpicking the bundle of factors that feed the process of motorisation.

Unpicking will require simultaneous action on a large number of fronts and over a long time period. Re-orienting space–time structures is a slow process. Rebuilding local communities, local services and attractive neighbourhoods is a slow process. It has taken almost 100 years to arrive at a position of car dominance and changes in lifestyle that continually demand more of the same. It is not unreasonable to expect that it will take at least 30–40 years to move towards a lifestyle that provides ample opportunity for local production links, local services, short distance trips, low energy using communities and very low polluting transportation systems.

This move will require targets and objectives, new kinds of investments and political priorities, but this has been done before in other areas of societal development in European history. The changes that took place in Europe to introduce sanitation and fresh water into cities, abolish child labour and establish social and healthcare provision for all were equally demanding and very successful.

Globalisation and Free Trade

Tim Lang and Colin Hines (1993) in their book *The New Protectionism* calculate that transnational corporations control 70 per cent of world trade. The top five companies direct 77 per cent of world cereal trade, the top three banana companies have 80 per cent of trade in bananas, the top three cocoa companies 83 per cent of world cocoa trade, the top three tea companies 85 per cent of tea trade, and the top four tobacco companies 87 per cent of world trade in tobacco.

This concentration of productive and trading capacity is responsible for the physical transport of commodities and manufactured products on a global scale that reap the benefits associated with this scale of operation (lower unit costs), and marshal a global advertising and product brand policy that makes very little room for smaller producers/manufacturers or local production/consumption links. Whilst this is not particularly surprising in the case of bananas and cocoa, the effects can be observed over a whole range of products and services and are a powerful source of non-sustainable long-distance transport.

The existence of the General Agreement on Trade and Tariffs (GATT) and the establishment of large free trade areas like the EU and NAFTA are intended to accelerate the process of globalisation and concentration of economic power into the hands of a small number of very large organisations. The activities of these large organisations are supported by the likes of the World Bank and the EU on the general logic that trade is good for economic development and economic development will solve the problems of poverty and inequality. In Europe, North America and globally the free trade areas of NAFTA and the EU are more likely to stimulate long-distance movement as part of the process of the capital exploitation of lower paid labour and low overhead costs which result from inadequate social security provision and inadequate environmental regulations, most often in developing countries. This is not always the case, however, and Britain has already made it clear within the EU that it will not accept the Social Chapter of Maastricht because this imposes too many cost burdens and will disadvantage UK industry and employment. The intention is to make UK employment cheaper than, say, Germany or Scandinavia, so as to attract inward investment. This will be achieved at the expense of lower welfare payments (which reduce the costs of employers) and inferior conditions for the retired (which reduces the costs of providing for this growing sector of the population). The result is a degree of success with inward investment, but only as part of the globalisation of production and consumption. This increases the amount of long-distance freight transport with resulting energy, ecological and pollution penalties.

In Europe there are numerous examples of 'useless' transport where long-distance road movements take place simply to take advantage of cheap labour or cheaper materials. Greenpeace, Zurich (1991) have described, for instance, the economics behind the road freighting of items of clothing from Sursee in Switzerland to Amares in northern Portugal, a journey of 2,000km that takes place each week to exploit wage differentials between the two countries. The garments are sent to Portugal for the sewing of seams and then returned to Switzerland for packing, marketing, quality control and sale as a quality Swiss product sold under the 'CALIDA' brand name.

This return journey consumes 1,500 litres of diesel fuel, produces 4,050kg of CO_2, 68kg of health damaging nitrogen dioxide, 1kg of carcinogenic particulates and 10kg of ozone-forming hydrocarbons. For CALIDA, the calculation does not need to be complicated by references to health, climate change or effects on trees, plants and animals. The calculation (in Swiss Francs) is shown in Table 12.1

Table 12.1: The Economics of Production and Transport (CALIDA)

	Swiss Francs
Labour costs including all overheads in Portugal at 21.45 Swiss Francs per hour and 3,300 hours work per lorry load of clothing	70,785
Labour costs for same work if done in Switzerland at 29 Swiss Francs per hour	95,700
Difference	24,915
Transport costs	6,765
Cost savings per return journey	18,150

Source: Eco-Logica (1994)

The example of CALIDA shows very clearly that long-distance transport is good for the economy of a company or transnational corporation. The environmental and social consequences of these long-distance trips are not factored into the calculation and there is currently no way of implementing the polluter pays principle and 'charging' the wider environmental costs directly to CALIDA. As long as this situation continues, road freight and air freight transport will show very high growth rates at the same time as exacting a very high environmental penalty.

Another European example of transport intensification and high environmental costs concerns the production of Parma ham. In 1989

Belgium exported 166,400 pigs to Italy (Parma) for slaughter. Two hundred animals were transported in 16 lorries per week which then returned empty. Before slaughter the pigs are fattened on skimmed milk powder which was manufactured in Hamburg, road freighted to Hartberg in Austria and then transported by more lorries across the Alps. After slaughter the pigs are converted into various products and exported to northern Europe as 'genuine' Italian ham, some of which would be consumed in Belgium.

Figure 12.1: Italian Ham

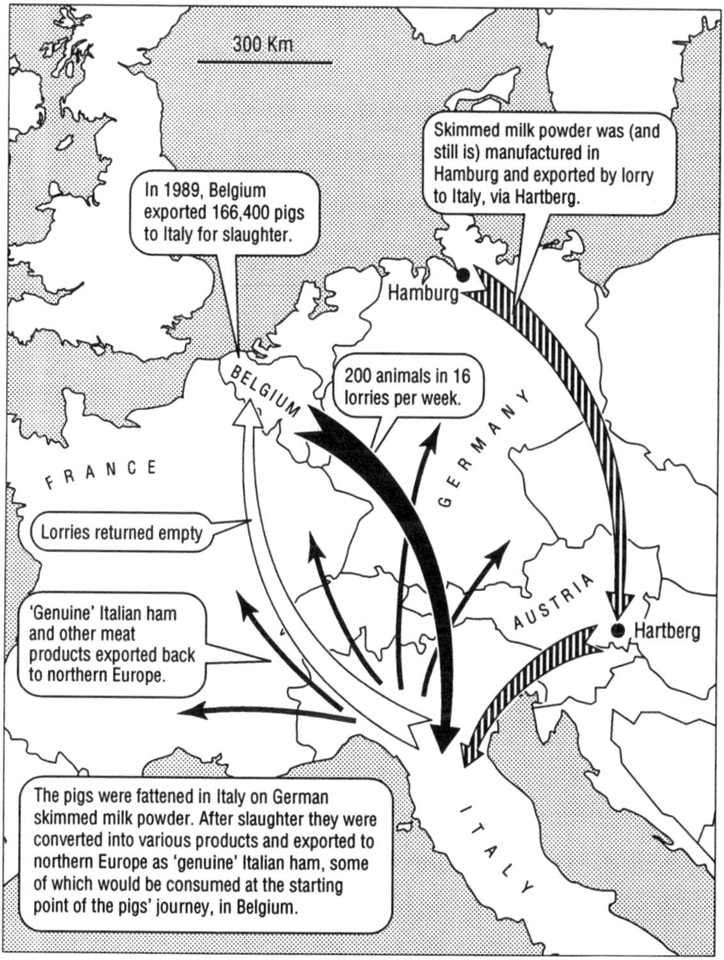

Source: Eco-Logica (1994)

Eco-Logica (1995) carried out a study for WWF (UK) identifying the basics of a solution to the growth of environmental damage and pollution by road freight. The solution takes as its starting point that a switch from road to rail will not solve the problem. As in the case of the car and personal lifestyles we have to unpick the web of factors that intensify the transportation element in production and consumption, and move to lower levels of demand. It was found that this can be done with no economic damage at the national level and with considerable benefits to local economies. Since freight is often identified as a more difficult sector in which to bring about change these suggestions for reducing demand are particularly important.

Demand Reduction

Hey *et al.* (1992) identify two main ways by which the demand for transport can be reduced:

i. procurement logistics involving the substitution of 'near suppliers' for 'far suppliers', and the minimisation of distances over which goods travel;
ii. distribution logistics involving the elimination of 'useless' transport (Eco-Logica, 1995). A great deal of road freight transport makes very circuitous journeys dictated by the pattern of distribution centres and national/international supply chains. It is possible to substitute direct for circuitous trips.

Holzapfel (1995) has identified a 67 per cent reduction potential in lorry kilometres in one sector of the food industry, 75 per cent of which is on motorways. Holzapfel takes the view that these savings underestimate the potential savings in a number of other industrial sectors:

> Compared with the potential savings in the yoghurt example, the potential savings in industrial sectors with a more complex supply structure, like for instance the car industry, are certainly much bigger. A theoretical analysis shows that the number of transport links grows with low integration of the production process and with high numbers of suppliers. The figures that were taken in the case of our yoghurt example (as for foodstuffs in general) to calculate the related potential savings were chosen in a way that they lead to an underestimate of feasible potential savings.

Strutynski (1995) has presented an argument for the reduction of freight transport through 'lean production'. He demonstrates how new forms of regional cooperation amongst suppliers and manufacturers in the car industry can substitute 'near' for 'far' and reduce distances over which goods are moved by at least 50 per cent. His conclusion is that a five-fold increase in the cost of road freight transport would produce this shift in organisation and spatial structure.

It is clear from the work of Strutynski (1995), Holzapfel (1995) and Böge (1995) that there is a potential of at least 50 per cent to reduce freight transport by road and that this potential has nothing to do with modal shift but is simply the result of substituting 'near' for 'far'. The implications of this could not be more significant.

Regionalised systems of production and consumption offer long-term economic benefits and a degree of spatial equity to Europe's local economies. The gains in environmental performance as a result of eliminating significant amounts of long-distance transport can be captured to ensure genuinely sustainable freight transport. No matter how successful our strategies for modal transfer are, they will be diluted over time as the volume of freight rises.

Towards A Sustainable Freight Transport System

The definition of sustainable freight transport in Werkgroep 2duizend (1993) calls for a 50 per cent reduction in CO_2 compared to 1990 levels. As Table 12.2 shows, this target was informed by the knowledge that freight transport activity would rise (in the basic scenario) to an indexed value of 148 in 2015 compared to 100 in 1990. A target of 50 per cent is, therefore, very difficult to achieve.

Table 12.2: The Environmental Effects of Basic Scenario 2015 and the New Course Scenario Set Off Against the Target for Sustainable Development

Environmental Effect	Basic Scenario 2015 (1990 = 100)	New Course Scenario (1990 = 100)	Sustainability Target (1990 = 100)
Energy consumption	147	54	50
CO_2 emissions	148	57	50
NO_x emissions	70	14	18

Source: Werkgroep 2duizend (1993)

In the UK context sustainability can be achieved by a three stage progression towards a similar reduction in CO_2 from the road freight sector:

i. utilising rail/road intermodalism and transferring 50–90 per cent of motorway road freight onto the railways;
ii. utilising port and waterway capacity to achieve higher levels of transfer away from road freight;
iii. reconstructing logistics and advancing the idea of regional production systems to minimise distance travelled by goods.

Each stage is associated with a timescale for implementation.

Figure 12.2 summarises stage one and reveals a potential reduction in CO_2 of 16.67 per cent. It is assumed that this can be achieved in one to five years. This reduction is approximately equal to the growth in road freight by the year 2000. The net effect therefore, in the absence of other measures, would be to wipe out this reduction and 'buy' about five years' grace in the growth of CO_2 emissions in this sector. This underlines the importance of approaches that go far beyond modal transfer from road to rail. Put more bluntly, a sustainable freight transport system cannot be built on shifting freight from road to rail.

Equally, the forecasts demonstrate that a functioning freight transport system cannot be based on the existing road system. Just-in-time transport rapidly loses its appeal if reliability levels drop. A sustainable freight transport system is one that can guarantee to maintain reliability and quality in a way that the present approach cannot.

Stage two is constructed over the longer time horizon of five to ten years. This stage takes the findings in British Maritime Charitable Foundation (1994) as its starting point. The UK port system is operating at 50 per cent of its capacity and with 300 ports there are very few parts of Britain not served in some way by a commercial port. The population centres in the Leeds, Doncaster and Sheffield area are in their turn well served by inland waterways.

It is not possible to make precise estimates of the likely transfer of freight from road to the port system for coastwise traffic or to the port system for international traffic. It is possible, however, to work to targets over a five to ten year planning period and given a 50 per cent estimate of spare capacity it is proposed that ports and inland waterways in combination with other segments of intermodal transport take up 10 per cent of the total vehicle-kilometres currently accounted for by goods vehicles. Table 12.3 summarises the impact of a 10 per cent transfer from road freight to shipping and inland waterways.

Figure 12.2: The Potential for Road/Rail Intermodalism (Stage 1)

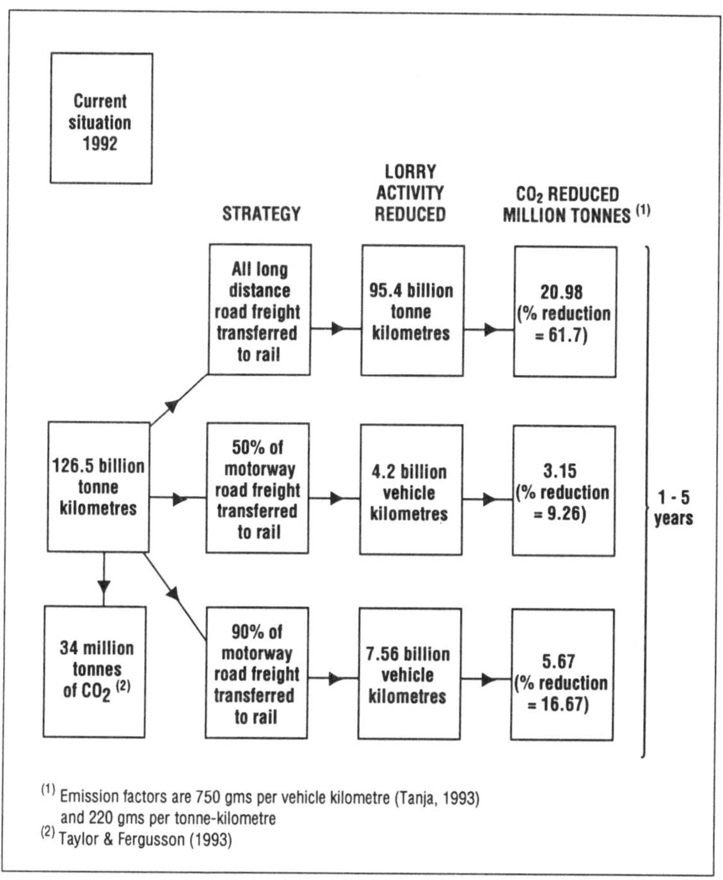

Source: Eco-Logica (1995)

A reduction of 2.13 million tonnes of CO_2 represents only 6.26 per cent of the 1992 CO_2 production in road freight. This contribution is, however, only a modest beginning. Ports and inland waterways can offer spare capacity for utilisation on a five to ten year time scale (and in some cases immediately). They also have much greater potential if regional production systems (Holzapfel, 1995) and lean production (Strutynski, 1995) become the norm.

Stage three takes freight transport into the area of 'strong' sustainability. Strong sustainability is defined here as the adoption of very clear strategies to resolve fundamental problems of growth and environmental impact. Modal transfer is categorised as 'weak' sustainability. This is because it does not tackle growth pressure in the sense of increasing amounts of distance travelled and freight movement, characteristic of contemporary European economies. Modal transfer does provide relief and is important. It will, for example, completely remove the perceived pressure for new road capacity across the Pennines. However, it only 'buys' time and itself cannot dampen down the growth in tonne-kilometres moved.

Table 12.3: Transfer of Road Freight to Shipping and Inland Waterways

Billion vehicle-kilometres by road (1992)	28.4
10% transfer	2.84
CO_2 reduction (million tonnes)	2.13

Strong sustainability involves a more ambitious strategy aimed at reducing the distances over which freight is moved by fundamentally altering the spatial relationships in production and consumption. It is designed to eliminate the illogical nature of logistics and substitute 'near' for 'far' wherever possible in the sourcing and production links of manufacturing, storage and distribution systems.

Holzapfel (1995) has calculated the potential for one category of food product and his results show that 67 per cent of vehicle-kilometres can be eliminated by using local/regional sources of inputs into the manufacture of, for example, yoghurt, rather than more distant sources. Strutynski (1995) supports this view with a case study in the field of motor vehicle manufacturing.

Clearly more work is needed on a range of products to test the sensitivity of these percentage reductions, but the principle is well established.

Stage three assumes that 50 per cent of vehicle-kilometres can be eliminated by removing geographical illogicalities in the distribution chain and by substituting near for far in sourcing decisions. For the purposes of this analysis a 50 per cent reduction in vehicle-kilometres will be equated with a 50 per cent reduction in CO_2 to be achieved by 2025. Figure 12.3 graphs the progressive implementation of the three stage reduction in CO_2 and the forecast of road freight to the year 2025.

The final reduction in CO_2 in Figure 12.3 is 60 per cent of the 1992 figure. This brings road freight very much into line with what is required of CO_2 reductions from all sectors. The IPCC

(1995) concluded that 60–80 per cent cuts in current emissions of CO_2 and other long-lived greenhouse gases are necessary merely to stabilise their concentrations in the atmosphere at 1990 levels.

Figure 12.3: Comparison of Strong Sustainability Scenarios (CO_2 reduction) with UK Business as Usual Scenarios

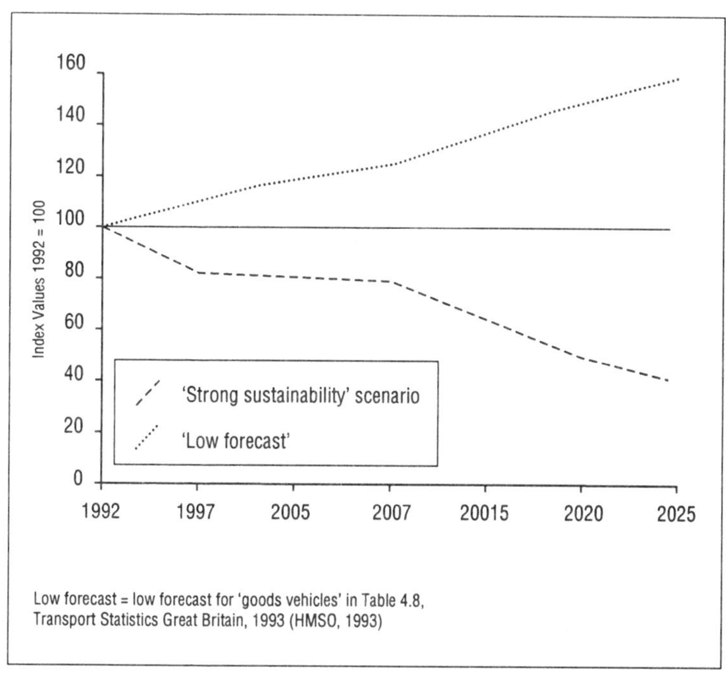

Source: Eco-Logica (1995)

The 60 per cent reduction implied by the strong sustainability scenario in Figure 12.3 would in practice be reduced in size by the robustness of the existing trajectory even if measures were adopted to implement the shift. No attempt has been made to superimpose the timing of reductions in the strong sustainability scenario on the timing of the growth in road freight. Hesse, however (1995), has identified three major fields of action to bring about a move to lower levels of dependency on private motorised transport. These are:

1. Structural change in the spatial distribution of origins and destinations of transport that have resulted from the low cost era of transport prices. This spatial structure is supported by

fossil fuels and cannot serve as a model for the world. Its energy and materials intensity produces not only environmental problems that affect the whole world but also real problems of global equity. Progress in developing countries depends on progress in the developed world.

2. An integrated transport policy is needed to maximise the use of non-polluting modes of transport and use low-polluting modes (for example, bus and rail) wherever appropriate. Integration means careful coordination, planning and fiscal systems that internalise external costs so that the costs of a 500m journey by car in a city really do reflect the environmental, health and social consequences of that trip, and the huge disparity between that damage and the damage caused by an equivalent trip on foot or by bike.
3. Vehicle technology, traffic flow and transport organisation ought to be optimised. Technology can make a contribution to environmental gain in the transition period to lower levels of demand, as can different kinds of organisation of passenger and freight transport, to reduce the amount of road transport and dampen the growth in demand.

The key to change is moving spatial structures towards a new state where the distances that have to be covered are much less than is currently the case. It also means increasing the attraction of cities, parts of cities and small settlements in rural areas so that the demand for travel can be satisfied locally if preferred. In the case of tourism, which is a significant source of travel demand, demand can be reduced (at least in part) by policies that set out to improve local environments. A large number of high quality local environments would offer more potential for local recreational and tourist activity as well as dampening the desire to flee degraded and unsatisfactory places.

Hesse's three principles find an echo in Zuckermann's 33 solutions. Both contributions lack a temporal element in the sense that some things will need to be done immediately (for example, car bans, car free residential areas and car free rural areas), some in the medium term (such as taxation and fiscal measures to make transport more expensive) and some in the long term (land use patterns that reduce the demand for transport and a high density of local facilities). Timing is important, and with sufficient vigour the time scale could be telescoped and different phases run simultaneously. Both Hesse and Zuckermann expect too much of technology in the form of more efficient vehicles or road pricing. Catalytic converters can only reduce emissions under very favourable circumstances (such as static or very low growth in vehicle-kilometres) and most forecasts of future emissions show a decline until about 2010 and then an increase. More vehicles and more vehicle-kilometres will cancel out the gains from catalytic converters and similar technology.

Technology can play a role in the transition towards sustainable mobility. For instance Europe is particularly badly affected by air pollution. A technological gain (for example, air pollution reduction through catalytic converters) should be welcomed as a 'breathing space' whilst other more fundamental measures have had sufficient time to bite. There is, however, a danger in this strategy. Technology can be very seductive and the tendancy is either to deny there is a problem or have complete faith in technology to solve a problem, should one exist. Going down a technological route leads in the direction of bio-fuels, electronic control systems, electric cars, compact cars or the carbon fibre, super fuel-efficient cars as advocated by Lovins. Technology can deliver improvements in individual vehicle performance but cannot deliver these improvements at each stage of the doubling of the car fleet or trebling of vehicle and truck kilometres.

> Technology reinforces a deep seated desire to reject anything that looks like 'eco-doom' and continue with the business as usual scenario. In the medium to long term technological advances might work to the disadvantage of a fundamental solution to transport intensity problems by perpetuating the myth that 'in the end it will be all right'. In the end it won't be all right. It isn't all right now unless widespread social inequity and poor air quality warnings on a warm sunny day are 'all right' and technology is unlikely to deliver a zero speed, zero mass, zero noise vehicle that has zero effect on health, community and land take.

On a global scale the fallacy of technology is very apparent. Two-and-a-half billion vehicles in 2030 will have a significant impact on energy use, materials consumption, urban form, health and the destruction of townscape and landscape. They will also kill a lot of people. Technology is (not surprisingly) quite silent on whether or not anyone would want to live in the kinds of towns and cities that will have to be remodelled to cope with the hyper-mobile and instant access high-performing vehicle.

The technology already exisits to control automatically and electronically the speed of every vehicle on every road in Europe. The problem is that this technology has negative associations. It would certainly give the advertising agencies problems in explaining the disparity between the 150kph capability and the less than 20kph reality. A restricted vehicle would save lives but it might not sell cars. Technology is ultimately the slave of consumerism, and some images just do not sell well.

Images and consumerism are even more important determinants of societal futures in developing countries and in eastern Europe, the former Soviet Union and China. The pressure amongst the Indian middle classes or the newly enriched entrepreneurs in Moscow to emulate the Western consumerist symbols is enormous. Car ownership is not a desire but an obsession, and it feeds on the complex web of media, advertising, film and television symbolism that has taken root in the thinking of the vast majority of the global population.

If the generous loans and inducements, institutional support for the introduction of free markets, new highways and car manufacturing plants are considered too the results will be fairly predictable. Under these circumstances the discussion about Hesse's three principles and Zuckermann's 33 solutions will become irrelevant. It often seems that the pressure is so great and the political momentum so overwhelming that the tide to a car-ridden future is unstoppable.

The situation in developing countries has parallels in the political debate in Britain. The Labour party has made a commitment to increase car ownership but not car use and has made it clear on many occasions that those of us who have already 'climbed the ladder of car ownership' should not 'pull it up behind us' to quote Anthony Crossland in his 1970 Fabian Lecture. The association of socialism with high levels of mass consumerism is an impediment to the achievement of sustainable development goals, and the articulation of policies that satisfy accessibility needs rather than mobility aspirations. Just as it is possible to run the domestic energy sector or industry's use of energy with much less electricity than in the past, and with reductions in costs and no loss of output, so it is possible to deliver a whole range of goods and services and quality of life objectives at much lower rates of transport intensity.

This brings the argument full circle and puts renewed emphasis on strategies and policies in Europe, North America and Australia to reduce car dependency and its associated energy and space intensity. It is fruitless from a position of high per capita incomes, CO_2 production and energy use to argue for restraint in developing countries. Such arguments will, quite rightly, be rejected. The Hesse and Zuckermann pointers are much more important because of the seriousness of the situation in developing countries, and the urgent need for those who have benefited from 150 years of resource and energy exploitation (irrespective of the consequences) to blaze a trail to lower levels of dependency. These lower levels must be associated with higher levels of welfare, health, quality of life and community vigour. No one would be interested in an environmentally wonderful future with high unemployment, poor health, inadequate housing, poor education but lots of trees and fields. There need not be any tension between environmental and economic objectives. It is possible to improve the environment and reduce pollution and strengthen the economy. The 'new' economy that would emerge might be different to the one we have grown used to since 1945, but it would be more successful at delivering jobs and a high quality environment than the present one.

Germany has created 750,000 jobs in the last ten years as a result of high environmental standards (von Weizsäcker, 1994). Walking, cycling and public transport investment creates more permanent and local jobs than highway investment. Environmentally high performing housing in terms of insulation, building practices and the local sourcing of materials and components creates more jobs than energy-inefficient housing serviced by large, centralised energy utilities that employ few and pollute the environment.

High environmental standards are associated with more job creation, not less, and by conserving resources can ensure that jobs are long term rather than transient. In developing countries, emphasis on rickshaws or cycles will generate and maintain more jobs than will capital-intensive highway developments, and emphasis on appropriate rural roads rather than tarmac and concrete highways will employ more local people in maintenance than would have been the case with the introduction of Western technologies.

A WWF report (Jacobs, 1994) 'Green Jobs: The Employment Implications of Environmental Policy' concludes that, in Europe, the environmental sector has created 962,000 jobs and that the environment and economy can operate together synergistically. An economy that cuts down on waste and energy consumption is more efficient, more innovative and has more resources to devote to research and development and the exploitation of further ideas for job creation involving high environmental standards. Environmentally high-performing transport systems reduce pollution costs, reduce waste, reduce raw material extraction costs, improve health and stimulate entrepreneurial and innovative developments in local economies. The organisation of industry and transport is likely to be less centralised, and therefore of greater benefit to job creation in peripheral regions than traditional policies.

Are There 33 Solutions and Three Principles for the Developing World?

The answer, quite simply, is yes, but it is particularly important that they should be articulated and broadcast by a national of a developing country who has been subjected to as wide debate as possible in developing countries. This condition can be met in

Europe, North America and Australia where there are a surfeit of analyses, critiques and good ideas about how to achieve sustainable mobility and sustainable development. They have risen above the developers knee-jerk response which is to accuse intelligent opposition to their ideas of NIMBY(ism), that is, 'Not In My Back Yard'. They have spelt out in some detail that transport policy is fundamentally flawed and that the construction and/or widening of the M65, M3, M25 and M62 will not solve traffic congestion problems and bring a tidal wave of well paid, secure jobs. The professionals and the politicians are lagging behind popular protest in Britain but are now showing welcome signs of a new dawn; what Phil Goodwin at University College London calls the 'new realism'.

This debate is under way in many parts of the developing world, for example, in determining the future of the Calcutta (India) tram system where politicians and professionals argue for its closure, and citizen groups oppose the closure and point out the basic social needs of Calcutta's poor which the tram serves well and the extreme space inefficiencies in a crowded city of replacing trams with cars or buses. The outcome of Calcutta's internal debate and other similar debates will produce home-grown Zuckermann lists.

India, China, the African continent, Poland and all other former territories of the Soviet Union and COMECON will have to go through the same process. It is of crucial importance that debate within these countries and within individual communities and constituencies identifies the nature of the problem and moves on to specify a solution. This cannot be done remotely from London, Brussels or Washington, and the residents of these newly motorising countries (NMCs) should be very wary indeed of transport investments dressed up as aid when the main impact will be to intensify the rate of motorisation.

This is not a counsel of despair. On the contrary, the NMCs can see what a mess the North has made and how inefficient are its very large investments in a transport system that fails to deliver health, social equity and regional equity. It is possible for an NMC to leapfrog the last 40 years of European and the last 70 years of North American transport development and move directly into a sustainable strategy that genuinely conserves resources, reduces pollution and pays great attention to the poorest when disbursing scarce cash. The probability that this will happen depends very much on the seriousness with which Europe and the other heavily motorised countries take steps to move in a different direction and reduce car dependency. This is where the prisoners dilemma is helpful.

The Prisoners Dilemma

The heavily motorised countries would like to retain current levels of motorisation, and possibly increase them. The general view is that technology will enable this situation to continue – though there are concerns that rises in the global population and increases in per capita income will lead to serious materials shortages, problems with the oil supply and with greenhouse gases and climate change. Nevertheless the global economic system is working towards the establishment of vehicle manufacturing capacity in developing countries and the associated infrastructure of highways.

From a developing country perspective the increasing stringency of environmental controls in the developed world and the calls for reductions in greenhouse gas emissions appear to be entirely selfish. Having achieved generally high per capita incomes and a standard of living well in excess of that in, say, India or Bangladesh, it is at the very least insensitive to argue for curtailment of the very thing that brought the achievements to Europe in the first place.

It is highly unlikely, therefore, that India or Bangladesh or China will be receptive to stringent targets set for greenhouse gas reduction and a range of other exhortations that seek to influence their lifestyle. Some reverse exhortation would at least enrich the debate and the time is right for intelligent Indian and Chinese critiques of European highway building and car ownership/use levels to come forward.

The prisoners dilemma (see Box on next page) highlights that there are substantial benefits to be had from pursuing a strategy that appears to be illogical, or at least not in the best interests of a very narrowly defined and selfish point of view. The reality is that policies and strategies that appear illogical are actually far more beneficial to the collective and individual welfare and quality of life than the selfish alternatives. The importance of the prisoners dilemma lies in its ability to reveal the choices that face us all individually and collectively, and to reveal that cooperation and collaboration provide a solution that benefits everyone.

The prisoners dilemma can be used to explain both the illogicality of seemingly rational decisions and the ways in which a new rationality can be shaped.

Barnes (1988) extrapolates from this example of two prisoners to farmers and pesticides. A new pesticide will increase a farmer's crop yield but pollute rivers and waterways if used in large quantities. If no one else uses the pesticide the farmer should use it since he would get more crop yield and suffer no loss. If everyone does the same thing and uses the pesticide he suffers the consequences anyway and using it gives him the benefit of more crops without making the situation tangibly worse. Thus, most farmers may well decide to follow self interest and use the pesticide to their mutual detriment.

Barnes then extrapolates further to society as a whole to suggest that rational self interested calculation in a social context is not

THE PRISONERS DILEMMA

Two women rob a bank and steal a car in which to escape. Police are in hot pursuit and rapidly gaining ground. As the chase goes over a bridge the robbers throw their money into the river so that when they are caught the sentence may well only be for car theft since the money is not there for evidence. The prisoners are caught and taken to separate cells for questioning. For clarity we will call the two prisoners 'A' and 'B' and follow the options that are open to them as they strive to get away with the smallest sentence.

The police suggest to A that if she makes a full confession and the confession is used to convict B then A goes scot-free. If B also confesses, so A's evidence is not needed to convict B, A's confession will still count in mitigation of her crime and a 21-year sentence will be reduced to 20 years. Against this A has to weigh the fact that if she does not confess she will in any case spend one year in prison for car theft. Moreover if B confesses and A does not confess, then B's confession could send her down for 21 years. If A thinks only in self-interested terms then the following would happen: if B confesses then A should confess; if B does not confess, then A still does better to confess.

In any case A should confess. This is summarised as follows:

A's sentence	A's policy	B's policy	B's sentence
20	Confess	Confess	20
21	Not confess	Confess	0
0	Confess	Not confess	21
1	Not confess	Not confess	1

In this dilemma B is logicking in a similar way to A and so will confess. This will result in the longest joint sentence shown above.

If both A and B had made an illogical calculation then neither would confess and would have gained the shortest possible joint sentence in the table. The conclusion is very clear. If both had acted against their individual best interests, they would have furthered those interests very effectively.

necessarily the best action for the good of society. One has to think more socially and altruistically.

The prisoners dilemma maps on to traffic and transport problems very well. At the regional and local level in the developed world the existence of significant health problems from vehicle exhaust emissions, serious and worsening traffic congestion and loss of valuable urban, rural and suburban green space and woodland is evidence of mutual detriment and significant loss where everyone suffers. This correlates to individual self-interested decisions about car ownership and use which have effectively maximised the 'prison sentence'.

The transport equivalent of both prisoners not confessing and both coming out with the lowest possible sentence is a situation where everyone comes out of their own individual and collective dilemma with very low air pollution, low noise, very high road safety, very high child freedoms and child health and very high community interaction based on a rich pattern of local facilities providing employment and diversity. In this scenario everyone can minimise travel demand whilst maximising accessibility and time availability for many purposes other than transport. The same scenario provides maximum availability of local goods and services whilst employing people locally and at the same time not inhibiting purchases and consumption of more distant objects where local availability is insufficient to meet demand. The same scenario reduces inequalities and provides high quality environments for low income people, something which is currently not possible.

The prisoners dilemma works globally as well as locally, and the high levels of motorisation now being pursued in large parts of the developing world are evidence of self-interested calculations influenced by the blatant example of 100 years of self-interested calculations in the developed world.

The prisoners dilemma shows us that globally we are once again on our way to maximising the joint sentence. In this case maximising the joint sentence equates with global warming, stratospheric ozone layer depletion and serious health problems from air pollution. The way out of this dilemma is through a fundamental restructuring of the parameters of decision making in such a way as to emphasise the collective, the social and the equity aspects of development. Sustainable development is part of this restructuring but still falters when exposed to the harsh treatment given out by supporters of economic development and supporters of sustainability, as long as it does not impede any development which has an economic objective. The prisoners dilemma is played out every day in Brussels and Washington and in most local authorities around the world and always in the direction of the first line of the list: mutual confession leading to mutual destruction.

The next section will explore how we can persuade these prisoners to recognise the mutual advantages stemming from cooperation.

A Non-Faustian Bargain

In Chapter 2 the discussion about Faustian bargains showed that there were at least two possible endings to the story. If we can accept the principle that the 'preferred' ending is one where we arrive at an equilibrium characterised by high levels of accessibility, strong local economies, much improved equity and a much improved environment then we can use the prisoners dilemma to get to that ending.

Unlike the original formulation of the prisoners dilemma, the situation presented by the choices available in transport and the environment can be discussed with shared information and an awareness about possible outcomes. The prisoners can communicate and choose a mutually advantageous future. From a global perspective the prisoners might first of all ponder on the choices that have to be made and the information that is available to aid those choices:

1. The advisability or otherwise of moving to lower levels of materials and energy intensity, transport intensity and pollution.
2. The availability of detailed design solutions in different geographical circumstances of how these lower levels of intensity translate into higher levels of social equity, health, welfare, economic success and the satisfaction of wants and need.

   (That is, improve accessibility to healthcare provision, improve availability of fresh water, sanitation and domestic cooking fuels, improve basic passenger transport by all modes that can provide widest possible social access, improve local production–consumption links to maximise proportion of goods and materials used that are locally sourced, discriminate against transport modes that are only relevant to the very wealthy, pursue environmental quality in urban and rural areas so that air quality, water quality, and noise quality are of the highest standard.)
3. The possibilities that exist to restructure the activities of multinational and transnational corporations so that they meet local and regional objectives in terms of environmental standards and 'level playing field' principles. Is there any merit in a general presumption against large-scale investments in technologies/ vehicles that will require large amounts of public subsidies (for example, highways and parking) to make them work?
4. The possibilities that exist to reform the activities of the multilateral lending agencies, for example the World Bank. Pursuing global markets in tobacco, medicines and cars with World Bank assistance (in the case of cars) is clearly in the interests of corporations who are responding to market saturation or market resistance in the developed world, but the developing world also has interests that should be articulated.
5. The advantages to be had from exploiting local democratic institutions to the full and linking citizen action groups in the North and the South as a means of increasing understanding and articulating mutually beneficial policies even if those policies are opposed by politicians and professionals.

Conclusion

The prisoners dilemma provides some insight into global problems and the potential of partnerships and cooperation. It also offers a great deal of insight at much more mundane levels. At the time of writing most of Europe's principal airports are involved in major expansion plans. This is justified on the crudest possible model of 'predict and provide' in an industry which has failed more than any other to understand concepts such as limits to growth, sustainability and environmental capacity. Each airport justifies its own plans on the grounds that if it does not expand then valuable business will be lost to competitors, and economic damage to the country will result. Heathrow, Frankfurt, Paris CDG, Schipol, Munich, Milan and many more have all adopted the same path and the same logic. The result will be airport expansion at every main airport and a further non-sustainable increase in air transport with all its damaging consequences for local health, ozone layer depletion and global warming. Airports and the airlines are locked in a resource-intensive and polluting competitive struggle that is reminiscent of the arms race and star wars. There is no interest at all within the industry in limits to growth or cooperation between airports. This lack of recognition of the advantages of a collective strategy will ultimately damage the airlines and will certainly damage the global environment.

At a more local geographical scale the absence of any appreciation of the prisoners dilemma is even more apparent. Most towns that are a regional focus and depend on attracting shopping trips from a wide hinterland are determined to win out in a competitive struggle with any adjacent towns. Salisbury in Wiltshire under its pre-May 1995 administration was determined to spend £8 million on a central car park to beat off competition from adjacent centres by giving car shoppers the best possible access to the heart of the town. This plan was the focus of electoral conflict; its supporters lost seats in the election and the plan was scrapped by the new administration.

In direct contravention of sustainable transport policies Lancaster City Council has provided a 120-space rooftop car park in the centre of the city directly above a new market hall. The developers, with the support of the City Council, are determined that car access will be of a high order to attract shoppers. This is necessary to beat off the competition in Kendal and Preston. The result is new car parking and car-attractive developments in Lancaster, Preston and Kendal adding to the growth in vehicle-kilometres and air pollution. The initial hope of a competitive advantage is lost as a result of other towns doing the same thing and everyone suffers from more traffic and more air pollution.

The Stockholm Environment Institute (SEI) in its 1994 report 'Measuring Sustainable Economic Welfare' has shown that increases in GNP do not necessarily mean the same things as increases in welfare, Jackson and Marks (1994). This is not a new discovery but it adds a very sharp focus to the transport debate in both North and South and to the interminable arguments about economic growth purchased by increase in trade and more transport. Traditional economic growth brings a whole range of negative consequences which are very costly. The SEI calculates the economic costs of commuting, personal pollution control, car accidents, water pollution, air pollution, noise pollution, ozone depletion and long-term environmental damage. The picture that emerges is of measurable and serious economic and environmental damage and an indicator of the degree to which consumption patterns are not sustainable. They are in fact very expensive – they threaten the health and welfare of future generations, they are socially inequitable and they do not even deliver economic security, health and community viability in developed countries.

This model of failure is now being marketed aggressively in developing countries. It may well succeed. The prisoners dilemma and the solution to the dilemma clearly show a way forward. It is now up to individuals and communities around the world to take the initiative and to question the model currently being marketed by transnational corporations, trading blocks and the proponents of free trade. The way forward is increasingly obvious to large numbers of individuals around the world involved in car free city activities, sustainable development, accessible city planning, safe routes to school, local exchange trading schemes, neighbourhood groups and anti-road building/anti-airport groups.

The extent of the failure of current transport policies has been revealed in this book and it centres on a major distortion of space–time relationships to create the illusion of freedom, choice, and heightened welfare whilst depleting the stock of quality environments and the opportunities for satisfying and healthy activities within our communities. In terms of the gathering momentum of argument, criticism, exploration of new ideas and the implementation of solutions we have now reached a critical mass that is big enough to feed a process of change that will slow down and then reverse this historic distortion of space–time relationships and substitute alternatives that deliver greater levels of satisfaction and greater levels of health and environmental quality. It will also deliver sustainable development.

Bibliography

Appleyard, D. (1981) *Livable Streets* (London: University of California Press).

Bannister, D. (1993) 'Policy Responses in the UK', in Bannister, D. and K. Button (eds) *Transport, the Environment and Sustainable Development* (London: E. & F.N. Spon).

Bannister, D. and K. Button (eds) (1993) *Transport, the Environment and Sustainable Development* (London: E. & F.N. Spon).

Barde, J.P. and K. Button (1990) *Transport Policy and the Environment: Six Case Studies* (London: Earthscan).

Barnes, B. (1988) *About Science* (Oxford: Blackwell).

Bertollini, R. *et al.* (1996) *Environment and Health 1: overview and main European issues* (Copenhagen: European Environment Agency).

Birol, F. and N. Guerer (1993) 'Modelling the transport sector fuel demand for developing economies', *Energy Policy* December 1993, pp. 1163–72.

Black, D. and M. Whitehead (eds) (1988) *The Health Divide – Inequalities of Health* (Harmondsworth: Penguin).

Blowers, A. (1980) *The Limits to Power* (Oxford: Pergamon Press).

Blumer, W., L. Blumer and L. Scherrer (1989) 'Messungen von feinsten Teerstaub an einer Autostrasse mit hoher Krebsmortalität', *Medicina Generalis Helvetica* vol. 9, no. 1, pp. 19–21.

Böge, S. (1995) 'The well-travelled yogurt pot: lessons for new freight transport policies and regional production', *World Transport Policy & Practice* vol. 1, no. 1, pp. 7–11.

Bolhuis, M. (1993) personal communication with the author (Ministry of Transport and Public Works, The Hague).

Bower, J.S. *et al.* (1994) 'A Winter NO_2 Smog Episode in the UK', *Atmospheric Environment* vol. 28, no. 3, pp. 461–75.

Boyden, S. (1987) *Western Civilization in Biological Perspective* (Oxford: Clarendon Press).

British Airport Authority (1994) *Heathrow Environmental Performance Report.*

British Maritime Charitable Foundation (1994) *UK Maritime Audit: Research Module No. 6 – Ports* (Cardiff: University of Wales Department of Maritime Studies and International Transport).

British Medical Association (1992) *Cycling: Towards Health and Safety* (Oxford: Oxford University Press).

Brög, W. (1996) Presentation to Car Free City Conference, May 1996 (Copenhagen: Commission of the European Communities).

Brown, L.R. *et al.* (1993) *Vital Signs 1993–94* (London: Earthscan/Worldwatch Institute).

—— (1994) *State of the World 1994* (New York: W.W. Norton/Worldwatch Institute).
—— (1995) *State of the World 1995* (London: Earthscan/Worldwatch Institute).
Brown, W. (1994) 'Dying from too much dust', *New Scientist* 141, pp. 12–13.
Bryceson, D. and J. Howe (1992) *African Rural Households and Transport: Reducing the Burden on Women?* (Delft: International Institute for Infrastructural, Hydraulic and Environmental Engineering).
Buchanan, C. *et al.* (1963) *Traffic in Towns: A Study of the Long Term Problems of Traffic in Urban Areas* (London: HMSO).
Bundesminister für Verkehr (1985), *Verkehr in Zahlen 1985*, (Bonn: DIW).
Centre for Exploitation of Science and Technology (1993) *Road Transport and the Environment – The Future Agenda in the UK* (London: HMSO).
Commission of the European Communities (1985) *The Assessment of the Effects of Certain Public and Private Projects on the Environment* Directive 85/337/EEC (Brussels: CEC).
—— (1990) *1992: The Environmental Dimension – the Task Force Report on the Environment and the Internal Market* (Brussels: CEC).
—— (1991a) *Draft Proposal for Directive on the Environmental Assessment of Policies, Plans and Programmes* XI/194/90-EN-REV.4 (Brussels: CEC).
—— (DG XI) (1991b) *Integrated Noise Policy at EC Level* (Brussels: CEC).
—— (1992a) *Green Paper on the Impact of Transport on the Environment – a Community Strategy for 'sustainable mobility'* COM(92) 46 final (Brussels: CEC).
—— (1992b) *Towards Sustainability – A European Community Action Programme of Policy and Action in Relation to the Environment and Sustainable Development* COM (92) 23 final – vol. II (Brussels: CEC).
—— (1992c) *European Community Environmental Legislation – Volume 2: Air* (Brussels: CEC).
—— (1993a) 'Resolution of the Council and the Representatives of the Governments of the member states, meeting with the Council of 1 February 1993 on a Community Programme of policy and action in relation to the environment and sustainable development', in *Official Journal of the European Communities* 138/1 (the same document is sometimes referred to as the *Fifth Environmental Action Plan: Towards Sustainability*) (Brussels: CEC).
—— (1993b) 'Growth, Competitiveness, Employment: the Challenges and Ways Forward into the 21st Century', White Paper, *Bulletin of the European Communities* Supplement 6/93 (Brussels: CEC).
—— (1993c) *Trans-European Networks: Towards a Master Plan for the Road Network and Road Traffic* (Brussels: CEC).
—— (1994a) *Strategic Environmental Assessment – Existing Methodology* (Brussels: CEC).
—— (1994b) *Progress Report on the Guidelines for the Trans-European Airport Network* (Brussels: CEC).
Department of the Environment (1990) *This Common Inheritance – Britain's Environmental Strategy* (London: HMSO).
—— (1994a) *Climate Change, The UK Programme* (London: HMSO).
—— (1994b) *Sustainable Development, The UK Strategy* (London: HMSO).

Department of the Environment and Department of Transport (1993) *Reducing Transport Emissions through Planning* (London: HMSO).
—— (1994) *Planning Policy Guidance: Note 13 – Transport* (London: HMSO).
Department of Transport (1989) *Roads for Prosperity* (London: HMSO).
—— (1993) *Transport Statistics Great Britain* (London: HMSO).
—— (1994) *National Travel Survey 1991/1993* (London: HMSO).
—— (1996) Transport Statistics Great Britain 1996 (London: HMSO).
Dicken, P. and P. Lloyd (1990) *Location in Space* (New York: Harper and Row).
Dimitriou, H. (1990) *Transport Planning for Third World Cities* (London: Routledge).
Dockery, D.W., J. Schwartz and J.D. Spengler (1992) 'Air pollution and daily mortality: associations with particulates and acid aerosols', *Environmental Research* 59, pp. 362–73.
Dockery, D.W., C.A. Pope, X. Xu *et al.* (1993) 'An association between air pollution and mortality in six U.S. cities', *New England Journal of Medicine* 329, pp. 1753–9.
Dowdeswell, E. (1994) 'Executive Director of UNEP addresses International Conference on Population and Development, Cairo, Egypt, 5–13 September 1994', Press release.
Eco-Logica (1994) *Driven to Destruction – Absurd Freight Movement and European Road Building* (London: Greenpeace).
—— (1995) *Freight Transport, Logistics and Sustainable Development* (Godalming: World Wide Fund for Nature).
ECOPLAN (1992) *Damage Costs of Air Pollution: A Survey of Existing Estimates* (Bern: ECOPLAN).
Elkin, T. *et al.* (1991) *Reviving the City – Towards Sustainable Urban Development* (London: Friends of the Earth).
Elsom, D. (1996) *Smog Alert – Managing Urban Air Quality* (London: Earthscan).
Environmental Resources Limited (ERL) (1992) *SAST – Local Pollution Study* (Brussels: CEC).
European Conference of Ministers of Transport (ECMT) (1993) *Transport Policy and Global Warming* (Paris: OECD).
—— (1995) *Urban Travel and Sustainable Development* (Paris: OECD).
European Information Service (1997) 'European environment' no. 495, section 1.
Faiz, A. *et al.* (1990) *Automotive Air Pollution: Issues and Options for Developing Countries* (Washington: The World Bank).
Fletcher, T. and A.J. McMichael (eds) (1997) *Health at the Crossroads* (Chichester: Wiley).
Flughafen Zurich (1991) 'Clean Air Program Control Zurich – Subproject "Airport"' Airport Authority (Zurich: Environmental Protection).
Ford, H. (1929) *My Philosophy of Industry* (London: Harrap).
Friends of the Earth (1990) *Benzene from Vehicles* (London: Friends of the Earth).
Gallagher, R. (1992) *The Rickshaws of Bangladesh* (Dhaka: The University Press).

Glendinning, C. and J. Millar (eds) (1992) *Women and Poverty in Britain: the 1990s* (Hemel Hempstead: Harvester Wheatsheaf).

Global 2000 (1982) *The Report to The President* (Harmondsworth: Penguin).

Goodlee, F. (1992) 'Transport: a public health issue', *British Medical Journal* 304, pp. 48–50.

Goodwin, P.B. (1994) 'Vehicle pollution and health: policy implications', in Read, C. (ed.) *How Vehicle Pollution Affects our Health* (London: Arden Trust).

—— (1997) 'Are transport policies driven by health concerns?', in Fletcher, T. and A.J. McMichael (eds) *Health at the Crossroads* (Chichester: Wiley).

Gordon, D. (1991) *Steering a New Course: Transportation, Energy and the Environment* (Washington: Island Press).

Gorham, E. (1989) 'Scientific Understanding of Ecosystem Acidification: A Historical Review', *Ambio* vol. 18, no. 3, pp. 150–3.

Gray, C.L. and J.A. Alson (1989) 'The case for methanol', *Scientific American* November 1989, pp. 86–92.

Greenpeace (1991) *EG-Transit Terror* (Zurich: Greenpeace Switzerland) with added data from Luzerner Newue Nachvielten (26 March 1992), *Die Vielbeklagte Lastwagen-Lauvine hat Vielgeldote Ursachen* LNN no. 72 (Lucerne: Luzerner Newue Nachvielten).

Gwilliam, K.M. and H. Geerlings (1992) *SAST 3 – Technology, Transport and the Environment* (Brussels: CEC).

Haq, G. (1994) 'Transport and environment: a Dutch perspective', in Wintle, M. and R. Reeve (eds) *Rhetoric and Reality in Environmental Policy* (Aldershot: Avebury Press).

Hameed, S. and J. Dignon (1992) 'Global emissions of nitrogen and sulphur oxides in fossil fuel combustion 1970–1986', *Journal of Air and Waste Management Association* vol. 42, pp. 159–63.

Harrison, D. (1992) *Tourism and Less Developed Countries* (London: Bellhaven Press).

Hartman, J. (1990) 'The Delft Bicycle Network', in Tolley, R. (ed.) *The Greening of Urban Transport* (London: Belhaven Press).

Harvey, D. (1973) *Social Justice and the City* (London: Edward Arnold).

Hesse, M. (1995) 'Urban space and logistics: on the road to sustainability?', in *World Transport Policy & Practice* vol. 1, no. 4.

Hey, C. *et al.* (1992) *Dead End Road – Climate Protection in European Freight Transport* (Zurich: Greenpeace).

Hilbers, H.D. and E.J. Verroen (1992) 'Mobility profiles and accessibility profiles, elaborated for a land use policy to reduce car use', paper presented at the PTRC, XX Summer Annual Meeting, University of Manchester (UMIST).

Hill, R., P. O'Keefe and C. Snape (1995) *The Future of Energy Use* (London: Earthscan/Worldwatch Institute).

Hillman, M., J. Adams and J. Whitelegg (1990) *One False Move: A Study of Children's Independent Mobility* (London: Policy Studies Institute).

Holman, C. (1991) *Air Pollution and Health* (London: Friends of the Earth).

Holmberg, J., K. Thomson and L. Timberlake (1993) *Facing the Future: Beyond the Earth Summit* (London: Earthscan).

Holzapfel, H. (1982) 'High speed systems of public transport – a positive trend?', proceedings of seminar, PTRC, Warwick, 14 July.

—— (1995) 'Potential forms of regional economic co-operation to reduce goods transport', in Koppen, I.J. and H.A. Arp (eds) *World Transport Policy & Practice* vol. 1, no. 2.

Howe, J. and R. Dennis (1993) 'The bicycle in Africa: luxury or necessity?', paper presented at the VELOCITY Conference: The Civilised City: Responses to New Transport Priorities, 6–10 September 1993, Nottingham.

Hughes, P. (1993) *Personal Travel and the Greenhouse Effect* (London: Earthscan).

IBG Women And Geography Study Group (1984) *Geography and Gender* (London: Hutchinson).

IEA (1993) *Cars and Climate Change* (Paris: OECD).

Intergovernmental Panel on Climate Change (1995) *IPCC Second Assessment Synthesis of Scientific-Technical Information Relevant to Interpreting Article 2 of the United Nations Framework Convention on Climate Change 1995* (Geneva: World Meteorological Organisation/United Nations Environment Programme).

International Civil Aviation Organisation (1995) *Report of the Data Bases and Forecasting Sub-group* (Bonn: ICAO).

International Institute for Energy Conservation (IIEC) (1995) *Sustainable Transport in Europe: A Key Agenda for Policy Makers at Sofia* (London: IIEC).

Ippen, M., R. Fehr and E.O. Krasemann (1989) 'Krebs bei Anwohnen verkehrsreicher Strassen', *Versicherungsmedizin*, 2, 39–42.

IUCN, UNEP and WWF (1991) *Caring For the Earth – A Strategy For Sustainable Living* (London: Earthscan).

Jackson, T. and N. Marks (1994) *Measuring Sustainable Economic Welfare – A Pilot Index 1950–1990* (London: New Economics Foundation and Stockholm Environment Institute).

Jacobs, J. (1961) *The Life and Death of American Cities* (London: Pelican).

Jacobs, M. (1991) *The Green Economy* (London: Pluto Press).

—— (1994) *Green Jobs? The Employment Implications of Environmental Policy* (Brussels: WWF).

James, N. and T. Pharaoh (1992) 'The Traffic Generation Game', in Roberts, J. *et al.* (eds) *Travel Sickness* (London: Lawrence & Wishart).

Janelle, D. (1969) 'Spatial reorganisation: a model and a concept', *Annals of the Association of American Geographers* 58, 348–64.

Jopling, J. and H. Girardet (1996) *Creating a Sustainable London* (London: Sustainable London Trust).

Kågeson, P. (1993) *Getting the Prices Right* (Brussels: T&E).

Koppen, I.J. and H.A. Arp (eds) (1995) *World Transport Policy & Practice* vol. 1, no. 2 (a special issue concerning freight transport in Europe).

Krippendorf, J. (1987) *The Holiday Makers: Understanding the Impact of Leisure and Travel* (London: Heinemann).

Krummenacher, B. (1993) 'Environmental impact of design and materials selection in cars', in United Nations Environmental Programme *Industry and Environment* vol. 16, no. 1–2, pp. 46–50.

Lancashire County Council (1994) 'Greening the Red Rose County' Technical Report No. 19 (Preston: LCC).
Lang, T. and C. Hines (1993) *The New Protectionism* (London: Earthscan).
Lee, N. (1983) 'Environmental Impact Assessment: A Review', *Applied Geography* vol. 3, pp. 5–27.
Lefohn, A.S. (1994) *The Special Issue of Atmospheric Environment on Surface Ozone Atmospheric Environment* vol. 28, no. 1, pp. 1–2. (a special issue on surface ozone).
Lewis, C.S. (1995) *Surprised by Joy – The Shape of My Early Life* (London: Geoffrey Bliss).
Local Government Management Board (1995) *Indicators for Local Agenda 21, A Summary* (Luton: LGMB).
London Borough of Hillingdon Environment Group (1994) *Air Quality Modelling Study for Heathrow and Surrounding Area Final Report* Appendix B, pp. B23, B26.
MacKenzie, J.J. and M.P. Walsh (1990) *Driving Forces: Motor Vehicle Trends and their Implications for Global Warming, Energy Strategies, and Transportation Planning* (New York: World Resources Institute).
Maddison, D. *et al.* (1996) *Blueprint 5 – The True Costs of Road Transport* (London: Earthscan).
Manchester Area Pollution Advisory Council (1993) *A Breathing Space: Vehicle Related Air Pollution in North West England* (Manchester: MAPAC).
Massey, D. (1994) *Space, Place and Gender* (Cambridge: Polity Press).
Meadows, D.H. *et al.* (1972) *The Limits to Growth* (New York: Universe Books).
Meadows, D.H. *et al.* (1992) *Beyond the Limits* (Post Mills, VT: Chelsea Publishing).
Mens, R. and A. Ruimte (1993) *The European High Speed Train Network: Environmental Impact Assessment – Executive Summary* (Brussels: CEC).
Ministry of Transport and Public Works (1987) *Evaluation of the Delft Bicycle Network Plan* (The Hague: Ministry of Transport and Public Works).
—— (1992) *Bicycles First: The Bicycle Master Plan* (The Hague: Ministry of Transport and Public Works).
Misch, A. (1994) 'Assessing Environmental Health Risks', in Worldwatch Institute *State of the World 1994* (New York: W.W. Norton).
Morgan, R. (1994) *Planet Gauge: The Real Facts of Life 1994* (London: Earthscan).
Munn, R. E. (1979) *Scope Report 5: Environmental Impact Assessment* (Chichester: Wiley).
Nadis, S. and J.J. MacKenzie (1993) *Car Trouble* (Boston: Beacon Press).
Odèn, S. (1968) 'The Acidification of Air and Precipitation and its Consequences in the Natural Environment', in *Ecology Committee Bulletin* no. 1 (Stockholm: Swedish National Research Council).
Organisation for Economic Co-operation and Development (1988) *Transport and the Environment* (Paris: OECD).
—— (1993a) *Cars and Climate Change* (Paris: OECD).
—— (1993b) *Electric Vehicles: Technology, Performance and Potential* (Paris: OECD).
—— (1994) *Environmental Impact Assessment of Roads* (Paris: OECD).

de Oliveira, A. (1991) 'Reassessing the Brazilian Alcohol Programme', *Energy Policy* January/February 1991, pp. 47–55.

O'Riordan, T. and W.R.D. Sewell (1992) *Project Appraisal and Policy Review* (Chichester: Wiley).

Pearce, D. *et al.* (1989) *Blueprint For A Green Economy* (London: Earthscan).

Peake, S. (1994) *Transport in Transition: Lessons from the History of Energy* (London: Earthscan).

Phillips, D. (1994) 'Can vehicle pollution cause cancer?', in Read, C. (ed.) *How Vehicle Pollution Affects our Health* (London: Ashden Trust).

Plowden, S. (1985) *Transport Reform: Changing the Rules* (London: Policy Studies Institute).

Public Health Alliance (1991) *Health on the Move – Policies for Health Promoting Transport* (London: PHA).

RAC (1992) *Cars and the Environment – A View to the Year 2020* (London: RAC).

Read, C. (ed.) (1994) *How Vehicle Pollution Affects our Health* (London: Ashden Trust).

Redclift, M. (1987) *Sustainable Development – Exploring the Contradictions* (London: Routledge).

Reese, R.A. *et al.* (1993) 'Herbaceous biomass feedstock production: the economic potential and impacts on US agriculture', *Energy Policy* July 1993, pp. 726–33.

Replogle, M. (1988) 'Sustainable Transportation Strategies for Third World Development', conference paper, Institute for Transportation and Development Policy, Washington.

Roberts, J. *et al.* (eds) (1992) *Travel Sickness* (London: Lawrence & Wishart).

Rodhe, H. (1989) 'Acidification in a global perspective', *Ambio* vol. 18, no. 3, pp. 155–60.

Royal Commission on Environmental Pollution (1994) *Eighteenth Report: Transport and the Environment* (London: HMSO).

SAST-Monitor (1992) *Research and Technology Strategy to Help Overcome the Environmental Problems in Relation to Transport – Resources Uses Study* (Brussels: CEC).

Satterthwaite, D. *et al.* (1996) *The Environment for Children* (London: Earthscan).

Savitz D.A. and L. Feingold (1989) 'Association of childhood cancer with residential traffic density', *Scandinavian Journal of Work and Environmental Health* 15, 360–3

Schallaböck, K.O. (1993) 'Zur Bedeutung des Luftverkehrs im klimapolitischen Verkehrsdiskurs', report to the Enquete-Kommission of the German Parliament (Wuppertal: Wuppertal Institut für Klima, Umwelt, Energie).

Scovazzi, T. and T. Treves (1992) *World Treaties for the Protection of the Environment* (Milan: Istituto Per L'Ambiente).

Seifried, D. (1990) *Gute Argumente: Verkehr, Beck'sche Reihe* (Munich: Beck).

Serageldin, I (1993). 'Environmentally sustainable urban transport: defining a global policy', *Public Transport International* vol. 2, pp. 17–24.

Sheate, W.R. (1992) 'Strategic environmental assessment in the transport sector', *Project Appraisal* vol. 7, no. 3, pp. 170–4.

Siemiatycki, J. *et al.* (1988) 'Associations between several sites of cancer and ten types of exhaust and combustion products', *Scandinavian Journal of Work and Environmental Health* 14, 79–90.
Smeed, R. (1964) *Road Pricing: The Economic and Technical Possibilities* (London: HMSO).
Sommerville, H. (1993) 'Airlines, aviation and the environment – the British Airways Programme', in United Nations Environmental Programme, *Industry and Environment* vol. 16, no. 1–2, pp. 54–9.
Stanners, D. and P. Bourdeau (eds) (1995) *Europe's Environment: The Dobris Assessment* (Copenhagen: European Environment Agency).
Stein, W. (1994) 'EIA methods for road planning: the EIA contribution for the Landesstrassenbedarfsplan Nordrhein-Westfalen', paper presented to the Third European Workshop on EIA Methodology and Research, Delphi, Greece, 6–8 October 1994.
Strutynski, P. (1995) 'A new approach to reducing road freight transport', in Koppen, I.J. and H.A. Arp (eds) *World Transport Policy & Practice* vol. 1, no. 1.
Swedish Environmental Protection Agency (1992) *ENVIRO – Magazine of Transboundary Air Pollution* no. 13.
Tanja, P.T. (1993) 'Towards an effective EC policy aiming to reduce CO_2 emissions in the transport sector', in *Transport Policy and Global Warming* (Paris: ECMT/OECD) pp. 155–94.
Taylor, D. and M. Fergusson (1993) *Energy Use and Air Pollution in UK Road Freight* (Godalming: World Wide Fund for Nature).
TEST (1991) *Wrong Side of the Tracks: Impacts of Road and Rail Transport on the Environment – a Basis for Discussion* (London: TEST).
Teufel, D. (1989) *Die Zukunft des Autoverkehrs* (Heidelberg: Umwelt und Prognose Institut).
Teufel, D. *et al.* (1993) *Öko-Bilanzen von Fahrzeugen* (Heidelberg: Umwelt und Prognose Institut).
—— (1995) *Folgen einer globalen Motorisierung* (Heidelberg: Umwelt und Prognose Institut).
Therivel, R. *et al.* (1993) *Strategic Environmental Assessment* (London: Earthscan).
Tivers, J. (1985) *Women Attached* (Canterbury: Croom Helm).
Tolba, M.K. *et al.* (1992) *The World Environment 1972–1992* (London: Chapman and Hall).
Tolley, R. (ed.) (1990) *The Greening of Urban Transport: Planning for Walking and Cycling in Western Cities* (London: Belhaven Press).
Transnet (1990) *Energy, Transport and Environment* (London: Transnet).
United Nations Conference on Environment and Development (1992) *Agenda 21* (Rio de Janeiro: UNCED).
United Nations Economic Commission for Europe (1979) *Convention on Long-range Transboundary Air Pollution* (Geneva: UNECE).
—— (1985) *Protocol to the 1979 Convention on Long-range Transboundary Air Pollution on the Reduction of Sulphur Emissions or their Transboundary Fluxes by at Least 30 Percent* (Geneva: UNECE).
—— (1988) *Protocol to the 1979 Convention of Long-range Transboundary Air Pollution Concerning the Control of Emissions of Nitrogen Oxides or their Transboundary Fluxes* (Geneva: UNECE).

—— (1991a) *Protocol to the 1979 Convention on Long-range Transboundary Air Pollution Concerning the Control of Emissions of Volatile Organic Compounds and their Transboundary Fluxes* (Geneva: UNECE).

—— (1991b) *Convention on Environmental Impact Assessment in a Transboundary Context* (Geneva: UNECE).

—— (1991c) *Policies and Systems of Environmental Impact Assessment* (Geneva: UNECE).

United Nations Economic and Social Commission for Asia and the Pacific (1984) *Fuels for the Transport Sector: Compressed Natural Gas* (Bangkok: UNESCAP).

United Nations Environment Programme (UNEP) (1991) *Environmental Data Report 1991/1992* (Oxford: Blackwell).

—— (1993a) *Industry and Environment* (a special issue on transport and the environment), vol. 16, no. 1–2.

—— (1993b) *Environmental Data Report 1993-94* (Oxford: Blackwell).

—— and World Health Organisation (1992) *Urban Air Pollution in the Megacities of the World* (Oxford: Blackwell).

Walters, S. (1994) 'What are the respiratory health effects of vehicle pollution?', in Read, C. (ed.) *How Vehicle Pollution Affects our Health* (London: Ashden Trust).

Wathern, P. (ed.) (1988) *Environmental Impact Assessment – Theory and Practice* (London: Unwin Hyman).

Watkins, L. (1991) *Air Pollution from Road Vehicles* (Crowthorne: Transport Research Laboratory).

Werkgroep 2duizend (1993) *A New Course in Freight Transport* (Amersfoort: Werkgroep 2duizend).

von Weizsäcker, E.U. and J. Jesinghaus (1992) *Ecological Taxation Reform* (London: Zed Books).

von Weizsäcker, E.U. (1994) *Earth Politics* (London: Zed Books).

Whitelegg, J. (1993) *Transport for a Sustainable Future – The Case For Europe* (London: Wiley).

Whitelegg, J., A. Gatrell and P. Naumann (1993) *Traffic and Health* (Lancaster: University of Lancaster Environmental Epidemiology Research Unit).

Whitelegg, J., S. Hultén and T. Flink (1993) *High Speed Trains: Fast Tracks to the Future* (Hawes: Leading Edge).

Whitelegg, J. (1995) 'Statement of evidence into the application for the development of a fifth terminal and associated facilities at Heathrow Airport' (Heathrow: Local Authorities Heathrow Terminal 5 Group).

Whittaker, S. (1995) *First Steps – Local Agenda 21 in Practice* (London: HMSO).

van Wijnen, J.H. *et al.* (1995) 'The exposure of cyclists, car drivers and pedestrians to traffic related air pollutants', in *International Archives of Occupational and Environmental Health* 67(3) pp. 187–93.

Wjst, M. *et al.* (1993) 'Road traffic and adverse effects on respiratory health in children', *British Medical Journal* 307, pp. 596–600.

Wolff, S.P. (1992) 'Correlation between car ownership and leukaemia: is non-occupational exposure to benzene from petrol and motor vehicle exhaust a causative factor in leukaemia and lymphoma?', *Experientia*, 48 301.

Wood, C. (1988) 'EIA in plan making', in Wathern, P. (ed.) *Environmental Impact Assessment – Theory and Practice* (London: Unwin Hyman).
Wood, C. and M. Dejeddour (1992) 'Strategic environmental assessment: environmental assessment of policies, plans and programmes', in *Impact Assessment Bulletin* vol. 10, no. 1, pp. 3–22.
World Bank (1994) *Transport Sector Policy Review* (Washington: World Bank).
World Commission on Environment and Development (1987) *Our Common Future* (Oxford: Oxford University Press).
World Health Organisation (1992a) *Motor Vehicle Air Pollution. Public Heath Impact and Control Measures* (Geneva: WHO).
—— (1992b) *Our Planet, Our Health: Report of the WHO Commission on Health and Environment* (Geneva: WHO).
—— (1993) *Community Noise. Environmental Health Criteria Document* (Copenhagen: WHO).
—— (1995a) *Update and Revision of the Air Quality Guidelines for Europe* (Copenhagen: WHO).
—— (1995b) *Concern for Europe's Tomorrow* (Copenhagen: WHO).
—— (1995c) *Bridging the Health Gap in Europe: A Focus on Non-communicable Disease Prevention and Control,* Environmental Action Plan, EUR/ICP/CIND 94 OZ/PV01 (Copenhagen: WHO).
WHO and UNEP (1992) *Urban Air Pollution in the Megacities of the World* (Oxford: Basil Blackwell).
World Resources Institute (WRI) (1992) *World Resources 1992–93* (Oxford: Oxford University Press).
—— (1994) *World Resources 1994–95* (Oxford: Oxford University Press).
—— (1996) *World Resources 1996–97 – The Urban Environment* (Oxford: Oxford University Press).
World Tourism Organisation (WTO) (1992) *Compendium of Tourist Statistics 1986–1990* (Madrid: WHO).
World Transport Policy and Practice (1995), Special Issue on Freight Transport, vol. 1, no. 2.
Wright, C.L. (1992) *Fast Wheels, Slow Traffic: Urban Transport Choices* (Philadelphia: Temple University Press).
Yago, G. (1984) *The Decline of Transit: Urban Transportation in German and US Cities, 1900–1970* (Cambridge: Cambridge University Press).
Zuckermann, W. (1991) *End of the Road: The World Car Crisis and How we can Solve it* (Cambridge: The Lutterworth Press).

Glossary and Abbbreviations

Biomass Crops grown as sources of energy for use in power stations and for the manufacture of fuels are known as biomass.

CFCs ChloroFluoroCarbons are industrial gases used in a variety of products. CFC-11 and CFC-12 are particularly harmful to the Ozone layer in the stratosphere. Their production, supply and use have been banned since 1995.

CNG Compressed Natural Gas.

CO Carbon Monoxide is one of many exhaust gases. It has a number of damaging effects on human health and can kill.

CO_2 Carbon Dioxide is one of the better known greenhouse gases.

Cohesion Policy As part of the deal to encourage acceptance of the Maastricht Treaty, in particular in the peripheral regions, the European Union introduced a policy whose objective was to improve the economies of the disadvantaged regions. The method used to implement this policy included the provision of large infrastructure projects and industrial development. See also Maastricht Treaty.

COMECON The Council for Mutual Economic Aid was an eastern bloc organisation set up to develop the member countries' economies on a complementary basis with the ultimate goal of achieving self-sufficiency.

Common Agricultural Policy One of two industry-wide policies (the other being transport) of the European Community. It is a protectionist mechanism for stabilising agricultural prices which has resulted in higher costs to the consumer.

dB(A) The 'A' weighted decibel scale is a standard metric for measuring noise in the range available to the human ear.

Demand Management Strategy An approach to transport planning that seeks to reduce the demand for travel and makes best use of all available transport modes. Sometimes referred to as 'Predict and Prevent'.

Earth Summit/Rio Declaration Most of the world's political leaders attended the Earth Summit (United Nations Conference on Environment and Development) which took place at Rio de Janeiro in 1992. The Rio Declaration was the outcome. This included the following:

- Agenda 21: a comprehensive programme of action needed throughout the world to achieve a more sustainable pattern of development for the next century;

- the Climate Change Convention (Framework Convention on the Atmosphere): an agreement committing the signatories to limiting their output of greenhouse gases;
- Convention on the Conservation of Biological Diversity – an agreement between countries designed to protect and preserve the variety of species and habitats from exploitation and harm;
- a Statement of Principles for the management, conservation and sustainable development of all the world's forests. See also Sustainability.

EBRD European Bank for Reconstruction and Development.

ECC Environmental Concept Car.

Ecological Footprint A term used to describe the global impact of a given level of consumption. For example, how much land globally is required to fulfil the needs of Perranporth for food, materials, energy, etc? For further information, see Wackernagel, M. and W. Rees (1996) *Our Ecological Footprint – Reducing Human Impact on the Earth* (Gabriola Island, B.C.: New Society Publishers).

EIA Environmental Impact Assessment.

EIB European Investment Bank.

EIS Environmental Impact Statement.

ENDS Report The Environmental Data Service Report is a highly regarded source of information about environmental matters.

EPAQS The UK Government's Expert Panel on Air Quality Standards.

ERT European Round Table of Industrialists.

ETR Ecological Taxation Reform.

EU European Union.

Friction of distance A geographical expression that describes a law-like tendency for the movement of goods and people to decrease in intensity as distances between origins and destinations increase.

GATT General Agreement on Tariffs and Trade.

Hand Pulled Carts These are vehicles used for local delivery in many places in the developing world, such as Calcutta. They are loaded up with a variety of goods, such as scaffolding, and are a highly sustainable mode of transport.

HCs Hydrocarbons are compounds of Carbon and Hydrogen. All fuels (methane, ethane, propane, butane, pentane, hexane, heptane, octane, diesel, coal, wood, etc.) are hydrocarbons.

HCFCs HydroChloroFluoroCarbons are the newer generation of CFCs. Although we are assured by industry that they are less environmentally damaging, a partial ban on their use has been emplaced.

IEA The aims of the International Energy Agency are to reduce members' dependence on oil supplies, to maintain information on international oil markets, to develop stable international energy trade and protect member countries from fluctuations in oil supplies.

IPCC The Intergovernmental Panel on Climate Change has predicted a possible rise in the mean global temperature of about 1°C by 2025 and 3°C before the end of the next century. These predictions have focused the minds of politicians and planners on the need to agree to limits on greenhouse gas emissions.

Ischaemic Heart Disease This is the correct term for coronary heart disease. It can be best treated by primary prevention, for example, clean air, diet and exercise.

IUCN International Union for the Conservation of Nature.

JIT Just-in-time delivery systems have developed in recent years. In the retail sector, for example, it allows firms to store less on the high street where rents and rates are high, and to fetch stock in just-in-time by using computerised ordering systems. It is totally dependent on uncongested roads.

Jitneys These are a privately owned, highly flexible form of free-market transport which provide cheap unregulated access to the public.

Kitting The storage of materials to await the moment when they will be used.

LPG Liquid Petroleum Gas.

Lead (Pb) Added to petrol as Lead tetraethyl. It improves the performance of an engine. It is harmful to human health. Most petrol sold today is lead-free and since its removal in the 1980s the levels of lead in humans have decreased dramatically.

Maastricht Treaty Signing this treaty resulted in the metamorphosis of the European Community into the European Union. This took place in Maastricht (Netherlands) in 1992. The initial aims of this was to allow the free movement of capital, services, goods and labour. The eventual aim of this treaty is to establish fully integrated common standards for industry, a common foreign policy, common economic policy and a common currency.

Mutagenicity The term used to describe the degree to which cells alter in response to external stimuli.

NAFTA North American Free Trade Agreement.

NGOs Non-governmental Organisations.

NMT Non-motorised Transport.

NO_x This is a generic term applied to a family of Oxides of Nitrogen. These include Nitric Oxide (NO), Nitrogen Dioxide (NO_2), and Nitrous Oxide (N_2O). They react with water in the air to form Nitric Acid, a particularly pungent and corrosive liquid.

OECD The Organisation Economic Co-operation and Development is, fundamentally, a club of the richest states. Its aims are to encourage economic growth and high employment with financial stability among its member countries, and to contribute to the economic development of the less advanced member and non-member countries and the expansion of world multilateral trade.

Ozone (O_3) Ozone is very beneficial in the stratosphere, as it shields us from ultraviolet radiation (UV) from the sun. It is being damaged by the release of a variety of greenhouse gases, especially CFCs and HCFCs. One consequence of this damage is 'the hole in the Ozone layer' over Antarctica.

Ozone is a greenhouse gas. It is increasing in the troposphere and decreasing in the stratosphere. In the troposphere it can affect animal and plant health, for example, aggravate asthma and reduce crop yield. Ozone is a secondary pollutant, which means that it is formed by other pollutants reacting together. Internal combustion engines (as in cars) produce NO which is oxidised to NO_2, which is then converted to Ozone. They also produce unburned hydrocarbons, thus continuing the cycle. Coal-fired power stations are another source of NO_2.

Particulates These microscopic particles (PM10s are <10μm in diameter, PM2.5s are < 2.5μm in diameter) of exhaust dust are visible as black smoke. They are small enough to be taken deeply into lung tissue. It has been estimated that PM10s are responsible for 10,000 deaths each year in the UK.
(1μm = 1 micron = 1 millionth of a metre)

Planning Policy Guidance Notes (PPG) Planning Policy Guidance Notes are issued by the Department of the Environment and refer to land use. They are a means of communicating current government policy.

PPG 13, published in March 1994, is unusual in that it was issued jointly by the Departments of the Environment and Transport. It focuses on Transport and stresses the importance of local facilities easily reached by bike, bus or foot. PPG 13 advises councils to reduce growth in the number and length of motorised journeys; encourage alternative means of travel with less environmental impact; reduce reliance on the private car, especially for commuting. Accordingly, PPG 13 is an important policy instrument for implementing demand management strategies.

PPG 6, revised in June 1996, is concerned with Town Centres and Retail Developments. After years of promoting out-of-town retailing it rediscovered, and now emphasises, the primacy of town centres for retailing. Local authorities are expected to clarify three key tests when assessing proposals for retail developments: the impact on the vitality and viability of town centres; accessibility by a choice of means of transport; impact on overall travel and car use.

See also SACTRA and the 18th Report of the Royal Commission on Environmental Pollution.

Predict and Provide A method used to decide that infrastructure developments are necessary. Predictions of the level of car ownership/airport use are made and, accordingly, we provide the necessary infrastructure. The result of this is self-perpetuating increases in car ownership and use and airport use. See Demand Management Strategy.

REHEX Regional Human Exposure Model.

Rickshaws These are tricycles which have accommodation for fare paying passengers.

Royal Commission on Environmental Pollution: 18th Report – Transport and the Environment This report, published in 1994, deals with the impact of transport on the environment:

> In the general survey of the environment which formed its First Report in 1971, the Royal Commission drew attention to the possible deterioration in air quality as a result of a forecast doubling in the number of motor vehicles by 1995. It also identified transport as 'the main menace' among sources of noise and discussed the effects of emissions of carbon dioxide and other substances on the global atmosphere. The Commission warned that it would be 'dangerously complacent' to ignore the potential implications of the increasing number of motor vehicles and commercial flights. The Fourth Report in 1974 returned to these subjects. By that time it was 'becoming increasingly apparent that it is not possible to cater for [the] unrestricted use [of vehicles] without engineering works on a scale that is socially unacceptable'. The Commission concluded: 'We may therefore expect that limitations on their use in some urban areas will be imposed in order to safeguard the local environment. This will lead to a reduction not only in their exhaust gases but also of their noise, which many regard as a worse problem'.(Para 1.1)
>
> The present system of transport is the consequence of policy choices over a period of a century or more. Their effect has been to transform the ways in which land is settled, people work and travel to work, and families live. (Para 14.120)
>
> The aim of future planning policies must be to reduce the need for movement. This will involve a gradual shift away from lifestyles which depend on high mobility and intensive use of cars. These changes of direction provide the essential foundation for a sustainable transport policy, and will make it possible for the economy to develop in ways which are compatible with preservation of the environment.

The report had many recommendations, the most important being the setting of targets to limit car use and increase public transport use. See also SACTRA and Planning Policy Guidance Notes.

SACTRA The Standing Advisory Committee on Trunk Road Assessment is a body which considers transport issues on behalf of the Department of Transport in the UK. In 1994, SACTRA produced a report 'Trunk Roads and the Generation of Traffic'. SACTRA posed itself four questions and came up with the following conclusions:

Is induced traffic a real phenomenon? 'Induced traffic can occur, probably quite extensively, though its size and significance is likely to vary in different circumstances.'

Does induced traffic matter? 'These studies demonstrate convincingly that the economic value of a scheme can be overestimated by the omission of even a small amount of induced traffic. We consider that this matter is of profound importance to the value for money assessment of the road programme.'

When and Where does induced traffic matter? In three sets of circumstances: where the road network is already congested; where travel behaviour has a high potential for change; where a scheme causes big changes in travel costs. In practice this means that traffic induction is most likely to occur on roads in and around urban areas, river crossings, and capacity-enhancing inter-urban schemes including motorway widening.

See also the Royal Commission on Environmental Pollution, Planning Policy Guidance Notes.

SEA Strategic Environmental Assessment.

Social Class Social classes in the UK are defined by the Office of Population Censuses and Surveys as follows:

I Professional (e.g. accountant, doctor, lawyer);

II Intermediate (e.g. manager, nurse, school teacher);

IIIn Skilled non-manual (e.g. clerical worker, secretary, shop assistant);

IIIm Skilled manual (e.g. bus driver, butcher, coalface worker, carpenter);

IV Partly skilled (e.g. agricultural worker, bus conductor, postman);

V Unskilled (e.g. labourer, cleaner, dock worker).

There are considerable problems attached to the use of any classification. Not only do occupational patterns change but many people cannot be classified by their occupation (e.g. retired, 'housewives'). The classification also ignores the unemployed and cannot cope with those who have several jobs. International variations in conventions will also render comparisons of social class attributes very difficult indeed.

Salting The application of chemicals to keep roads and paths free of ice.

SO_x The generic term for Oxides of Sulphur. These include Sulphur Dioxide (SO_2) which reacts with water in the atmosphere to form Sulphuric Acid, one of the main components of Acid Rain. Sulphates are derivatives of the above.

Stratosphere This is the upper section of the atmosphere ranging from approximately 15km to 50km above the earth. It is where the protective Ozone Layer resides.

Sustainability/Sustainable Development Defined by the Brundtland Report (Our Common Future) as 'development that meets the needs of the present without compromising the ability of future generations to meet their own needs'. Another definition is 'Improving the quality of life while living within the carrying capacity of supporting ecosystems'. There are four fundamental principles required for sustainable development. These involve:

- Future Generations: Our actions should not have an adverse impact on the lives of those who will come after us. Therefore we should be careful in our use and abuse of finite resources;
- Participation: People should be able to share in decisions that affect their quality of life and the environment through proper consultation which suits people and not planners;

- Fairness: Resources should be used to provide for the needs of the whole of the community without exclusion or disadvantage to any group. There is a pressing need to reduce social inequalities particularly with respect to global disparities in income, wealth and health;
- Environmental Protection: We all depend on the earth's resources to live. These resources should be protected by reducing our levels of consumption of raw materials and energy.

All in all, sustainability can be effectively summarised as 'we do not inherit the planet from our ancestors, we borrow it from our children'.

TENS Trans-European Network Strategy.

TERN Trans-European Road Network.

Transport and Energy Intensity These terms refer to the total amount of energy or transport required to manufacture or deliver a given unit of a particular product. An example is given in the work of Böge (1995) who shows that one pot of yoghurt weighing 150g has 'consumed' an amount of transport equivalent to moving one lorry 9.2 metres. The production of food products and consumer durables is consuming increasing amounts of transport and energy over time, that is, the transport intensity/energy intensity of our production systems is increasing. For a fuller discussion of these trends see Peake (1994).

Transport and Health Study Group This Study Group, now defunct, has produced some excellent material on the health impacts associated with transport. This is available from Transport 2000 in London.

Troposphere This is the lowest layer of the atmosphere extending to approximately 15km above the earth.

Twyford Down A major road project near Winchester (UK) from 1993 to 1995 involving a huge cutting through protected landscape. Now a symbol of the damaging effect of UK road building policies.

UNCED United Nations Conference on Environment and Development. See Earth Summit.

UNECE United Nations Economic Commission for Europe.

UNEP United Nations Environment Programme.

VOCs Volatile Organic Compounds are damaging to human health. They include benzenes, toluenes, ketones (such as acetone), alcohols, ethers, esters, formaldehyde, etc.

WHO The World Health Organisation is a UN agency charged with responsibility for global health issues and for setting standards.

WMO The World Meteorological Organisation is an agency of the United Nations.

WTO World Tourism Organisation.

WWF World Wide Fund for Nature.

Index

AA (Automobile Association), 24, 142
access, accessibility, 2, 4, 7, 16, 20, 22, 35, 48, 49, 51, 57, 62, 70–1, 73–4, 77, 79, 91, 92, 97, 110, 111–12, 126, 128, 132–3, 135–9, 144, 146, 169–70, 192–3, 199, 217–8, 223–6
acid deposition, acidification, 119, 120, 121, 203
Africa, 5, 6, 27, 44–6, 54, 73, 96, 118, 144, 148, 220
Agenda 21, 101, 128, 173, 174, 175
aircraft, aeroplanes, 29, 32, 73, 120, 123, 203
airports, 9, 13, 76–7, 88, 90–6, 126–7, 147, 166, 173, 225–6
alternative fuels, 177, 179, 180–2, 184, 217
American Lung Association, 153
Antarctica, 83
Appleyard, D., 140, 149
Australia, 4, 20, 37, 67, 68, 72, 84, 108, 196, 218, 220
auto-dependency, car dependency, 4, 17, 21, 68, 111–13, 126–7, 141, 169, 170, 205, 209, 218, 220
aviation, air travel, air freight, 33–5, 39, 43–4, 56, 60, 62, 76–96, 98–9, 148, 166, 200, 208

Bangkok, 44, 51, 81, 122, 130, 165
Bangladesh, 39, 44–8, 115, 129, 144, 221
benzene, 27, 151, 156
Berlin, 3, 55, 57, 70, 143, 201
biodiversity, 29, 76, 90–1, 96, 103, 109, 124
biomass, fuel crops, 180, 181–4
Birmingham, 11–12, 15, 46, 61, 125, 130, 202
Boracay, 80–1
Britain, 88, 103, 130, 142, 156, 159, 168, 196, 198, 218, 220
see also United Kingdom
British Airways, 89, 90, 95
British Medical Association (BMA), 150
Brundtland Report, 99–100
Brussels, 16, 71, 167, 220, 223
Buchanan, C., 191
buses, 4, 10, 22, 36, 54, 71, 110, 135, 141, 205, 220

Calcutta, 3, 43, 220
Calida, 208
California, 176–8, 182, 196
Canada, 3, 68, 79, 118, 152, 182
cancer, carcinogen, 27, 151, 152, 156, 158, 159, 180
carbon dioxide (CO_2), 5, 27, 43, 56, 68, 89, 93, 94, 104–9, 111–12, 114–15, 118–20, 124–5, 129–30, 175, 178–9, 181, 183–5, 192, 197, 211–15, 218
carbon monoxide (CO), 27, 43, 114, 120, 122, 153, 155–6, 159, 161, 176–9
carbon tax, 11, 64
car-free developments, 141–2, 204, 226
catalytic convertors, 27, 119, 125, 127, 161–3, 177, 179, 197, 216–7
children, future generations, 3–8, 12–3, 16, 19, 23, 26, 28, 31, 37, 44, 46, 51, 57, 61, 71, 80–2, 96, 98–9, 103, 108, 110, 113, 134–5, 142–3, 148, 151, 155, 160, 203–4, 226

China, 5, 6, 7, 8, 26, 27, 47, 62, 103, 115, 119, 130, 143–4, 148, 184–5, 218, 220–1
choice, 34–5, 37, 39, 59, 71, 112, 113, 199, 224, 226
climate change, 8, 27, 90, 101, 104, 115–19, 129, 148, 171, 173–4, 203, 221
climate change convention, 8, 104, 173
common transport policy, 57 *see also* trans European networks, European Union
community, 13, 15, 18, 20, 57, 60, 76, 86, 92, 96, 101, 106–7, 109, 127, 145, 149–50, 165, 201, 205, 217, 223
community cohesion, 10, 11, 75
community disruption, 12, 29, 86, 136, 140, 163
community viability and vitality, 5, 141, 218, 226
company cars, 188
Concorde, 73
consultation, participation, 13, 105, 108, 132, 145–6, 199, 201–2 *see also* local democracy
consumption, 6–7, 15, 34, 50, 66, 68, 83, 98, 102, 104, 108, 132, 178–9, 206, 218 , distance, 59 –75, 76, 144 , energy, 5, 13, 25–6, 39, 43–4, 52, 60–1, 65, 67–9, 75, 76, 84–5, 96, 103, 108, 111–12, 114, 122, 124–6, 129–30, 173, 175, 184–5, 187, 200, 204–7, 216–17, 219, 224 , fossil fuel dependence, 4, 6, 20, 25, 57, 110, 112, 114–19, 125, 130 , food, 5, 6 , materials extraction, resource depletion, 6, 25–6, 52, 57, 60–1, 65, 96, 102–3, 105, 107, 123, 128–30, 174, 177, 184, 187, 204, 216–7, 219, 221, 224–5 , production, 6, 39, 49, 179, 186
Convention on Long-range Transboundary Air Pollution (LRTAP), 171 *see also* regulatory intervention
corner shops, 18, 205
Cornwall, 1, 2, 6, 8, 9, 11
cost-benefit analysis (COBA), 13
crime, personal attack, 36, 108, 112, 140, 149 *see also* fear of crime, safety
critical mass, 4, 5, 13, 16, 226
cycling, cyclists, 4, 10, 22, 30, 35–7, 46, 49, 57, 71, 105, 110, 112, 114, 124–7, 133, 136–7, 141, 150, 169, 173, 187–8, 190–3, 200, 205–6, 216, 219

Delft, 20, 146, 190, 202
demand management, 76, 91, 96, 97, 106, 122, 170, 173, 185, 192, 198–9, 204, 205, 216
Denmark, 137, 164, 203
Department of the Environment, 31, 125, 192
Department of Transport, 14, 36, 43, 125, 159
deregulation, 12, 35, 54
desertification, 98–9
developing countries, 34, 79, 97, 111, 121–2, 127, 128–9, 131, 136, 174–5, 203–5, 218–9, 221, 224, 226
Directives (EU) EIA, 176, 195 *see also* regulatory intervention
distance intensity, 59, 60, 66, 75, 126
distinctiveness, 60, 76, 83, 96, 140
Dobris Report, 119
duplicated transport, 19

Earth Summit, 99, 101
ecological footprint, lifecycle analysis, 130, 184, 200
ecological taxation reform, 187
economic development, 1–4, 6–7, 14–5, 34, 48–9, 77, 83–4, 96, 112, 147, 170, 207, 221, 223

economic growth, 1–3, 12, 17, 26, 51, 52, 57, 86, 88, 96, 97, 188
economic welfare, 3, 56, 210, 224, 226
economies of scale, 65, 67, 131, 207–8
ECOPLAN, 30
Edinburgh, 15, 70, 72, 141
Eeklo, 3, 4, 6
electric vehicles, 177, 179, 182, 184, 198
emissions directives – EU, 176 *see also* California, climate change convention, directives, regulatory intervention
environmental capacity, carrying capacity, 6, 76, 96, 100, 105, 225
environmental degeneration, 4, 11, 18, 25, 33, 35, 59, 83, 98, 109, 114–27, 129, 131–2, 147, 170, 174, 176, 195–6, 198, 202–3, 207–8, 218–19, 222, 224–6
Environmental Impact Assessment (EIA), 172, 176, 194–5, 196, 198
environmental quality, 1, 2, 4, 18, 31, 80
equitable distribution of resources, wealth, etc., 102, 128, 131, 139, 185
equity, 7, 54, 56, 57, 61, 102, 131, 184, 185, 189, 200, 220, 224 *see also* inequality, social inequality, social justice
Espoo Convention, 172
Europe, 1, 5, 10, 26, 35, 39, 46, 54–8, 59, 62, 64, 78, 84–5, 93, 96, 118–19, 123, 147, 161–2, 165, 171, 182, 189, 200, 206, 217–18, 220–1
European Bank of Reconstruction and Development, 50, 55–8
European Commission, 26, 119, 182
European Federation of Transport and the Environment, 32
European Investment Bank, 50, 55–6, 58
European Round Table of Industrialists, 50
European Union, European Community (EU), 3, 5, 8–9, 11, 31–2, 50, 56–8, 88, 90, 103, 104, 123, 129, 147, 153, 154, 167, 179, 188, 196, 202, 207,
exercise, 150, 169
external benefits of transport, 26–33
external costs of transport, 11, 16, 26–33, 126 *see also* internalising the external costs, true costs of private transport

Faust, 17–33, 223
fear of crime, personal attack, security, 16, 24, 36, 75, 91, 110, 138, 148 *see also* crime, safety
Fifth Environmental Action Plan, 9, 11, 31, 91, 168, 176, 186, 188
Ford, H., 18, 65
Ford Motor Company, 56
freedom, 15, 17, 20, 23, 26, 29, 30, 32, 34, 36, 37, 90, 96, 97, 135, 142, 144, 199, 203, 205, 223, 226
free market economy, 8, 57, 126
freight, 8, 19, 21, 33, 39, 43, 45, 50, 55, 57–8, 62–6, 69, 86, 103, 110–11, 115, 131, 187, 189, 196–7, 200, 203, 206–8, 210–16, 217 *see also* rail freight, aviation, maritime transport
friction of distance, 59–75
fuel taxation, 88, 89, 90, 188, 205
fuelwood, cooking fuel, home heat, 34–5, 45–6, 84–5, 129, 224

GATT, 207
Germany, 3, 37, 39, 55, 73, 78, 89, 119, 125, 133, 139, 142, 148, 152, 16–22, 167, 182, 187, 196, 206–7, 219
global warming, 18, 27, 86, 90, 92, 114–19, 148, 185, 223, 225
Greece, 3, 9, 55, 83
greenhouse gases, 11, 20–1, 52, 55, 56, 60, 76, 88, 99, 103, 105, 111, 118, 129, 168, 184
Greenpeace, 15, 208, 215, 221
Growth, Competitiveness, Employment (Delors white paper), 26

health, 3, 4, 6–8, 10, 16, 18, 23, 28–9, 35–6, 39, 46, 48, 51–2, 57, 60, 68, 71, 76, 83, 86, 90, 92, 95–6, 98, 107, 109–10, 114–15, 122–3, 127, 131, 139–43, 144, 147–69, 172–3, 184, 187, 199, 201, 203, 217–219, 220, 222–6
Heathrow, 22, 34, 76, 88, 90, 93–5, 202, 225 *see also* airports
heavy metal emissions, 179
Heidelberg (Environmental Forecasting Institute/Umwelt-und Prognos Institut), 26–9, 148, 187
Hesse, M., 206–15, 216, 218
high-speed rail, trains, 9, 13, 60, 72, 123, 126, 167, 196
homelessness, home loss (due to progress), housing, 1, 35, 52, 58, 125, 219
Hungary, 3, 4, 6, 54
hydrocarbons, *see* volatile organic compounds
hyper-mobility, 3, 15, 18, 33, 60, 76, 169, 217

India, 4, 5, 6, 8, 27, 44–5, 62, 84, 96, 103, 115, 144, 148, 184–5, 218, 220–1
industrial location grants, 67–8
inequality, 16, 70, 131, 137, 188, 207, 223 *see also* Equity, social inequality, social justice
Intergovernmental Panel on Climate Change (IPCC), 104, 107, 115, 214,
integrated ticketing, 139, 205.
internalising the external costs, 31–2, 187–8, 194 *see also* external costs of transport, true costs of private transport
International Institute for Energy Conservation (IIEC), 54
International Road Federation, 3
invisibility of vulnerable, non-motorised road users, 19, 46–9, 143

Jacobs, J., 149
Janelle, D., 74–5
Japan, 15, 78, 118–19, 182, 196
JIT (Just-In-Time), 66, 67, 212 *see also* logistics
jobs and employment, 2, 4, 6, 7–10, 12–14, 29, 35, 52, 55, 65, 67–9, 71, 72, 75, 80–1, 108, 110, 132, 134–5, 137, 140, 150, 187–8, 192, 201, 207–8, 219, 223
jitneys, 54
Just-In-Time, *see* JIT

Kenya, 39, 43, 59, 130, 147
Krippendorf, J., 84

Lancashire, 9, 11, 13–14, 73
Lancashire County Council, 8, 9, 48
Lancaster, 8, 9, 46, 225
Lancaster Study, 154
Lancaster Western Bypass, 8, 14, 46
landscape consumption, 84, 96
landscape depletion, habitat loss, 8, 16, 75, 86, 92, 96, 106, 111, 124
Latin America, 6, 43, 79, 148, 155
lead, 155, 176, 179, 181

Lewis, C. S., 144
liberalisation, 35, 51, 54
Liverpool, 12, 15, 44
Local Agenda 21 (LA21), 101, 199
local communities, neighbourhoods, 1–4, 7, 12, 16, 75, 112, 124, 202–3, 206
local democracy, 5, 16, 145 *see also* consultation, participation
local economies, 2, 3, 7, 8, 57, 65, 72, 75, 107, 109, 111, 210
local facilities, services, 4, 22, 35, 49, 61, 70–1, 112, 127, 206, 223
local production–consumption relationships, 5, 7, 21–2, 39, 49, 75, 111, 127, 187, 204, 206–7, 223–4
logistics, 13, 20, 43–4, 55, 65–67, 203, 208–12, 214, 219 *see also* JIT
London, 16, 44, 47, 61, 69, 71–2, 130, 134–6, 151, 156, 165, 167, 201, 220
long distance transport, travel, 2–4, 5, 7, 8, 15, 19–21, 56–57, 59, 66, 67, 73, 75, 76, 90, 96, 97, 106, 110–11, 133, 142, 187, 200, 201, 207–8, 211

Maastricht Treaty, 56, 57, 207
Manchester, 22, 44, 54, 71, 76, 88, 90, 92, 95, 130, 143
maritime transport, 11, 55–6, 63, 98, 212–3
market forces, 12, 34, 50, 70, 73, 97, 188
mobility, 4–5, 7, 13, 16, 20, 50–51, 54, 57, 66, 71, 96, 97, 105, 107, 111–12, 115, 127, 132–5, 139, 146, 164, 199, 203, 206, 217, 218, 220
modernisation, 3, 47–8, 66, 80

National Environmental Protection Act (US), 194–5
'near for far' procurement, 210–11, 214
Nepal, 84, 85
North America, 4, 5, 26, 73, 78, 84, 118–19, 171, 189, 207, 218, 220
NAFTA, 3, 147, 202, 207
Netherlands, 106, 139, 146, 168, 182, 188, 190, 192–3, 196–7, 206
New Scientist, 156
New Zealand, 39, 67, 182, 196
nitrogen oxides (NO_x), 27, 43, 88, 90, 95, 106, 109, 114, 118–22, 151, 153, 156, 158–9, 161–2, 176–9, 181–3, 197
noise, 10, 28–31, 52, 67, 71, 76, 83, 86, 90, 92, 95, 106, 110, 113, 121–7, 130, 132, 140–2, 147–8, 155, 163–8, 171, 183, 187, 189–90, 201, 202, 217, 223, 224, 226
non-motorised transport, 46–9, 54, 111, 138, 173, 199, 205
nuclear power, 183–4

OECD (Organization of Economic Co-operation and Development), 32, 103, 115, 118, 122, 164, 184, 196
opportunity, 128, 132, 139, 149
Öresund, 50, 202
ozone (O_3), 27, 76, 86, 88, 90, 99, 103, 105, 109, 114, 119–20, 151–3, 158–61, 171–2, 176, 179, 181, 203, 223, 225–6

Paris, 73, 167, 201, 225
parking, 6, 18, 19, 22, 24, 37, 39, 84, 91, 108, 110, 123–4, 126–7, 130, 142, 178, 188, 192, 202
particulates, 121, 122, 147, 152, 155–9, 176–7
pedestrians, *see* walking
Perranporth, 1, 2, 3, 4, 6, 9, 13
Planning Policy Guidance Note 13 (PPG 13), 125, 192

polluter pays principle, 186, 188, 208
pollution, pollutants, 1, 4, 8, 16, 20–3, 26–31, 36, 39, 43–4, 51–2, 55, 59–61, 68–71, 75, 76, 83, 84, 86, 88, 90, 92, 95, 102, 106, 108–10, 113, 114, 118–19, 121–2, 124, 127, 130, 132, 140–2, 147–8, 150–5, 167–8, 171–2, 174, 177–9, 187, 189, 190, 193, 201–2, 204, 206–7, 217, 219–20, 222–6
pollution protocols, *see* regulatory intervention, California
poverty, 51–2, 58, 102, 127, 129–31, 140, 142–3, 154, 187, 207, 220, 223
precautionary principle, 52
predict and provide, 88, 91, 97, 111, 200, 225
Preston (Lancashire), 16, 48
prisoners' dilemma, 204, 220–6
privatisation, 35, 51, 54
progress, 17, 26, 53, 144, 216
public transport, 2, 4, 10, 30, 35, 37, 54, 69, 70, 97, 105, 110, 114, 122, 125, 126, 127, 131, 133, 134, 135, 136, 137, 138, 140, 141, 173, 174, 187–8, 190, 192–3, 205–6, 219

quality of life, 1, 16, 22, 71, 100, 106–9, 111, 124, 127, 128–9, 137, 139, 141, 168, 170, 194, 199, 218, 221

RAC (Royal Automobile Club), 17
rail freight, 4, 22, 35, 205, 210, 212–13 *see also* freight
rail, railways, trains, 3, 11, 35, 54–6, 63–5, 67, 69, 71, 91, 135, 168, 173, 196, 205, 206
regulatory intervention, protocols, 8, 104, 171–3, 198 see *also* emissions directives
ribbon development, 70
rickshaws, 3, 46–7, 49, 200, 219
Rio Declaration, 99, 173, 175
road, traffic danger, 30, 46–9, 71, 125, 127, 130, 136, 140, 143, 146, 147–8, 183, 190
Roads for Prosperity, 14
road pricing, 188, 189, 205, 216
road safety, 30, 170, 190, 223
road traffic accidents, 23, 27–9, 31, 37, 48, 51, 76, 107, 110, 122, 141–4, 147–8, 163, 187, 201, 217, 226
Royal Commission on Environmental Pollution, 29, 67, 155–6

SACTRA, 14
safe routes to school, 137, 190, 226
safety, 24, 110, 138, 140, 141, 146 *see also* crime, fear of crime
Salisbury, 4, 6–8, 225
schools, schooling, school run, 4, 18, 23, 29, 35, 60, 68, 70, 71, 83–4, 95–6, 109, 110, 131, 133–4, 137, 165, 167, 168, 187, 202
sea level, 115
shopping, retailing, 34, 39–41, 43–4, 59, 61, 68, 71, 109–10, 126, 133–5, 169, 191, 200, 202, 225
slavery, 5, 31
Smeed Report, 189
smog, 27, 119, 156, 159, 162, 172, 176
social benefits, 17–33, 34
social cohesion, instability, 12, 18, 33, 65, 76, 102, 140
social costs, 17–33, 50
social inequality, 2, 8, 15, 49, 51, 127, 216, 226 *see also* equity, inequality, social justice
social isolation, 138, 147–8
social justice, 2, 7, 10, 32, 49, 54, 57, 142 *see also* equity, inequality
soil erosion, 85, 102–3, 106
South America, 44–5, 73, 79, 118, 144

space, space intensity, spatial organisation, 4, 5, 53, 55, 59, 126, 204, 214, 218
space-time relationships, 4, 15–16, 21–3, 60, 74, 144, 171, 206, 226
space compression, 144
Spain, 9, 56, 83
speed, 17, 19, 23, 37, 65, 75, 76, 96, 97, 112, 143, 163, 171, 190, 217
Stockholm Environmental Institute, 226
Stockton to Darlington railway, 69
Strategic Environmental Assessment (SEA), 196, 197, 198, 199
strong sustainability, 199, 213–16
subsidies to private transport, 10, 30, 188, 205, 224
sulphur dioxide (SO_2), Sulphates (SO_x), 109, 119–20, 154, 156, 157, 161–2, 176, 180, 183
Sustainable Seattle Initiative, 108–9
Sweden, 145, 182, 188, 203
Swedish EPA, 179

target setting and monitoring, 107–8, 198, 199, 221
taxation, 32, 88–90
technical change, innovation, development, 62–75, 97, 105, 111, 119, 131, 170, 177–82, 184, 189, 197–8, 216–7
telecommunications, 72, 98
telecommuting, 205
Thailand, 35, 81–3, 147
time, 19, 20–1, 44, 46–7, 59–75, 112
time savings, compression, 14, 18, 61, 75, 76, 96, 97, 132–3, 136, 138, 146, 203, 223
time penalties, losses, 46, 132–4, 135, 138
tourism, 1, 35, 75, 76–96, 99, 132, 216
Traditional Economic Growth Model, 9, 10, 49, 50, 53, 57, 201
traffic generation, 1, 6, 12–14, 90, 92, 126, 201
trams, 3, 22, 70, 91, 141, 205, 220
transboundary air pollution, 119, 120, 161–2, 171
transboundary environmental impacts, 172
Trans European Networks (TENs), 50, 91, 123, 147
Trans European Road Networks (TERN), 9, 11, 55–7, 123, 196
transnational corporations (TNCs), 5, 50, 103, 207–8, 224, 226.
trans-Pennine motorway (M65), 8, 11, 14, 43, 214, 220
Transport and Health Study Group, 149–50
true costs of private transport, 186–7, 204 *see also* external costs of transport, internalising the external costs
Twyford Down (M3), 43, 56, 61, 96, 196, 220

United Kingdom (OK), 4, 8, 10, 31, 78, 98, 104, 125, 129–30, 133, 137, 145, 155, 157–9, 162, 177, 182, 190, 194, 203, 206 *see also* Britain
United Nations (UN), 101, 104, 175
United Nations Economic Commission for Europe (UNECE), 171–2, 176, 196–7
United States of America (USA), 3, 6, 32, 37, 59, 68, 78–9, 98, 103, 104, 108, 118–9, 121, 129–30, 147, 151–2, 156, 159, 164, 176, 181–2, 194

volatile organic compounds, hydrocarbons, 27, 36, 43, 106, 109, 114, 119, 120, 122, 152, 155, 158–9, 162, 171, 176–9, 181, 183, 197
Volkswagen, 27, 54, 56

walking (and pedestrians), 4, 10, 22, 30, 35–6, 37, 46, 49, 57, 69, 71, 105, 110, 112, 114, 125, 126–7, 133, 135–6, 137, 141, 150, 165, 169, 173, 187–8, 190–3, 200, 205–6, 216, 219,
war, 148, 155
waste generation and disposal, 2, 5, 80–1, 84–5, 90, 102, 107–9, 181, 186–7, 219
water, water pollution, 29, 72, 74, 76, 80–1, 84, 86, 90, 98, 103, 105, 186, 206, 224, 226
Wolff, S., 151
World Bank, 3, 5, 50–8, 147, 207, 224
World Health Organization (WHO), 23, 51, 90, 121–3, 148, 154, 156, 161–6, 199
World Resources Institute (WRI), 115, 119, 122, 147
World Tourist Organization (WTO), 77–9
Worldwatch Institute, 6, 8, 151
World Wide Fund for Nature (WWF), 21, 100, 210, 219
Wuppertal Institute for Climate, Energy and the Environment, 19, 25, 31, 39, 89, 187, 206

Yago, G., 37
yoghurt, 39–42, 210, 214
York, 191

Zuckerman, W., 204–5, 216, 218, 220